# ONE NATION UNDER SURVEILLANCE

# One Nation Under Surveillance

## Surveillance

*A New Social Contract to Defend Freedom
Without Sacrificing Liberty*

SIMON CHESTERMAN

**OXFORD**

UNIVERSITY PRESS

# OXFORD
## UNIVERSITY PRESS
Great Clarendon Street, Oxford ox2 6DP

Oxford University Press is a department of the University of Oxford.
It furthers the University's objective of excellence in research, scholarship,
and education by publishing worldwide in

Oxford  New York

Auckland  Cape Town  Dar es Salaam  Hong Kong  Karachi
Kuala Lumpur  Madrid  Melbourne  Mexico City  Nairobi
New Delhi  Shanghai  Taipei  Toronto

With offices in

Argentina  Austria  Brazil  Chile  Czech Republic  France  Greece
Guatemala  Hungary  Italy  Japan  Poland  Portugal  Singapore
South Korea  Switzerland  Thailand  Turkey  Ukraine  Vietnam

Oxford is a registered trade mark of Oxford University Press
in the UK and in certain other countries

Published in the United States
by Oxford University Press Inc., New York

© Simon Chesterman 2011

British Library Cataloguing in Publication Data
Data available
Library of Congress Cataloging in Publication Data
Data available

Typeset by SPI Publisher Services, Pondicherry, India
Printed in Great Britain
on acid-free paper by
Clays Ltd, St Ives plc

ISBN 978-0-19-958037-8

1 3 5 7 9 10 8 6 4 2

*Was he free? Was he happy? The question is absurd;*
*Had anything been wrong, we should certainly have heard.*

WH Auden, 'The Unknown Citizen'

# Acknowledgements

The nature of this research calls for some measure of discretion. In 1998, the *Washington Times* reported that US intelligence services were able to monitor Osama bin Laden's satellite phone. A CIA agent later argued that bin Laden stopped using the phone because of the story, and that a causal link joined the decision to publish to the September 11 attacks on the United States. As I suggest in Chapter three, the account somewhat exaggerates this particular incident, but one must accept that the subject matter is sensitive. For present purposes, it is sufficient to note that certain details of past and current operations will be glossed over and that most interviews were on a not-for-attribution or off-the-record basis and thus will not be identified. Since the book is primarily forward-looking, it is hoped that this will not unduly distort either analysis or prose.

I am, nonetheless, extremely grateful to the many current and past practitioners who were kind enough to share their time and their insights with me in New York, Washington, DC, London, Ottawa, Canberra, Singapore, and elsewhere. In addition, I received valuable comments on various parts of the text from William Abresch, Rueban Balasubramaniam, Gary Bell, Curtis Bradley, Tom Donnelly, Michael Dowdle, Michael Ewing-Chow, Trevor Findlay, Adrian Friedman, Michael Fullilove, Richard Goldstone, Allan Gyngell, Stephen Humphreys, David Jordan, Liliana Jubilut, Richard Junnier, Benedict Kingsbury, Chia Lehnardt, Lim Yee Fen, Karin Loevy, David Malone, Madan Mohan, Paul Monk, Muhammad Aidil Bin Zulkifli, Roland Paris, Sharanjeet Parmar, Joost Pauwelyn, Danielle Louise Pereira, Priya Pillai, Victor Ramraj, Lakshmi Ravindran, David Tan, Tan Hsien-Li, Patricia Tan Shuming, Tan Teck Boon, Teo Yu Chou, Laura Thomas, and Ludwig Ureel. Errors, omissions, and violations of Official Secrets Acts are the responsibility of the author alone.

Thanks also to the many students from New York University School of Law and the National University of Singapore who have participated in the Intelligence Law seminar that I have taught for the past few years. Their insights and their questions frequently helped shape my own views on this topic.

The book develops certain ideas first published elsewhere. These earlier works include *Shared Secrets: Intelligence and Collective Security* (Sydney: Lowy Institute for International Policy, 2006); 'The Spy Who Came In from the Cold War: Intelligence and International Law', *Michigan Journal of International Law* 27 (2006) 1071; 'Secrets and Lies: Intelligence Activities and the Rule of Law in Times of Crisis', *Michigan Journal of International Law* 28 (2007) 553; ' "We Can't Spy... If We Can't Buy!": The Privatization of US Intelligence Services', *European Journal of International Law* 19 (2008) 1055; 'I Spy', *Survival* 50(3) (2008) 163; 'Deny Everything: Intelligence Activities and the Rule of Law', in Victor V Ramraj (ed), *Emergencies and the Limits of Legality* (Cambridge University Press, 2008) 314; 'Secret Intelligence', in Rüdiger Wolfrum (ed), *The Max Planck Encyclopedia of Public International Law* (Oxford University Press, 2009); and 'Intelligence Cooperation in International Operations: Peacekeeping, Weapons Inspections, and the Apprehension and Prosecution of War Criminals', in Hans Born, Ian Leigh, and Aidan Wills (eds), *International Intelligence Cooperation and Accountability* (Routledge, forthcoming). Permission to reproduce the relevant passages is gratefully acknowledged.

My final thanks go to Ming and our family, for showing me what is really worth watching closely.

# Contents

# Abbreviations

| | |
|---|---|
| ANZUS | Australia, New Zealand, and the United States Security Treaty |
| ASIO | Australian Security Intelligence Organisation |
| ASIS | Australian Secret Intelligence Service |
| CCTV | closed-circuit television |
| CIA | Central Intelligence Agency (US) |
| CIFA | Counterintelligence Field Activity (US) |
| CSEC | Communications Security Establishment Canada |
| CSIS | Canadian Security Intelligence Service |
| CTC | Counterterrorist Center (US) |
| DIA | Defense Intelligence Agency (US) |
| DSD | Defence Signals Directorate (Australia) |
| EISAS | Executive Committee on Peace and Security Information and Strategic Analysis Secretariat (UN) |
| FBI | Federal Bureau of Investigation (US) |
| FISA | Foreign Intelligence Surveillance Act (US) |
| FOIA | Freedom of Information Act (US) |
| FISC | Foreign Intelligence Surveillance Court (US) |
| GA Res | General Assembly resolution (UN) |
| GAO | Government Accountability Office (US) |
| GCHQ | Government Communications Headquarters (Britain) |
| GCSB | Government Communications Security Bureau (New Zealand) |
| GSS | General Security Service (Israel) |
| GWOT | global war on terror |
| HUMINT | human intelligence |
| IAEA | International Atomic Energy Agency |
| ICC | International Criminal Court |
| ICCPR | International Covenant on Civil and Political Rights |
| ICRC | International Committee of the Red Cross |

| | |
|---|---|
| ICTR | International Criminal Tribunal for Rwanda |
| ICTY | International Criminal Tribunal for the former Yugoslavia |
| IGIS | Inspector-General of Intelligence and Security (Australia) |
| IMINT | imagery intelligence |
| IPT | Investigatory Powers Tribunal (Britain) |
| IRA | Irish Republican Army |
| KGB | Committee for State Security [*Komitet Gosudarstvennoy Bezopasnosti*] (Soviet Union) |
| MI5 | Security Service (Britain) |
| MI6 | Secret Intelligence Service (Britain) |
| NATO | North Atlantic Treaty Organization |
| NRO | National Reconnaissance Office (US) |
| NSA | National Security Agency (US) |
| NZSIS | New Zealand Security Intelligence Service |
| ODNI | Office of the Director of National Intelligence (US) |
| OMB | Office of Management and Budget (US) |
| ONA | Office of National Assessments (Australia) |
| OPCW | Organisation for the Prohibition of Chemical Weapons |
| ORCI | Office for Research and the Collection of Information (UN) |
| OSI | Office of Strategic Influence (US) |
| PMSC | private military and security company |
| PSI | Proliferation Security Initiative |
| RCMP | Royal Canadian Mounted Police |
| SAIC | Science Applications International Corporation |
| SC Res | Security Council resolution (UN) |
| SIGINT | signals intelligence |
| SVR | Foreign Intelligence Service [*Sluzhba Vneshney Razvedki*] (Russia) |
| SWIFT | Society for Worldwide Interbank Financial Transactions |
| UKUSA | United Kingdom–USA Intelligence Agreement |
| UN | United Nations |
| UNAMIR | UN Assistance Mission for Rwanda |
| UNMOVIC | UN Monitoring Verification and Inspection Commission |

| | |
|---|---|
| UNPROFOR | UN Protection Force |
| UNSCOM | UN Special Commission in Iraq |
| US | United States |
| USC | United States Code |
| USSR | Union of Soviet Socialist Republics |
| WMD | weapons of mass destruction |

# Introduction: The End of Privacy

> There was of course no way of knowing whether you were being
> watched at any given moment.... It was even conceivable that they
> watched everybody all the time.
>
> George Orwell, *Nineteen Eighty-Four*[1]

Soon after his appointment as US Secretary of State in 1929, Henry Stimson
was shown several Japanese communications that had been intercepted
and deciphered by the State Department's small, highly classified Cipher
Bureau, known informally as the Black Chamber. His immediate and
violent reaction was that such subterfuge was 'highly unethical' and that
the State Department could have nothing to do with it. The annual budget
of $25,000 was effectively cut off, its six staff retrenched, and the Black
Chamber was forced to close. Writing in his memoirs some years later,
Stimson explained his firm belief that 'Gentlemen do not read each other's
mail.'[2]

Eighty years later, the National Security Agency (NSA) is the successor to
the Black Chamber. Its staff now number more than 30,000, with a classified
budget estimated at well over ten billion dollars. Created soon after the
Second World War, most Americans had never heard of it until the mid-1970s.
(For decades its acronym was said to stand for 'No Such Agency'.) NSA
activities were long the subject of hyperbolic speculation, but a few years
after the end of the Cold War a comparatively sober report to the European
Parliament noted that all e-mail, telephone, and fax communications on

---

[1] George Orwell, *Nineteen Eighty-Four* (London: Secker and Warburg, 1949), 9.
[2] Herny L Stimson and McGeorge Bundy, *On Active Service in Peace and War* (New York: Harper and Brothers, 1947), 188; William F Friedman, 'From the Archives: A Brief History of the Signal Intelligence Service (June 1942; declassified 1979)', *Cryptologia* 15(3) (1991) 263 at 266–8.

the continent were routinely intercepted.[3] Working with allies such as Britain and Australia, and with much of the world's Internet traffic passing through US territory, the United States now enjoys a level of information superiority unprecedented in the history of espionage.

Spying on foreigners has long been regarded as an unseemly but necessary enterprise. The laws of war, for example, allow for the use of spies—but if those spies are captured they are not entitled to prisoner-of-war status and may be executed. International law tolerates intelligence activities and even, in areas such as arms control, protects it. Spying on one's own citizens in a democracy, by contrast, has historically been subject to various forms of domestic legal and political restraint. For most of the twentieth century these regimes were kept distinct organizationally and legally, with foreign and domestic intelligence pursued by separate agencies governed by different rules. The US Central Intelligence Agency (CIA) and Britain's Secret Intelligence Service (MI6) operated abroad with few constraints; their domestic counterparts, the intelligence element of the Federal Bureau of Investigation (FBI) and Britain's Security Service (MI5) had more restrictions on their activities and cooperated to varying degrees with the regular police. Surveillance of agents of foreign powers was permissible; spying on citizens generally was not. There were, to be sure, violations of these principles—spectacularly culminating in Watergate and the resignation of President Nixon. Such scandals reinforced the view that foreign and domestic intelligence should and could be kept apart.

That position is no longer tenable. Three factors are driving the erosion of the distinction. First, and most obviously, many of the threats facing modern democracies do not respect national borders. It is important not to overstate the threat posed by terrorism: over the past four decades, the number of Americans killed by international terrorists was about the same as the number killed by lightning strikes or allergic reactions to peanuts.[4] Nevertheless, for the foreseeable future, the most significant

---

[3] Steve Wright, An Appraisal of the Technologies of Political Control (Brussels: European Parliament, STOA Interim Study, PE 166.499/INT.ST, 1998). See generally James Bamford, *The Puzzle Palace: A Report on America's Most Secret Agency* (Boston: Houghton Mifflin, 1982); James Bamford, *The Shadow Factory: The Ultra-Secret NSA from 9/11 to the Eavesdropping on America* (New York: Doubleday, 2008).

[4] Philip Bobbitt, *Terror and Consent: The Wars for the Twenty-First Century* (New York: Allen Lane, 2008), 7.

threat of violence on US or British soil will come from terrorists who do not have an obvious state sponsor that could be deterred or coerced: the targets of intelligence services will therefore be individuals rather than states.

The second factor is the revolution in technology and communications. Linked to developments in transportation and the enmeshing of diverse economies described by the loose term 'globalization', the increased use of electronic communications has been matched by the development of ever more sophisticated tools of surveillance. It has also blurred the distinction between what is foreign and what is domestic. The idea that the NSA, for example, can intercept e-mails sent by foreigners but not by US citizens poses—apart from anything else—technical challenges: when a message is routed through strings of Internet service providers, it is not always clear what is 'foreign' and what is 'local'. In any case, there are frequent reports citing analysts within the NSA to the effect that restrictions are not rigorously enforced.[5]

Thirdly, changes in culture are progressively reducing the sphere of activity that citizens can reasonably expect to be kept from government eyes. This is most obvious in the amount of information voluntarily disclosed through social-networking Web sites and the use of loyalty cards, as well as the increased toleration of closed-circuit television (CCTV) in public spaces. It is also implicit in the use of e-mail, credit cards, and other everyday transactions where significant amounts of personal information are passed on to corporations, the government, or both. The trend is likely to grow as personal data are increasingly stored online or 'in the cloud', facilitating access to information by users from a variety of devices, but also placing that information in the hands of an ever-widening circle of actors.[6]

The main casualty of this transformed environment will be privacy. Though privacy is invoked with respect to many aspects of life, the term is used here primarily in the sense of information. Assertions of a *right* to privacy can be understood as the claim of an individual to determine for

---

[5] See, eg, James Risen and Eric Lichtblau, 'E-mail Surveillance Renews Concerns in Congress', *New York Times*, 16 June 2009.

[6] See Jonathan Zittrain, *The Future of the Internet—and How to Stop It* (New Haven, CT: Yale University Press, 2008).

him- or herself when, how, and to what extent information about him or her is communicated to others.[7] Though the desire to keep certain information about oneself private has ancient origins, the modern 'right' is commonly traced to late nineteenth century developments in the United States, where it was the legal response to changed threats, technology, and culture: the rise of sensationalistic journalism, the invention of the hand-held camera, and changing views on the proper role of mass media.[8]

Similar factors were at work through the twentieth century as different balances were struck between the desire of the state to understand and pre-empt threats and the desire of individuals 'to be let alone'.[9] The latter half of the century saw an explosion in literature dealing with the question, with prescient warnings about computerization increasing the amount of information available to governments and other actors, as well as the ease of accessing it.[10] Revelations of abuse or constitutional upheavals periodically slowed it down, but the inexorable trend has been towards greater collection and aggregation of data. That trend only accelerated with the rise of the Internet.

In recent years, the battleground of privacy has been dominated by fights over warrantless electronic surveillance in the United States and CCTV in Britain; the coming years will see further debates over DNA databases, data mining, and biometric identification. There will be protests and lawsuits, editorials and elections resisting these attacks on privacy.

Those battles are worthy. But the war will be lost. Efforts to prevent governments from collecting such information are doomed to failure because modern threats increasingly require that governments collect it, governments are increasingly able to collect it, and citizens increasingly accept that they *will* collect it.

---

[7] Alan F Westin, *Privacy and Freedom* (New York: Atheneum, 1967), 7. Cf James B Rule, *Privacy in Peril* (Oxford: Oxford University Press, 2007), 3; Jon L Mills, *Privacy: The Lost Right* (Oxford: Oxford University Press, 2008), 13–27.

[8] Samuel D Warren and Louis D Brandeis, 'The Right to Privacy', *Harvard Law Review* 4 (1890) 193; Westin, *Privacy and Freedom*, 8–22; Richard F Hixson, *Privacy in a Public Society* (Oxford: Oxford University Press, 1987), 3–25. Some European jurisdictions had embraced similar rights earlier than this. See, eg, *L'affaire Rachel* (Tribunal civil de la Seine, 16 June 1858). See further Chapter eight, section 4.

[9] This formulation derives from Thomas M Cooley, *A Treatise on the Law of Torts, or the Wrongs Which Arise Independent of Contract*, 2nd edn (Chicago: Callaghan & Co, 1888), 29.

[10] See, eg, Westin, *Privacy and Freedom*, 158.

There are, of course, limits to what citizens will tolerate. In 2002, for example, the Pentagon developed plans to fund research projects aimed at using information technology to identify and counter threats from terrorist actors. The plans were largely to draw on information already in the hands of government, but some bad choices doomed the project: labelling the goal as 'Total Information Awareness', adopting a logo with the all-seeing Eye of Providence from the pyramid on the Great Seal of the United States, and putting in charge an official who had been indicted for his role in the 1980s Iran–Contra affair.[11]

Nevertheless, the clear progression is towards ever greater government collection of information on the citizenry, and broad—though hardly universal—acceptance of that reality. The argument here is not that this is good or bad: it is, in many ways, an inevitable consequence of a modern and globalized life. Rather, the point of this book is to shift the focus away from questions of whether and how governments should *collect* information and onto more problematic and relevant questions concerning its *use*.

## 1. UNDERSTANDING INTELLIGENCE

In the shelf-straining literature on intelligence, three broad questions have dominated for over half a century. The first, given the secretive nature of much of the subject, is simply 'what happened?' Such books tend to cluster around the self-serving memoirs of former spies on the one hand, and the breathless accounts of outsiders on the other.[12] The second question concerns how to make sure that intelligence services have sufficient powers to do their job effectively, without acquiring so much power that they undermine or corrupt democratic government. These volumes lean

---

[11] Bobbitt, *Terror and Consent*, 261–3. One of the first articles raising the alarm against the programme was William Safire, 'You Are a Suspect', *New York Times*, 14 November 2002.

[12] Prominent examples include Bamford, *Puzzle Palace*; Peter Wright, *Spycatcher: The Candid Autobiography of a Senior Intelligence Officer* (New York: Viking, 1987); Stephen Dorril, *MI6: Inside the Covert World of Her Majesty's Secret Intelligence Service* (New York: Free Press, 2000); Robert Baer, *See No Evil: The True Story of a Ground Soldier in the CIA's War on Terrorism* (New York: Three Rivers, 2002); Bamford, *Shadow Factory*.

towards either paternalistic expositions of the national security threats that civil libertarians cannot or will not understand, or the recitation of scandals and abuses of power that national security enthusiasts conveniently overlook.[13] Thirdly, there is a growing body of what one might call 'reform literature' that identifies systemic problems of analysis and coordination between agencies in the hope of improving the output of intelligence services without necessarily increasing the input. Here the dominant themes tend to be the need to liberate agents and analysts from bureaucracy and encourage individual excellence, or else to strengthen that bureaucracy in order to ensure that coordinated and coherent advice reaches policymakers.[14]

The result has been more heat than light, with surprisingly little serious academic treatment of the subject of intelligence.[15] What is missing in this literature is a clear-eyed account of how one can and should balance oversight and operational freedom—legitimacy and effectiveness—in the activities of intelligence services. This book addresses that tension directly and seeks to map out a new way of understanding intelligence in its modern context. Similar efforts have been undertaken with respect to particular questions—the US approach to torture, for example, or preventive detention—but the present work aims to cover a wider range of subjects (including electronic surveillance and information sharing between governments) across a spectrum of cases (notably comparing

---

[13] See, eg, Hans Born, Loch K Johnson, and Ian Leigh (eds), *Who's Watching the Spies: Establishing Intelligence Service Accountability* (Washington, DC: Potomac Books, 2005); Hans Born and Marina Caparini (eds), *Democratic Control of Intelligence Services: Containing Rogue Elephants* (Aldershot: Ashgate, 2007); Bobbitt, *Terror and Consent*; John Yoo, *Crisis and Command: A History of Executive Power from George Washington to George W Bush* (New York: Kaplan, 2010).

[14] See, eg, Richard A Posner, *Preventing Surprise Attacks: Intelligence Reform in the Wake of 9/11* (Stanford, CA: Hoover, 2005); Richard K Betts, *Enemies of Intelligence: Knowledge and Power in American National Security* (New York: Columbia University Press, 2007); Robert M Clark, *Intelligence Analysis: A Target-Centric Approach*, 2nd edn (Washington, DC: CQ Press, 2007); Thomas E Copeland, *Fool Me Twice: Intelligence Failure and Mass Casualty Terrorism* (Leiden: Koninklijke Brill NV, 2007); Richard L Russell, *Sharpening Strategic Intelligence: Why the CIA Gets It Wrong and What Needs to Be Done to Get It Right* (Cambridge: Cambridge University Press, 2007); Amy B Zegart, *Spying Blind: The CIA, the FBI, and the Origins of 9/11* (Princeton: Princeton University Press, 2007); Robert Jervis, *Why Intelligence Fails: Lessons from the Iranian Revolution and the Iraq War* (Ithaca, NY: Cornell University Press, 2010).

[15] Amy B Zegart, 'Cloaks, Daggers, and Ivory Towers: Why Academics Don't Study US Intelligence', in Loch K Johnson (ed), *Strategic Intelligence* (Westport, CT: Praeger, 2007), 21.

the United States, Britain, and intelligence sharing within the United Nations).

'Intelligence' is understood here in two senses. In the abstract, it will be used to refer to information obtained covertly—that is, without the consent of the person or entity that controls the information. This is sometimes referred to as 'secret intelligence'. Within this heading, two subcategories of intelligence that have remained essentially unchanged since the Second World War are intelligence obtained wittingly or unwittingly from individuals, known as human intelligence or HUMINT, and signals intelligence or SIGINT, which comprises communications intercepts and other electronic intelligence. A newer subcategory is photographic or imagery intelligence (IMINT), now dominated by satellite reconnaissance. Many more -INTs appear in the literature, but these three will be the focus here.[16]

The abstract definition of intelligence is complemented by a broader understanding of the term as the analytical product of intelligence services, best understood as a risk assessment intended to guide action. These two definitions highlight an important distinction that must be made between the collection and the analysis of intelligence. Though collection may be covert, analysis should generally draw upon a far wider range of sources, most of which—frequently the vast majority—will be publicly available or 'open'. These discrete functions are reflected in the structure of most Western intelligence services: more by accident than design, the principle has evolved that those who collect and process raw intelligence should not also have final responsibility for evaluating it. The top-level product of such analysis is known in Britain as an assessment; in the United States the term estimate is used. This is distinct from how such analysis should inform policy—a far broader topic.[17]

These two uses of intelligence correspond roughly to a distinction sometimes made between 'secrets' and 'mysteries'. A secret is a knowable fact that can be stolen by a spy or intercepted by a technical sensor, such as

---

[16] See Michael Herman, *Intelligence Power in Peace and War* (Cambridge: Cambridge University Press, 1996), 61–81. Wider definitions of intelligence are sometimes used, such as 'information designed for action', but this would appear to encompass any data informing policy at any level of decision-making. See generally Michael Warner, 'Wanted: A Definition of Intelligence', *Studies in Intelligence (Unclassified Edition)* 46(3) (2002) 15.

[17] Herman, *Intelligence Power*, 111–12.

the number of nuclear weapons possessed by a given country. A mystery is a puzzle to which no one can be sure of the answer, such as the likely response of a political leader to future events: no one can steal that answer; the leader may not know him- or herself.[18]

Intelligence services may have other functions such as covert action and counter-intelligence, but the focus here is on the acquisition of secrets and the resolution of mysteries. A key finding is that the increasing transparency of many aspects of modern life is reducing the number of secrets it is possible to keep from anyone.

## 2. OUTLINE OF THE BOOK

The book is organized into three parts. Part I addresses the modern political and legal context within which intelligence services operate, with the first Chapter reviewing the changing role of intelligence during and after the Cold War. Understanding the intentions and capacities of other actors has always been an important part of statecraft. Recent technological advances have increased the risks of ignorance, with ever more powerful weapons falling into ever more unpredictable hands. At the same time, other advances have lowered the price of knowledge: vastly more information is freely available and can be accessed by far more people than at any point in history. 'Secret intelligence', in the sense of information being obtained covertly, is thus both more and less important than it was during the Cold War.

The following two chapters address basic questions that run through the volume. *Should* intelligence activities by the state be constrained when those activities are intended to protect the life of the nation? And, regardless of how one answers that question, *can* intelligence activities be constrained in a meaningful way when those activities will necessarily be undertaken secretly?

Chapter two examines the unresolved debates over how democracies should respond to crises such as the 'ticking time-bomb' scenario, in which a terrorist knows the location of a bomb but will not talk. This is an

---

[18] Joseph S Nye, 'Peering into the Future', *Foreign Affairs* 73(4) (1994) 82 at 86–8.

extreme example of an emergency that may cause a state to bend or break its own laws. As Bruce Ackerman has wryly noted, only one major thinker of the twentieth century treated emergencies as a central theme of his work: 'and he, alas, turned out to be a Nazi'.[19] Debates over the limits of legality precede the writings of Carl Schmitt, however, and the Third Reich now offers a salutary warning of the dangers of excessive state power. Indeed, one of the most interesting aspects of twentieth century intelligence is that even as the powers of agencies tended to expand, so did the view that they should be grounded in law. This turn to law was severely challenged following the September 11 attacks on the United States.

Even if one concludes that intelligence services should be subject to the rule of law, it is generally accepted that some degree of secrecy is appropriate for their activities. The sociologist Edward Shils, writing soon after the McCarthy hearings had shaken the United States, argued that liberal democracy rested on protecting privacy for individuals and rejecting it for government.[20] The following half-century has seen the opposite happen: in addition to the erosion of privacy for individuals, governments have become ever more secretive. This is true with respect to the classification of information that governments now deem 'secret', but also with respect to efforts at oversight by other branches of government. Norman Mineta, who served on the House Intelligence Committee under Ronald Reagan, famously commented that legislative overseers were like mushrooms: the intelligence community kept them in the dark and fed them a lot of manure.[21] Chapter three discusses the limits of appropriate secrecy and the challenges it poses for effective accountability.

Part II turns to three cases that illustrate evolution in the practice of intelligence. The intention is not to provide an exhaustive account of intelligence practices in each jurisdiction, but rather to use them to examine how threats, technology, and culture have shaped that practice. Chapter four describes the United States and the upheavals caused by the response to September 11. Demands for effective responses by government to the threat of terrorism exerted understandable pressure towards a freer hand

[19] Bruce Ackerman, *Before the Next Attack: Preserving Civil Liberties in an Age of Terrorism* (New Haven, CT: Yale University Press, 2006), 56.
[20] Edward A Shils, *The Torment of Secrecy: The Background and Consequences of American Security Policies* (London: Heinemann, 1956), 21–5.
[21] David M Alpern, 'America's Secret Warriors', *Newsweek*, 10 October 1983, 38.

for intelligence services, with legal and political consequences that are still being revealed. One of the most troubling aspects of the contemporary US intelligence community is the extent to which these archetypically 'public' functions are now being carried out by private actors.

Chapter five examines the political and legal status of Britain's intelligence services, which were only formally established by law beginning in 1989. Until that time, the legal fiction was that intelligence officers were merely 'ordinary citizens'. The passage of legislation was largely a response to challenges that stemmed from Britain's accession to the European Convention on Human Rights. Britain therefore provides a useful case study of the turn to law, but also of the danger of formalizing the activities of intelligence services if mandates are not drawn carefully, and of the limited effect legislation may have on entrenched practices. The risks are particularly evident in the belated efforts to apply privacy rights to video surveillance after some four million CCTV cameras (about one for every 14 citizens) had been installed across the country.

Chapter six turns to the manner in which the response to transnational threats has led to a reassessment of how intelligence can be shared through international organizations. During the Cold War, intelligence was a 'dirty word' within the United Nations, but international cooperation on counterterrorism and other issues now depends on reliable and timely intelligence that is normally collected by states. The topic rose in prominence following the presentation of intelligence by the United States when attempting to justify the 2003 Iraq war, but is also relevant to targeted financial sanctions and international criminal prosecutions. The use of intelligence at the multilateral level is essential to address threats that do not respect borders, but reluctance to share sensitive information creates practical barriers that discourage sharing and poses legal problems when sharing does take place.

The three cases are interesting in themselves but also suggest broad themes for effective and legitimate intelligence: the essentially public nature of the power being exercised, the need to ground that power in the rule of law, and the importance of addressing not merely the collection of intelligence but its use by the state and all those with whom the intelligence is shared. The third and final part of the book draws on these themes to map out appropriate structures of accountability, the functions that can and should be subjected to those structures, and a framework to understand the changed role of intelligence and respond to the challenges that it poses.

Chapter seven examines the most appropriate structures for ensuring the accountability of intelligence services. An important distinction must be made between control, oversight, and review, and the different roles that may be played by the executive, the legislature, and the judiciary, as well as civil society actors such as the media. Few accountability structures are established in a vacuum: indeed, a key determinant of the structures adopted in a given jurisdiction is the context in which reforms are undertaken. Change most commonly takes place after a scandal, with predictable consequences if that scandal was failure to prevent a terrorist attack, or overzealous efforts to prevent one.

Chapter eight considers whether the focus of accountability should be on the collection of intelligence or its use. Here it is important to distinguish the functions of law enforcement agencies from those of intelligence services, and to consider how the relationship between such governmental agencies should be managed. When secret intelligence would be useful in a criminal proceeding, what safeguards, if any, should be put in place to protect the rights of the accused? What safeguards should protect the sources and methods of the intelligence service? Increasingly, where such information is collected, it is unrealistic to assume that law enforcement agencies will not have access to it, regardless of any safeguards. Again, the better question appears to focus on the use of that information, with new safeguards required in a post-privacy world.

The final Chapter returns to the theme of whether and how intelligence activities can be regulated effectively, linking this to larger questions of the diminishing sphere of truly private activity and the growing coercive powers of the state. Historically, that relationship was thought of as a public/private dichotomy, marking a distinction between the political and the personal: under liberal theory the former was subject to legal regulation; the latter was not. The transformations of threats, technology, and culture described in this book show that the relationship between public and private no longer makes sense as a dichotomy and is instead best thought of as a dynamic. With the emergence of the modern state, philosophers such as Hobbes, Locke, Kant, and Rousseau posited a social contract that explained how the legitimacy of political authority derived from the consent of the governed: in essence, people give a centralized political entity coercive powers in order to make organized society possible. What we are witnessing now is the emergence of a new social contract, in which individuals give the state (and, frequently, many other actors) power over information in exchange for security and the conveniences of living in the modern world.

## 3. FREEDOM AND LIBERTY

The surveillance state described in George Orwell's dystopian novel *Nineteen Eighty-Four* was perpetuated through coercion and deception. Orwell explicitly set his novel in Britain in order to emphasize that it was not an attack on communism and fascism alone, but a warning that 'totalitarianism, *if not fought against*, could triumph anywhere.'[22] It is revealing that 'Big Brother' was, in the late twentieth century, a warning cry used by civil libertarians to deplore attacks on privacy reminiscent of Orwell's surveillance state.[23] By the first decade of the twenty-first century, however, the term was most commonly linked to a reality television programme of the same name in which housemates are continually watched by television cameras.[24] 'The innocent have nothing to fear' was once the patronizing mantra of an authoritarian state. Increasingly, a new media savvy generation appears to embrace the view that 'the fearless have nothing to hide'. The change is not confined to young people or those ignorant of security protocols. In July 2009, it was revealed that the wife of the incoming head of MI6 had posted compromising information on a Facebook account, including the location of their London flat and the whereabouts of their three adult children.[25]

[22] George Orwell, Letter to Francis A. Henson, dated 16 June 1949, reprinted in Ralph Thompson, 'In and Out of Books', *New York Times*, 31 July 1949.

[23] See, eg, Shannon E Martin, *Bits, Bytes, and Big Brother: Federal Information Control in the Technological Age* (Westport, CT: Praeger, 1995); Simon Davies, *Big Brother: Britain's Web of Surveillance and the New Technological Order* (London: Pan Books, 1996).

[24] See, eg, Toni Johnson-Woods, *Big Bother: Why Did That Reality TV Show Become Such a Phenomenon?* (Brisbane: University of Queensland Press, 2002); Jonathan Bignell, *Big Brother: Reality TV in the Twenty-First Century* (New York: Palgrave Macmillan, 2005).

[25] Jason Lewis, 'MI6 Chief Blows His Cover as Wife's Facebook Account Reveals Family Holidays, Showbiz Friends and Links to David Irving', *Mail on Sunday* (London), 5 July 2009.

Arguments over the appropriate balance between liberty and security have a long pedigree in political theory.[26] During debates on the Patriot Act, for example, a US senator invoked the words of one of the founding fathers: 'As Ben Franklin once noted, "if we surrender our liberty in the name of security, we shall have neither." '[27] In fact Franklin's words were more nuanced: 'Those who would give up *essential* Liberty, to purchase a little *temporary* Safety, deserve neither Liberty nor Safety.'[28] This volume will not be the last word on how that balance should be struck. But it is hoped that by reframing the relationship between privacy and security in the language of a social contract, mediated by a citizenry who are active participants rather than passive targets, the book offers a framework to defend freedom without sacrificing liberty.

[26] See Chapter two, section 1.2.

[27] Patrick Leahy, 'The Uniting and Strengthening America Act of 2001', *Congressional Record (Senate)* 147(134) (2001) S10365 at S10366.

[28] Benjamin Franklin, 'Pennsylvania Assembly: Reply to the Governor, November 11, 1755', in Leonard W Labaree (ed), *The Papers of Benjamin Franklin* (New Haven, CT: Yale University Press, 1963) vol 6, 242 (emphasis added). See also Michael J Woods, 'Counterintelligence and Access to Transactional Records: A Practical History of USA PATRIOT Act Section 215', *Journal of National Security Law & Policy* 1(1) (2005) 37 at 71; Bobbitt, *Terror and Consent*, 286.

# Part I

# Theory

# 1

# The Spy Who Came In from the Cold War

'The ethic of our work, as I understand it, is based on a single assumption. That is, we are never going to be aggressors.... Thus we do disagreeable things, but we are *defensive*. That, I think, is still fair. We do disagreeable things so that ordinary people here and elsewhere can sleep safely in their beds at night. Is that too romantic? Of course, we occasionally do very wicked things.' He grinned like a schoolboy. 'And in weighing up the moralities, we go in for dishonest comparisons; after all, you can't compare the ideals of one side with the methods of the other, can you now?...

'I mean, you've got to compare method with method, and ideal with ideal. I would say that since the war, our methods—ours and those of the opposition—have become much the same. I mean, you can't be less ruthless than the opposition simply because your government's *policy* is benevolent, can you now?' He laughed quietly to himself. 'That would *never* do,' he said.

John le Carré, *The Spy Who Came In from the Cold*[1]

Oleg Danilovich Kalugin first entered the United States in 1958 to study as a Fulbright Scholar at Columbia University. Posing as a journalist, he worked for Radio Moscow at the United Nations in New York, later moving to become deputy press officer at the Soviet Embassy in Washington, DC. In reality he was one of the most senior KGB officers in the country, later promoted as the youngest general in the intelligence organization's history. Today, Kalugin works with David Major, a retired FBI agent who was a counter-intelligence advisor in the Reagan White House—essentially responsible for tracking, turning, or expelling spies like Kalugin—and now runs the Centre for Counterintelligence and Security Studies. From

---

[1] John le Carré, *The Spy Who Came In from the Cold* (London: Gollancz, 1963), 23–4.

the mid-1990s, they began offering a 'SpyDrive' tour of Washington to corporate executives and government officials. Opened to the public in 2001, gawking busloads can now see the 'signal sites, dead drops, meeting places' and other attractions for about $35 a head.[2]

The fact that a KGB operative now partners with his FBI tracker is suggestive of how much intelligence has changed since the end of the Cold War. That is obviously true at the level of geopolitics, but the craft has also been transformed by business. Satellite reconnaissance, for example, used to be one of the most highly classified elements of US and Soviet intelligence; today, high quality photographs are available commercially or even free through such services as Google Earth. Similarly, the popularity of SpyDrive (recently expanded to 'SpyTrek®: Espionage Themed Excursions' in three continents) reflects longstanding interest in the world of intelligence—as well as unprecedented openness on the part of its practitioners. This Chapter examines how such changes in threats, technology, and culture have shaped the political and legal context within which intelligence services now operate.

## 1. THE RISE AND FALL OF INTELLIGENCE

Spying, as the cliché has it, is the world's second-oldest profession. Nevertheless, governments have long been profoundly ambivalent about intelligence activities during peacetime. Many of the major intelligence services now operating had the outlines of their structure and mandate defined during war. Britain's Security Service and Secret Intelligence Service, better known as MI5 and MI6, derive their popular acronyms from Military Intelligence, Sections 5 and 6 respectively. Both date back to the First World War. Government Communications Headquarters (GCHQ), rationalized the signals intelligence capacity in Britain's army and navy from the First World War, adopting its current name soon after the Second. In the United States, the CIA is the successor of the Office of Strategic Services, which coordinated espionage activities of US military services during the Second World War. The National Security Agency (NSA)

---

[2] Duncan Spencer, 'Spymasters Flog Past Exploits', *The Hill*, 10 January 2001.

was established within the Department of Defense to coordinate signals intelligence by the same services.

The Second World War also made possible the 1947 United Kingdom–USA Intelligence Agreement, known by the shorthand 'UKUSA'. The agreement forms the basis for a signals intelligence alliance that links the collection capacities of the NSA, GCHQ, and their counterparts in Australia, Canada, and New Zealand.[3] Comparable to the burden sharing by the United States and Britain in the Second World War, the 'Five Eyes' countries assumed responsibility for surveillance of different parts of the globe. They also agreed to adopt common procedures for identifying targets, collecting intelligence, and maintaining security; on this basis, they would normally share raw signals intelligence as well as end product reports and analyses.[4] Other countries later joined, but it is the five original members whose relationship is the closest—so close that it is said that 'home' and 'foreign' contributions can be difficult to distinguish.[5] Though it is only one of the codenames used, the popular name for the operation intercepting global telecommunications through this network is Echelon.[6]

## 1.1. The Cold War

While hot wars led to their creation, it was the Cold War and the threat posed by Communism that justified the expanding powers and budgets of these agencies. Their record, however, was patchy. Despite periodic claims that it won the Cold War, for example, the CIA failed to predict the break-up of the Soviet Union. Indeed, the few identifiable human intelligence

---

[3] The counterpart agencies are Australia's Defence Signals Directorate (DSD), the Communications Security Establishment Canada (CSEC), and New Zealand's Government Communications Security Bureau (GCSB).

[4] See generally Jeffrey T Richelson and Desmond Ball, *The Ties that Bind: Intelligence Cooperation Between the UKUSA Countries, the United Kingdom, the United States of America, Canada, Australia, and New Zealand* (Sydney: Allen & Unwin, 1985).

[5] Michael Herman, *Intelligence Power in Peace and War* (Cambridge: Cambridge University Press, 1996), 203.

[6] See generally Patrick Radden Keefe, *Chatter: Inside the Secret World of Global Eavesdropping* (New York: Random House, 2005); James Bamford, *The Shadow Factory: The Ultra-Secret NSA from 9/11 to the Eavesdropping on America* (New York: Doubleday, 2008).

successes during the confrontation with Moscow came from 'walk-ins'—notably Soviet and Polish agents who volunteered their services to the CIA, rather than being spotted, assessed, developed, and recruited in the manner of spy folklore. In the entire confrontation with the Soviets, the CIA never succeeded in running an agent deep inside the Kremlin, while the CIA was itself penetrated at least once with devastating effect by Aldrich Ames. *All* of its important Cuban sources appear to have been double-agents.[7]

The effectiveness of an intelligence service is notoriously difficult to judge. If the achievement is preventing an attack, there may be no evidence and no story; if the success is turning a high-level spy, there may be a tactical advantage in keeping the defection quiet. The NSA broke the codes of something like 40 countries during the Cold War and intercepted personal conversations of Soviet Premier Leonid Brezhnev, though it was understandably reticent about trumpeting these achievements.[8] The timeframe also matters: the CIA's role in overthrowing the Iranian government in 1953 and installing the Shah, or its efforts to recruit and train mujahedeen in Afghanistan to fight the Soviets in the 1980s were, in a narrow sense, operational successes.[9] Yet these successes also sowed the seeds of the Iranian revolution of 1979 and the rise of the Taliban and al Qaeda in Afghanistan in the 1990s.

Failures, by contrast, tend to be spectacular: not predicting the invasion of South Korea by North Korea in 1950; the Bay of Pigs debacle of 1961. The politicization of intelligence during the Vietnam War led to a re-examination of the deference shown to intelligence services during the Cold War, coinciding with revelations of political sabotage and criminal cover-ups in the Watergate scandal and investigations into the domestic activities of the CIA, FBI, and NSA. These investigations revealed breaches of the law and abuses of power, many of which had been documented by the CIA itself in the 'Family Jewels' report commissioned in 1973, following allegations of Agency involvement in Watergate.[10] The abuses ranged from

[7] Richard L Russell, *Sharpening Strategic Intelligence: Why the CIA Gets It Wrong and What Needs to Be Done to Get It Right* (Cambridge: Cambridge University Press, 2007), 29, 97; Tim Weiner, *Legacy of Ashes: The History of the CIA* (New York: Doubleday, 2007), xv.

[8] James Bamford, *Body of Secrets: Anatomy of the Ultra-Secret National Security Agency from the Cold War Through the Dawn of a New Century* (New York: Doubleday, 2001), 369.

[9] Weiner, *Legacy of Ashes*, 81–92, 420–2.

[10] The report was declassified in 2007. 'Family Jewels' (Internal CIA report commissioned in 1973) (Langley, VA: Central Intelligence Agency, FOIA Electronic Reading Room, 2007).

unlawful mail opening, domestic wiretapping and spying on journalists, to failed assassination plots and experiments with mind-control drugs. Senate and House committees were constituted to look into possible illegality by the intelligence services, now known by the surnames of their respective chairmen, Senator Frank Church and Congressman Otis Pike.

The 1975 Church and Pike hearings led to a transformed legal regime intended to increase accountability,[11] but also to a cultural shift. Speaking three decades later, the former head of the NSA recounted that since the mid-1970s the agency had 'played a bit back from the line so as not to get close to anything that got the agency's fingers burned in the Church–Pike era'.[12] This trend continued over the next two decades. The Iranian revolution of 1979 was both an intelligence failure and a cause of further difficulties: among other things it led to the closure of two posts in northern Iran that had been used to monitor Soviet missile tests. The Iran–Contra scandal (1986–87), in which the Reagan administration linked two illegal covert operations—using the proceeds of unauthorized missile sales to Iran to fund the Nicaraguan Contras in violation of congressional restrictions on such aid—demonstrated the difficulty of constraining a determined executive, yet at the same time reinforced the view of intelligence as something to be contained rather than exploited.

## 1.2. After the Thaw

Wariness of intelligence on the part of policymakers and reticence on the part of agencies themselves were compounded by a new era of uncertainty ushered in by the fall of the Berlin Wall and the collapse of the Soviet Union. During the 1990s, Senator Daniel Patrick Moynihan twice introduced legislation that would have abolished the CIA entirely, assigning its functions to the State Department.[13] Abandoning intelligence completely

---

[11] See Chapter eight, section 2.

[12] Hearing of the Senate Select Committee on Intelligence: Nomination of Lieutenant General Michael V Hayden, USAF, to be the Director of the Central Intelligence Agency (Washington, DC: Senate Select Committee on Intelligence, 18 May 2006).

[13] Elaine Sciolino, 'CIA Casting About for New Missions', *New York Times*, 4 February 1992; Vernon Loeb, 'Inside Information', *Washington Post*, 1 November 1999. See generally Daniel Patrick Moynihan, *Secrecy: The American Experience* (New Haven, CT: Yale University Press, 1998).

was never a realistic option, but intelligence did come to be seen as less important, less necessary, and less tolerable.

The end of the Cold War greatly reduced the threat of global conflict and saw a significant reduction in the standing armies of states. Defence budgets fell by around one-third in the 1990s. Intelligence budgets, which typically constitute around 10 per cent of a defence budget, also fell.[14] Though there was some interest in the possible use of government services in industrial or economic espionage, foreign corporations tended to be targeted for surveillance by government agencies mainly to track bribery, enforce sanctions, and monitor the proliferation of weapons of mass destruction.[15] Industrial espionage in the sense of stealing trade secrets tended to be undertaken by companies themselves, with the main response of governments directed at protecting their own companies against foreign spies.[16] There was also some movement in the direction of greater intelligence cooperation for collective security through the United Nations,[17] but the overall trajectory was towards a more modest role for intelligence.

In the same period the necessity of certain forms of intelligence was also called into question. For much of the twentieth century it was human intelligence that captured the imagination of writers and conspiracy theorists, placing spies and double agents in locations sometimes more exotic and action-packed than their real world counterparts.[18] By the beginning of the twenty-first, however, the spread of electronic communications led to increased reliance on signals intelligence. Following the report mentioned in the Introduction,[19] the European Union committed to developing secure communications based on quantum cryptography, which would theoretically be unbreakable by any surveillance system, specifically including the

[14] Derek Braddon, *Exploding the Myth? The Peace Dividend, Regions and Market Adjustment* (New York: Routledge, 2000); Douglas Jehl, 'Caution and Years of Budget Cuts Are Seen to Limit CIA', *New York Times*, 11 May 2004.

[15] James Woolsey, 'Intelligence Gathering and Democracies: The Issue of Economic and Industrial Espionage', *Foreign Press Center Briefing Transcript*, 7 March 2000.

[16] See, eg, Economic Espionage Act 1996 (US).      [17] See Chapter six.

[18] Frederick P Hitz, *The Great Game: The Myth and Reality of Espionage* (New York: Alfred A Knopf, 2004).

[19] Steve Wright, An Appraisal of the Technologies of Political Control (Brussels: European Parliament, STOA Interim Study, PE 166.499/INT.ST, 1998).

Echelon network.[20] Rumours of omnipotence were thus counterbalanced by new technical challenges: the United States eventually gave up its futile efforts to stop the export of encryption software; fibre-optic cables now required physically tapping into networks rather than just vacuuming up satellite transmissions; and the sheer volume of users and data threatened to overwhelm the NSA—indeed, its entire system crashed for three days in late January 2000.[21]

The 1990s was also the decade in which public perception turned on spies. Moves to increase the transparency of government threatened the classified budgets of intelligence services. The expansion of the Internet led to greater worries about eavesdropping and created the perfect medium through which to share paranoid obsessions. Today, a quick search can locate once highly classified information, as well as lists of suggested words for e-mail attacks designed to crash the NSA again. Though popular with paranoiacs, concerns about 'Big Brother' became mainstream with the 1998 film *Enemy of the State*, in which an everyman played by Will Smith is caught up in a murderous plot directed by the NSA. General Michael Hayden saw the film just before taking the position as director of the agency and realized that he had something of an image problem. Speaking in 2000—on-the-record, itself indicative of the change in culture—he told James Bamford that the film was inaccurate but entertaining: 'I'm not too uncomfortable with a society that makes its boogeymen secrecy and power...making secrecy and power the boogeymen of political culture, that's not a bad society.'[22] Bamford's first book on the NSA, published in 1982, led the Reagan administration to threaten prosecution for espionage if he did not return documents given to him under Freedom of Information Act requests. (The administration later backed down.) After publication of his second book in early 2001, he was invited to sign copies at the NSA's Cryptologic Museum.[23]

---

[20] See Soyoung Ho, 'EU's Quantum Leap', *Foreign Policy* 144, September 2004, 92; Alexander Sergienko, Saverio Pascazio, and Paolo Villoresi (eds), *Quantum Communication and Quantum Networking* (Berlin: Springer, 2010).

[21] Walter Pincus, 'NSA System Inoperative for Four Days; Computer Glitch Halted Data Interpretation', *Washington Post*, 30 January 2000; Keefe, *Chatter*, 109–11.

[22] Bamford, *Shadow Factory*, 31.

[23] Vernon Loeb, 'Crypto City Lifts the Drawbridge; Author Basks in Post-Cold-War Thaw', *Washington Post*, 28 April 2001.

By the turn of the century, then, many intelligence services faced existential challenges as to their purpose and their morale. Popular culture offered something of a barometer: the villains in the last two James Bond films of the 1990s were a media tycoon and an oil heiress;[24] the English novelist and former spy John le Carré's first book of the new millennium based its typically byzantine plot on the machinations of a pharmaceutical company.[25]

Despite their wartime origins, the culture of US intelligence services had become more bureaucratic than military. The quality and quantity of human intelligence had fallen; the agencies struggled to retain staff. Though hindsight easily gives the illusion of wisdom, it is difficult not to see these problems as limiting the ability of the intelligence community to do its job. In the course of 2001 the CIA trailed two al Qaeda suspects and future hijackers into the United States and then dropped the case without informing the FBI. The FBI later declined to seek a search warrant to investigate the computer files of another suspected terrorist who had been detained after suspicious behaviour at a flight training school in August. And the NSA intercepted messages between pay phones in Afghanistan and Saudi Arabia stating that 'Tomorrow is zero hour' and 'The match begins tomorrow', but it took two days before they were translated and distributed on 12 September 2001.[26]

## 2. THE RULES OF THE GAME

The Cold War demonstrated some of the consequences of failing to regulate intelligence services, as well as the practical difficulties of doing so effectively. It was also a period of experimentation in the international legal regime governing intelligence. Just as the end of the nuclear stand-off radically changed the political context for intelligence, it also raised serious questions about the legal framework that had been developed.

---

[24] *Tomorrow Never Dies* (1997); *The World Is Not Enough* (1999).

[25] John le Carré, *The Constant Gardener* (London: Hodder & Stoughton, 2001).

[26] Jane Mayer, *The Dark Side: The Inside Story of How the War on Terror Turned Into a War on American Ideals* (New York: Doubleday, 2008), 11; Bamford, *Shadow Factory*, 92. See also Chapter two, section 2.2.

Despite its relative importance in the conduct of international affairs there are few treaties that deal with intelligence directly. The academic literature on international law typically omits the subject entirely, or includes a paragraph or two defining a spy and describing his unhappy fate if captured.[27] For the most part, intelligence is dealt with explicitly only in special regimes such as the laws of war. Beyond this, it looms large but almost silent in the legal regimes dealing with diplomatic protection and arms control. Much of international law derives from custom, determined by a combination of consistent state practice and the belief that a practice is obligatory (*opinio juris*). As the vast majority of states both engage in intelligence and yet denounce similar activities by other states, the two components of custom appear to be running in opposing directions.

The scope of activities covered by the term intelligence is, of course, crucial and enables some obvious cases to be dispensed with quickly. Clearly where espionage (the running of spies or covert agents) or territorially intrusive surveillance, such as aerial incursions, rises to the level of an armed attack a target state may invoke its right of self-defence.[28] Similarly, covert action that causes property damage to the target state or harms its nationals might properly be the subject of state responsibility.[29] Some classified information might also be protected as intellectual property: certain intelligence activities might therefore breach the World Trade Organization-brokered agreement on Trade-Related Aspects of Intellectual Property Rights (TRIPS);[30] it might also conceivably be protected by the right to privacy enshrined in some human rights treaties.[31] The majority of intelligence analysis, by contrast, which relies on open source information, is legally unproblematic.

---

[27] See, eg, Richard A Falk, 'Foreword', in Roland J Stanger (ed), *Essays on Espionage and International Law* (Columbus, OH: Ohio State University Press, 1962), v.

[28] UN Charter, art 51. See Ingrid Delupis, 'Foreign Warships and Immunity for Espionage', *American Journal of International Law* 78 (1984) 53.

[29] See generally W Michael Reisman and James E Baker, *Regulating Covert Action: Practices, Contexts, and Policies of Covert Coercion Abroad in International and American Law* (New Haven, CT: Yale University Press, 1992).

[30] Agreement on Trade-Related Aspects of Intellectual Property Rights (TRIPS), 15 April 1994, WTO Agreement, Annex 1C, arts 39(2), 73.

[31] Francesca Bignami, 'Transgovernmental Networks vs Democracy: The Case of the European Information Privacy Network', *Michigan Journal of International Law* 26 (2005) 807. See also Chapter eight, section 4.

## 2.1. Wartime Treatment of Spies

Hugo Grotius, writing in the seventeenth century, observed that the sending of spies in war is 'beyond doubt permitted by the law of nations.' If any state refused to make use of spies, it was to be attributed to their loftiness of mind and confidence in acting openly, rather than to their view of what was just or unjust. In the event that any of these spies were caught, however, Grotius noted that they were usually treated 'most severely...in accordance with that impunity which the law of war accords'.[32]

This apparent contradiction—allowing one state to send spies and another state to kill them—reflects the legal limbo in which spies operate, a status closely related to the dubious honour associated with covert activities generally.[33] The brutality of the response also indicated the danger posed by espionage and the difficulty of guarding against it. Some authors thus argued that states, though they might conscript individuals to fight in a standing army, could not compel anyone to act as a spy.[34] From around the time of the US Civil War, this was supplemented by an unusual and quite literal escape clause: if caught in the act of espionage, spies were subject to grave punishments; if they managed to return to their armies before being captured, however, they were entitled to be treated as prisoners of war and were immune from the penalties meted out to spies.[35]

Spies therefore bear personal liability for their acts, but are not war criminals as such and do not engage the international responsibility of the state that sends them.[36] This highly unusual situation is compounded by a kind of statute of limitations that rewards success if the spy rejoins the

[32] Hugo Grotius, *De iure belli ac pacis libri tres* [1646], translated by Francis W Kelsey, Classics of International Law (Oxford: Clarendon Press, 1925), bk III, ch iv.

[33] Geoffrey Best, *War and Law Since 1945* (Oxford: Oxford University Press, 1994), 291.

[34] See, eg, HW Halleck, *International Law; or, Rules Regulating the Intercourse of States in Peace and War*, 1st edn (San Francisco: H Bancroft, 1861), 406.

[35] Instructions for the Government of the Armies of the United States in the Field, prepared by Francis Lieber, promulgated as General Orders No 100 by President Lincoln (Lieber Code) (Washington, DC: Adjutant Generals' Office, 24 April 1863), art 104. Cf Protocol Additional to the Geneva Conventions of 12 August 1949, and relating to the Protection of Victims of International Armed Conflicts (Additional Protocol I), 8 June 1977, art 46.

[36] Yves Sandoz, Christophe Swinarski, and Bruno Zimmerman (eds), *Commentary on the Additional Protocols of 8 June 1977 to the Geneva Conventions of 12 August 1949* (Geneva: Martinus Nijhoff, 1987), 562.

regular armed forces. Such apparent inconsistencies may be attributed to the unusual nature of the laws of war, a body of rules that exists in an uneasy tension between complicity in and irrelevance to its subject matter. It also reflects the necessary hypocrisy of states decrying the spies of their enemies while maintaining agents of their own.

## 2.2. Non-Intervention in Peacetime

The laws of war say nothing of espionage during peacetime. Espionage itself, it should be noted, is merely a subset of human intelligence: it would seem that signals intelligence (such as intercepting telecommunications) and imagery intelligence (such as aerial photography) are either accepted as ruses of war or at least not prohibited by the relevant conventions.[37]

The foundational rules of sovereignty, however, provide some guidance on what restrictions, if any, might be placed on different forms of intelligence gathering that do not rise to the level of an armed attack or violate other specific norms. The basic rule was articulated by the Permanent Court of International Justice in 1927 as follows: 'the first and foremost restriction imposed by international law upon a State is that—failing the existence of a permissive rule to the contrary—it may not exercise its power in any form in the territory of another State.'[38] The rule would clearly cover unauthorized entry into territory; it would also cover unauthorized use of territory, such as Italian claims that CIA agents abducted an Egyptian cleric in Milan in February 2003 in order to send him to Egypt for questioning regarding alleged terrorist activities, as well as the use of airspace to transfer such persons as part of a programme of 'extraordinary rendition'.[39]

A key question, therefore, is how far that territory extends. In addition to land, this includes the territorial waters of a country, which may extend up to 12 nautical miles from the coast. The UN Convention on the Law

---

[37] Cf Rules Concerning the Control of Wireless Telegraphy in Time of War and Air Warfare (1923 Hague Rules) (The Hague: Drafted by a Commission of Jurists at the Hague, December 1922–February 1923), arts 11, 27–9.

[38] *Case of the SS "Lotus" (France v Turkey) (Merits)* (Permanent Court of International Justice, 1927) PCIJ Series A, No 10, 18.

[39] See Chapter three, section 3.2; Chapter four, section 3.1.2.

of the Sea, for example, protects innocent passage through territorial waters but specifically excludes ships 'collecting information to the prejudice of the defence or security of the coastal State'.[40] On the high seas—that is, beyond the territorial waters—there is no restriction on such activities.

The Chicago Convention on International Civil Aviation affirms that every state enjoys complete and exclusive sovereignty over the airspace above its territory, understood as the land and territorial waters.[41] Though the convention deals primarily with civilian aircraft, there is a general prohibition on state aircraft flying over or landing on the territory of another state without authorization.[42] Deliberate trespass by military aircraft other than in cases of distress may, it seems, be met with the use of force without warning: when the Soviet Union shot down a US reconnaissance aircraft 20,000 metres above Soviet territory in 1960, the United States protested neither the shooting down nor the subsequent trial of the pilot.[43] When a US Navy EP-3 surveillance plane collided with a Chinese F-8 fighter jet over the South China Sea in April 2001, China claimed that such surveillance even beyond its territorial waters was a violation of the UN Convention on the Law of the Sea, which requires that a state flying over or navigating through the exclusive economic zone of a country (extending up to 200 nautical miles beyond the coastline) have 'due regard to the rights and duties of the coastal State'.[44] The distressed plane was allowed to land on Chinese territory but its crew was detained for 11 days and much of the plane was dismantled by Chinese authorities.[45] The same

[40] United Nations Convention on the Law of the Sea (UNCLOS), done at Montego Bay, 10 December 1982, in force 16 November 1994, art 19(2)(c).
[41] Convention on International Civil Aviation (Chicago Convention), done at Chicago, 7 December 1944, in force 4 April 1947, arts 1–2.      [42] Ibid, art 3.
[43] Quincy Wright, 'Legal Aspects of the U-2 Incident', *American Journal of International Law* 54 (1960) 836; Major John T Phelps, 'Aerial Intrusions by Civil and Military Aircraft in Time of Peace', *Military Law Review* 107 (1985) 255 at 291–2.
[44] UNCLOS, art 58(3). See, eg, US Seriously Violates International Law (Washington, DC: Embassy of the People's Republic of China in the United States, 15 April 2001).
[45] China demanded an apology and $1 million in reparations; the United States replied with a letter that it was 'very sorry for the incident' and a 'non-negotiable' offer of $34,567. See Margaret K Lewis, 'Note: An Analysis of State Responsibility for the Chinese-American Airplane Collision Incident', *New York University Law Review* 77 (2002) 1404; Eric Donnelly, 'The United States-China EP-3 Incident: Legality and Realpolitik', *Journal of Conflict and Security Law* 9 (2004) 25.

norms would apply to unmanned aerial vehicles, such as the two US craft that crashed in Iran during 2005.[46]

There is no prohibition, however, on spying from orbit. The Outer Space Treaty provides that 'space, including the moon and other celestial bodies, is not subject to national appropriation by claim of sovereignty, by means of use or occupation, or by any other means.'[47] Surveillance satellites are not prohibited by the treaty and no state has formally protested against their use. A problem that has emerged with new generations of aircraft such as scramjets going ever higher and faster is that there is no agreed definition of where airspace ends and outer space begins.[48]

Alternative approaches to regulating such activities have had limited success. A separate convention requires the registration of satellites and other objects launched into space. Basic information is to be deposited 'as soon as practicable' with the UN Secretary-General concerning the basic orbital parameters of the object and its 'general function'.[49] The regime provides considerable leeway for reporting on spy satellites and the information provided tends to be very general indeed: in 2009, the United States registered 29 objects, all of which were described as 'Spacecraft engaged in practical applications and uses of space technology such as weather or communications.'[50]

In 1986, the UN General Assembly adopted 15 'Principles Relating to Remote Sensing of the Earth from Outer Space', though these applied only to remote sensing 'for the purpose of improving natural resources management, land use and the protection of the environment.' Such activities are to be conducted on the basis of respect for sovereignty and in a manner

[46] Letter dated 26 October 2005 from the Chargé d'affaires a.i. of the Permanent Mission of the Islamic Republic of Iran to the United Nations addressed to the Secretary-General, UN Doc S/2005/692 (2005).

[47] Treaty on Principles Governing the Activities of States in the Exploration and Use of Outer Space, including the Moon and Other Celestial Bodies (Outer Space Treaty), done at London, Moscow, and Washington, 27 January 1967, in force 10 October 1967, art 2.

[48] See, eg, D Goedhuis, 'The Changing Legal Regime of Air and Outer Space', *International and Comparative Law Quarterly* 27 (1978) 576 at 590; Committee on the Peaceful Uses of Outer Space, Historical Summary on the Consideration of the Question on the Definition and Delimitation of Outer Space, UN Doc A/AC.105/769 (2002).

[49] Convention on Registration of Objects Launched into Outer Space, 14 January 1975, in force 15 September 1976, art 4.

[50] See Online Index of Objects Launched into Outer Space, available at <http://www.oosa.unvienna.org>.

not detrimental to the legitimate rights and interests of the state whose territory is the subject of investigation. The scope of the principles was clearly intended to exclude, among other things, surveillance and military satellites.[51] The commercial availability of satellite imagery has made at least some of these concerns moot. Though some states have occasionally expressed concerns about the prudence of making such images available, there appears to be no suggestion that either the collection or dissemination of the material is itself illegal.

Interception of electronic communications raises more complicated issues. The International Telecommunications Convention of 1973 provides, on the one hand, that members will take 'all possible measures, compatible with the system of telecommunication used, with a view to ensuring the secrecy of international correspondence.' Nevertheless, they 'reserve the right to communicate such correspondence to the competent authorities in order to ensure the application of their internal laws or the execution of international conventions to which they are parties.'[52]

## 2.3. Diplomatic and Consular Relations

Diplomacy and intelligence gathering have always gone hand in hand. The emergence of modern diplomacy in Renaissance Italy recognized the importance of having agents to serve as negotiators with foreign powers, but a chief function of the resident ambassador soon came to be ensuring the flow of a continuous stream of foreign political news to his home government.[53]

This practice is reflected in the current treaty law on diplomatic relations, which implicitly acknowledges the intelligence component of diplomacy and seeks to define some of the limits of what is acceptable. Thus the 1961 Vienna Convention on Diplomatic Relations includes among

---

[51]  GA Res 41/65 (1986), Annex.

[52]  International Telecommunication Convention, done at Malaga-Torremolinos, 25 October 1973, in force 1 January 1975, art 22.

[53]  Garrett Mattingly, *Renaissance Diplomacy* (London: Jonathan Cape, 1962), 67; Van Dinh Tran, *Communication and Diplomacy in a Changing World* (Norwood, NJ: Ablex, 1987), 89–92; Keith Hamilton and Richard Langhorne, *The Practice of Diplomacy: Its Evolution and Administration* (New York: Routledge, 1995), 217–21; Herman, *Intelligence Power*, 9–10.

the functions of a diplomatic mission 'ascertaining *by all lawful means* conditions and developments in the receiving State, and reporting thereon to the Government of the sending State.'[54] The Convention also provides for receiving state approval of military attachés, presumably in order to ascertain their intelligence function.[55] This is consistent with the relatively common practice of having identified intelligence officials in certain diplomatic missions for liaison purposes.

Other provisions are clearly intended to prevent or at least limit intelligence gathering. The receiving state may limit a mission's size and composition; its consent is required to install a wireless transmitter or establish regional offices. The freedom of movement of diplomats may be restricted for reasons of national security.[56] More generally, diplomats have a duty to respect the laws and regulations of the receiving state and not to interfere in its internal affairs. In addition, the premises of the mission are not to be used 'in any manner incompatible with the functions of the mission as laid down in the present Convention or by other rules of general international law or by any special agreements in force between the sending and the receiving State.'[57]

Regardless of their activities, the person of the diplomat, the mission's premises, and diplomatic communications are inviolable.[58] Temporary detention of diplomats accused of espionage is not uncommon, but there are no recorded cases of prosecution for espionage.[59] The traditional remedy for overstepping the explicit and implicit boundaries of diplomacy is to declare a diplomat *persona non grata*, normally prompting a swift recall of the person to the sending state.[60] Though the Vienna

---

[54] Vienna Convention on Diplomatic Relations, done at Vienna, 18 April 1961, in force 24 April 1964, art 3(d) (emphasis added).

[55] Ibid, art 7. See also Michael Hardy, *Modern Diplomatic Law* (Manchester: Manchester University Press, 1968), 28.

[56] Vienna Convention on Diplomatic Relations, arts 11, 27(1), 12, 26. See Grant V McClanahan, *Diplomatic Immunity: Principles, Practices, Problems* (New York: St Martin's Press, 1989), 163.

[57] Vienna Convention on Diplomatic Relations, art 41.      [58] Ibid, arts 22, 27, 29, 31.

[59] Paul Lewis, 'France Proposes 2 Sides Evacuate Embassy Staffs', *New York Times*, 19 July 1987; Michael R Gordon, 'Russians Briefly Detain US Diplomat, Calling Her a Spy', *New York Times*, 1 December 1999; Ian Fisher, 'In Serbia, Politics in Turmoil as US Diplomat Is Detained', *New York Times*, 16 March 2002.

[60] Vienna Convention on Diplomatic Relations, art 9(1). See generally Eileen Denza, *Diplomatic Law: A Commentary on the Vienna Convention on Diplomatic Relations* [1976], 2nd edn (Oxford: Clarendon Press, 1998), 64.

Convention does not require reasons to be given, the formula typically used by the receiving state is that a diplomat has engaged in 'activities incompatible with his or her diplomatic status.'[61] Beyond this remedy, a receiving state may have recourse to the 'more radical remedy' of breaking off diplomatic relations and calling for the immediate closure of the offending mission.[62]

The norms in place, then, both implicitly accept limited intelligence gathering as a necessary part of diplomacy and explicitly grant an absolute discretion to terminate that relationship at will. A practice has, nevertheless, emerged of states justifying their actions with reference to appropriate and inappropriate activities. The possible normative content of this practice is most evident in the cases of retaliatory expulsions (technically the naming of diplomats *persona non grata* prior to recall).[63] In early 2001, for example, following revelations of espionage by Robert Hanssen, the United States demanded that four Russian diplomats leave Washington in ten days and a further 46 alleged spies depart by 1 July 2001. The Russian government swiftly identified four US diplomats in Moscow who were required to leave within ten days and a further 46 required to exit by the same July deadline. The US diplomats appear to have been chosen at random, but pointedly excluded the CIA's Moscow station chief who would continue to serve his liaison function.[64]

Such arrangements may be extended to situations where diplomatic immunity does not apply: though the days of trading spies across Berlin's Glienicke Bridge at midnight appear to be over, foreign agents may still be expelled by the target state rather than prosecuted in order to ensure that the state's own agents will be treated similarly.[65]

[61] See, eg, Irvin Molotsky, 'US Expels Cuban Diplomat Who Is Linked to Spy Case', *New York Times*, 20 February 2000.      [62] *Tehran Hostages case (Merits)*, para 85.

[63] Delupis, 'Foreign Warships', 59; McClanahan, *Diplomatic Immunity*, 163; Denza, *Diplomatic Law*, 66.

[64] Patrick E Tyler, 'Russia's Spy Riposte: Film Catches Americans in the Act', *New York Times*, 28 March 2001. The United States did not expel the station chief of Russia's Foreign Intelligence Service (SVR) in Washington either.

[65] Steven Erlanger, 'US Will Ask Former Soviet Republic to Lift Diplomat's Immunity in Fatal Car Crash', *New York Times*, 6 January 1997.

## 2.4. Arms Control

One of the reasons for the unusual treatment of espionage in diplomatic relations is the principle of reciprocity—the recognition that what one does to another state's spies will affect the treatment of one's own agents. The underlying assumption of this arrangement is that intelligence collection is an important or at least an unavoidable component of diplomatic relations. These considerations are even more relevant to a fourth body of international law that casts light on the regulation of intelligence gathering: arms control. Arms control poses a classic prisoners' dilemma, where a key mechanism for avoiding the negative costs associated with a lack of trust is to seek information about the other party's capacity and intentions.[66] Intelligence can provide this information and arms control regimes exhibit innovative means of protecting it.

In the late 1960s and early 1970s, intelligence became essential to strategic arms limitations negotiations then underway between the United States and the Soviet Union.[67] The inability to reach agreement on a verification regime, such as on-site inspections, had for some time stalled agreement on a test ban and arms control treaties even as space-based surveillance increased access to information on the conduct of the other party. Eventual agreement depended not on a verification regime but rather on protection of that surveillance capacity. In the end, the same text was used in the two agreements concluded in Moscow in May 1972: the Anti-Ballistic Missile Treaty and the first Strategic Arms Limitation Talks (SALT I) Agreement. Both embraced the euphemism 'national technical means of verification' for the intelligence services of the two parties:

1. For the purpose of providing assurance of compliance with the provisions of this Treaty, each Party shall use national technical means of verification at its disposal in a manner consistent with generally recognized principles of international law.

---

[66] Joseph Frankel, *Contemporary International Theory and the Behavior of States* (Oxford: Oxford University Press, 1973), 93ff; John K Setear, 'Responses to Breach of a Treaty and Rationalist International Relations Theory: The Rules of Release and Remediation in the Law of Treaties and the Law of State Responsibility', *Virginia Law Review* 83 (1997) 1 at 27–32.

[67] Herman, *Intelligence Power*, 158–9.

2. Each Party undertakes not to interfere with the national technical means of verification of the other Party operating in accordance with paragraph 1 of this Article.

3. Each Party undertakes not to use deliberate concealment measures which impede verification by national technical means of compliance with the provisions of this Treaty. This obligation shall not require changes in current construction, assembly, conversion, or overhaul practices.[68]

The text effectively establishes a right to collect intelligence—at least with respect to assessing compliance with arms control obligations. Although there is no formal elaboration of such a right, the text strongly implies that such activity is or can be consistent with 'generally recognized principles of international law'. It then prohibits interference with such activities and limits concealment from them. Drawing on Wesley Newcomb Hohfeld's analytical approach to rights, this amounts to a *claim-right* (or a 'right' in the strict sense of the word) for state A to collect intelligence on state B, as state B is under a corresponding duty not to interfere with state A's actions. The situation may be contrasted with the treatment of spies in the laws of war, discussed earlier, where state A may have a *liberty* to use spies—state B is unable to demand that A refrain from using spies, but is not prevented from interfering in their activities.[69]

Subsequent US–Soviet arms control treaties tended to follow or extend the approach used in the ABM Treaty. The 1987 Intermediate-Range Nuclear Forces Treaty (INF), for example, affirmed the basic text quoted above and added a right to make six requests a year for the implementation of 'cooperative measures' to enable inspection of deployment bases for certain road-mobile missiles. These measures consisted of opening the roofs of all fixed structures and displaying the missiles on launchers in the open; this was to happen within six hours of the request and the weapons were to remain displayed in the open for a period of twelve hours,

---

[68] Anti-Ballistic Missile Systems (ABM Treaty), done at Moscow, 26 May 1972, in force 3 October 1972 (United States announced its withdrawal on 13 December 2001), art XII; SALT I Agreement, done at Moscow, 26 May 1972, in force 3 October 1972, art V.

[69] Wesley Newcomb Hohfeld, *Fundamental Legal Conceptions as Applied in Judicial Reasoning and Other Legal Essays* (New Haven, CT: Yale University Press, 1923), 27–64. Hohfeld distinguishes two separate uses of the word right: (i) a *claim-right*, which has an enforceable *duty* as its correlative, and (ii) a *privilege* (commonly renamed 'liberty' in the subsequent literature), which corresponds not to a duty but to a *no-right* (ie, the lack of a claim-right that something not be done).

presumably to enable satellite observation.[70] The 1991 Strategic Arms
Reduction Treaty (START I) required the parties to limit the use of
encryption or jamming during test flights of certain missiles.[71]

A more regulated approach was followed in the Treaty on Open
Skies, which established a regime of unarmed aerial observation flights
over the entire territory of its participants. Rather than guaranteeing non-
interference with unilateral intelligence collection, the agreement provides
for a defined quota of flights using specific airplanes and photographic
technology that must be commercially available to all states parties.
Imagery collected is made available to any other state party.[72]

The use of intelligence in the ways described here serves two functions.
In addition to being an important check on specific factual questions,
such as compliance with disarmament obligations, ensuring a regular
supply of intelligence itself may serve as a confidence-building measure.
The United States has demonstrated a willingness to use its own intelligence in this way in conflict mediation, as when Secretary of State Henry
Kissinger offered Egypt and Israel U-2 overflight imagery as a means of
guarding against surprise attack following the 1973 Yom Kippur War,[73] or
using intelligence briefings of both sides in order to avert war between
India and Pakistan over Kashmir in 1990.[74]

## 2.5. Regulating Intelligence

Intelligence, then, is touched on by a number of international legal
regimes but typically through indirection and at times with contradictory effects. In the laws of war, intelligence is allowed but so is the severe
punishment of its practitioners; the norm of non-intervention limits
the activities of one state in the territory of another but has failed to
keep pace with technological advancements that render traditional

---

[70] Intermediate-Range Nuclear Forces (INF) Treaty, done at Washington, DC, 8 December 1987, in force 1 June 1988, art XII.
[71] Strategic Arms Reduction Treaty Text (START I), done at Moscow, 31 July 1991, in force December 1994, art X.
[72] Treaty on Open Skies, done at Helsinki, 24 March 1992, in force 1 January 2002, arts I(1), II(4), III–VI, IX.
[73] Henry Kissinger, *Years of Upheaval* (Boston: Little, Brown, 1982), 828.
[74] Herman, *Intelligence Power*, 157.

territorial limits irrelevant; diplomacy has long tolerated intelligence but established guidelines for limiting its intrusion; and arms control effectively establishes a right to collect specific intelligence necessary to the success of the relevant agreement. In each case, intelligence collection is recognized as a necessary evil, something to be mitigated rather than prohibited. This is reflected in the remedies for violation of the different norms: spies in war may be punished without the state that sent them incurring responsibility; violations of the norm of non-intervention are limited to traditional conceptions of territorial sovereignty; diplomatic impropriety is addressed by the removal of the diplomatic status; interference in intelligence collection undertaken as part of an arms control regime would undermine the main intended product of that regime—trust.

Practice has very much led theory in this area and states have obviously been reluctant to establish a single regime that would impose undesirable limits on their own freedom of action. It is apparent, nonetheless, that the piecemeal and indirect approach to regulation of intelligence collection does establish some normative guidelines that add to the domestic legal constraints that are the primary source of rules for intelligence services.

The significance of these guidelines might be considered in at least two different ways. The first is that they provide a set of basic red lines that, even if unenforced, help to avoid anarchy. An analogy might be drawn with speed limits that are loosely enforced: even without policing, heavy traffic on a highway with a theoretical speed limit of 55 miles per hour may assume an actual average speed of, say, 65 miles per hour. Such 'rules of the road' might correspond to the treatment of territorial borders during the Cold War, when Soviet and US surveillance aircraft would push at the limits of what was acceptable by making slight incursions on one another's airspace—a practice subsequently legitimized and regulated more formally in the Treaty on Open Skies. It may also be a useful analogy for the manner in which diplomats have sometimes pushed the boundaries of acceptable conduct without being declared *persona non grata*.

A second way in which the guidelines might be interpreted is as providing 'rules of the game'. The metaphor of a game is appropriate not simply because it is one frequently embraced by the intelligence literature and the actors themselves,[75] but also because it suggests a kind of community that generates, adapts, and internalizes rules. The notion of spies and other intelligence actors developing their own norms has lagged far behind the traditional military conceptions of honour, chivalry, and so on because espionage was long held to be suspect in precisely these areas. As intelligence became a more common and accepted part of foreign policy—notably as it moved from being a wartime activity to one conducted in peacetime, or at least in cold as opposed to hot wars—communities of intelligence officials began to emerge.

Shared understandings of the 'rules of the game' also derive from the interaction of opposing intelligence services. This is epitomized by the practice of exchanging captured agents during the Cold War,[76] but also helps to explain the manner in which diplomats with an intelligence function are treated—in particular the expulsion of 'innocent' diplomats as a reprisal for the perceived illegitimate treatment of one's own diplomats. In addition, anecdotal evidence suggests the existence of shared sensibilities on the part of these diverse actors, if not explicitly in the form of a code of conduct then at least as a kind of professional ethic.[77]

Many of these developments were tied, however, to a period of great power rivalry. The Cold War 'game' of espionage was played by the United States and the Soviet Union in conditions of relative equilibrium with an expectation of repeat encounters: each side had a clear interest in maintaining stability and cultivating norms that would protect their own agents in the event of capture. The end of that equilibrium was destabilizing in two ways.

First, as indicated in the previous section, intelligence services to varying degrees lost their sense of purpose. Secondly, however, the emergence of asymmetric threats such as terrorism offered no doctrine comparable to balance of power or containment; there is little prospect of prisoner exchanges with al Qaeda, let alone of establishing any kind of diplomatic

---

[75] See, eg, James Rusbridger, *The Intelligence Game* (New York: New Amsterdam, 1989); Scott Ritter, *Endgame: Solving the Iraq Problem—Once and for All* (New York: Simon & Schuster, 1999); Hitz, *The Great Game*.

[76] See Craig R Whitney, *Spy Trader: Germany's Devil's Advocate and the Darkest Secrets of the Cold War* (New York: Random House, 1993).

[77] Cf Myres S McDougal, Harold D Lasswell, and W Michael Reisman, 'The Intelligence Function and World Public Order', *Temple Law Quarterly* 46 (1973) 365 at 372.

relations. This may be compared with the cautious handling of the stand-off with China over the downed surveillance plane and a subsequent incident in March 2009 involving the US ocean surveillance vessel *Impeccable*'s activities in the South China Sea.[78] Such differences may go some way towards explaining US policies such as official challenges to the applicability of the Geneva Conventions to alleged terrorists and open discussion of whether to allow US agents or their proxies to engage in torture. It is noteworthy that these policies were protested most strongly by the uniformed military—in significant part due to concerns that such decisions may impact on US servicemen and women captured in the field, who may themselves one day be termed 'unlawful combatants' and subjected to 'enhanced interrogation methods'.[79]

## 3. NEW THREATS, NEW PARADIGMS

*The Spy Who Came In from the Cold*, John le Carré's novel of Cold War espionage and betrayal, paints a bleak picture of intelligence as a question of ends rather than means. Control, the head of Britain's MI6, explains the 'ethic of our work' to Alec Leamas in the course of recruiting him to protect an important East German spy. In the film version, when Leamas realizes that he has been manipulated into condemning a good man and saving a bad one, he resigns himself to the changed moral context in more terse language: 'Before, he was evil and my enemy; now, he is evil and my friend.' After a final double-cross, however, in which his lover is killed, Leamas turns his back on a waiting colleague and allows himself to be gunned down on the eastern side of the Berlin Wall.[80]

The factors shaping intelligence collection are more complicated than the ends simply justifying the means. Throughout its modern history, intelligence collection in liberal democracies has been subject to political and legal restrictions—driven by threats, enabled by technology, but also shaped by culture. At the end of its 1975 report on plots by the CIA to

---

[78] Ann Scott Tyson, 'China Draws US Protest over Shadowing of Ships', *Washington Post*, 10 March 2009.     [79] See Chapter four, section 1.2.
[80] le Carré, *Spy Who Came In*, chs 25–6.

assassinate leaders in three continents, the Church Committee added an epilogue in which it noted that the Committee did not believe that the acts that it had examined represent 'the real American character':

The United States must not adopt the tactics of the enemy. Means are as important as ends. Crisis makes it tempting to ignore the wise restraints that make men free. But each time we do so, each time the means we use are wrong, our inner strength, the strength which makes us free, is lessened.[81]

As a result of the report, President Gerald Ford issued a ban on assassinations, later renewed by President Ronald Reagan.[82]

The recurring influences on how much power and discretion are granted to intelligence services appear to be trust and fear. Where faith in government is strong, as it was in the United States during and after the Second World War, the activities of the CIA and other actors were minimally restrained. That trust was violated, and from the mid-1970s there were greater efforts at oversight. The end of the Cold War reduced fears of conflict and further constrained the budgets and authority of the intelligence services. Following the September 11 attacks, however, fear of future attacks escalated and intelligence services were—for a time—given a free hand. Six days after the attacks, for example, President George W Bush signed an intelligence order secretly lifting the ban on assassinations.[83] Only when that fear began to dissipate and revelations of excesses and abuses by the intelligence services were widely known did the legislature and the judiciary begin to reassert their role in checking the executive.

A similar dynamic is evident at the international level. Trust is clearly a key component of any international legal regime and laid the foundation for the basic rules that applied during the Cold War. The post-September 11 terrorist threat, by contrast, was not counterbalanced by fears of any consequences for violating the law. During the proxy conflicts of the Cold

---

[81] Interim Report: Alleged Assassination Plots Involving Foreign Leaders (Church Committee Interim Report) (Washington, DC: Senate Select Committee to Study Governmental Operations with Respect to Intelligence Activities, Report 94–465, 20 November 1975), 285.

[82] Executive Order 12333: United States Intelligence Activities (Washington, DC: White House, 4 December 1981).

[83] Mayer, *Dark Side*, 41–3; Mark Mazzetti and Scott Shane, 'CIA Had Plan to Assassinate Qaeda Leaders', *New York Times*, 13 July 2009.

War international humanitarian law was, generally, respected; Soviet agents were not—or at least not routinely—tortured.[84] This respect was driven partly by considerations of humanity, but primarily by self-interest: protecting one's own soldiers and agents, as well as the norms that offered a degree of international stability. All of this was thrown into doubt when the United States suffered the deadliest terrorist attack in its history and responded by declaring a global war on terror.

[84] Noah Feldman, 'Ugly Americans', in Karen J Greenberg (ed), *The Torture Debate in America* (Cambridge: Cambridge University Press, 2006), 267 at 277. Cf *KUBARK Counter-intelligence Interrogation* (Langley, VA: Central Intelligence Agency, July 1963).

# 2

## The Exception and the Rule

The question you propose, whether circumstances do not sometimes occur, which make it a duty in officers of high trust, to assume authorities beyond the law, is easy of solution in principle, but sometimes embarrassing in practice. A strict observance of the written laws is doubtless *one* of the high duties of a good citizen, but it is not *the highest*. The laws of necessity, of self-preservation, of saving our country when in danger, are of higher obligation. To lose our country by a scrupulous adherence to written law, would be to lose the law itself, with life, liberty, property and all those who are enjoying them with us; thus absurdly sacrificing the end to the means.

Thomas Jefferson[1]

The exception is more interesting than the rule. The rule proves nothing; the exception proves everything: It confirms not only the rule but also its existence, which derives only from the exception. In the exception the power of real life breaks through the crust of a mechanism that has become torpid by repetition.

Carl Schmitt[2]

In the days after the September 11 attacks, smoke still rising from where a Boeing 757 had crashed into the Pentagon, the Bush White House was negotiating with Congress on the breadth of the authorization for a military response. Under the US Constitution, the President is Commander in Chief of the armed forces, but Congress is given the power to declare war,

---

[1] Thomas Jefferson, 'Letter from Thomas Jefferson to John B Colvin, 20 September 1810', in Paul Leicester Ford (ed), *The Works of Thomas Jefferson* (New York: GP Putnam's Sons, 1905), vol 11, 146.
[2] Carl Schmitt, *Political Theology: Four Chapters on the Concept of Sovereignty* [1922], translated by George Schwab (Cambridge, MA: MIT Press, 1985), 15.

maintain the armed forces, and regulate the taking of prisoners. On 14 September 2001, the Senate and House authorized President Bush to use 'all necessary and appropriate force against those nations, organizations, or persons he determines planned, authorized, committed, or aided the terrorist attacks', including those who harboured such organizations or persons in order to prevent future acts of terrorism. Congress had earlier resisted an effort to expand the definition of the enemy beyond those who had struck New York and Washington to include anyone whom the President deemed a terrorist. Minutes before the vote, the White House proposed inserting language that would allow the President to conduct the coming war within the territory of the United States. This, too, was resisted and the more limited language passed with only a single dissenting vote.[3]

On the same day, however, the President's lawyers sought advice from the Justice Department on doing exactly what Congress had refused to support. A week later, a 20-page memorandum essentially offered the President a blank cheque: should the President decide that the threat justified deploying the military within the United States, the memo argued, constitutional limitations on executive authority would be no more relevant than in cases of invasion or insurrection. Among other things, the President could legally set up military checkpoints, use surveillance methods 'more sophisticated than those available to law enforcement', and use military force to shoot down hijacked airliners or 'attack dwellings where terrorists were thought to be, despite risks that third parties could be killed or injured by exchanges of fire.'[4]

The memorandum and many other legal opinions drafted during the Bush administration were subsequently repudiated. But the episode highlights a longstanding debate over the extent to which a government should be constrained from acting in defence of the life of the nation. Writing to a Maryland correspondent a year after stepping down as President, Thomas Jefferson observed that the laws of necessity, of 'saving our

---

[3] Authorization for Use of Military Force Against Terrorists 2001 (US); Jane Mayer, *The Dark Side: The Inside Story of How the War on Terror Turned Into a War on American Ideals* (New York: Doubleday, 2008), 44–5.

[4] Tim Golden, 'After Terror, a Secret Rewriting of Military Law', *New York Times*, 24 October 2004; Mayer, *Dark Side*, 44–7.

country when in danger', constitute a higher obligation than strict observance of the written laws; to lose one's country by scrupulous adherence to that law would be 'absurdly sacrificing the end to the means'.[5] A century later, Carl Schmitt built a jurisprudence around the foundational question of determining who is an enemy of the state, and the ability of a sovereign to act against such an enemy without being constrained by the rule of law. The slide towards National Socialism that Schmitt legitimized suggested that there was more than one way to 'lose one's country'.

This Chapter considers the evolution of arguments over emergency powers before turning to whether the intelligence services that are tasked with evaluating threats to the countries should themselves be governed by law. It concludes with a discussion of what happens when an agent of the state nevertheless follows Jefferson's injunction and adheres to what he or she perceives to be the higher obligations of saving the country at the expense of adherence to law.

## 1. EMERGENCIES AND POWER

How should law deal with crises, epitomized by the hypothetical 'ticking time-bomb'? The scenario is exceedingly rare in real life, yet remains a staple of television shows such as *24*: a terrorist has planted a bomb that will detonate within a fixed time period and kill large numbers of people; the terrorist is apprehended but will not reveal the location of the bomb.[6] Should legal restrictions apply to the interrogation? Can the suspect be tortured? Torture is the most prominent focus of this debate, though it is far from the only example of conduct that would normally be illegal but is claimed to be justified by extraordinary circumstances. In a situation of increased threat there is understandable pressure to augment the ability of the state to gather information through surveillance and other collection techniques; where there is a perceived need to prevent an attack there may be calls to detain individuals or groups without being able to convict them

---

[5] Jefferson, 'Letter to John B Colvin'.
[6] Jane Mayer, 'Whatever It Takes: The Politics of the Man Behind "24"', *New Yorker*, 19 February 2007, 66.

of an offence under the criminal law. Not surprisingly, these questions have confronted many societies that otherwise embrace the rule of law, and challenged theorists who have sought to make sense of the tensions thus exposed.

## 1.1. In Practice

The history of what are now called emergency powers is commonly traced back to the early Roman institution of the dictatorship. During a crisis, the consuls who normally governed with coequal status could be authorized by the Senate to appoint a dictator with extraordinary powers for a period of six months. This period could not be extended and the Senate retained control of finances, but during that time the dictator had power over life and death. He was tasked with protecting against foreign attack and suppressing domestic upheaval, but could not launch offensive wars. Importantly, though his discretion was unfettered and he was immune from responsibility for his actions, the dictator was unable to make new laws. The institution lasted from the end of the sixth century BC to the end of the third century BC, with about 90 dictators being named.[7]

Though Julius Caesar's later appointment as dictator in perpetuity led to his assassination and the discrediting of the institution, the model of a regularized departure from the normal functioning of the state continues in many legal orders. The powers available tend not to be as extreme as those granted to the Roman dictator, but human rights treaties negotiated in the twentieth century generally provide for the possibility of derogating from certain obligations in times of emergency. The International Covenant on Civil and Political Rights, for example, allows a state to declare the existence of a 'public emergency which threatens the life of the nation' and to derogate from, among other things, privacy protections and limits

---

[7] Clinton Lawrence Rossiter, *Constitutional Dictatorship: Crisis Government in the Modern Democracies* [1948] (New Brunswick, NJ: Transaction Publishers, 2006), 15–28; Oren Gross and Fionnuala Ní Aoláin, *Law in Times of Crisis: Emergency Powers in Theory and Practice* (Cambridge: Cambridge University Press, 2006), 17–26. See generally Frederick M Watkins, 'The Problem of Constitutional Dictatorship', *Public Policy* 1 (1940) 324; Arthur Kaplan, *Dictatorships and 'Ultimate' Decrees in the Early Roman Republic, 501–202 BC* (New York: Revisionist Press, 1977).

on arbitrary detention. Certain rights, however, are non-derogable: notably the right to life, and the right not be subjected to torture.[8]

Provision for the declaration of a state of emergency is commonly found in a constitution. An early precursor was the French 'state of siege', which sought to extrapolate from the powers of the military commander of a fortress under siege to a political model for the state as a whole.[9] This model is now reflected in many constitutions, but the conservative aspects of the Roman dictatorship remain: the assertion of extraordinary powers is on a temporary basis intended to restore the normal order; during that period laws applicable beyond the duration of the crisis are not to be passed (in particular, there is to be no change to the constitution on the basis of which an emergency was first declared). A key difference is that the powers tend not to be invested in someone from outside government; frequently they are granted to an elected president.[10] Some constitutions establish classes of emergencies: a state of 'siege' or 'war' where the constitutional order is directly threatened by foreign aggression, serious disturbance of the domestic order, or public calamity; and a state of 'emergency' when confronting lesser threats.[11]

While the state of siege located its foundations in a constitution or basic law, the English common law tradition approached emergencies through the invocation of martial law. This complex doctrine is grounded on the common law right of the sovereign to protect its existence, with analogies sometimes drawn to an individual's right of self-defence.[12] The decline of the prerogative power and the rise of parliamentary supremacy has put greater emphasis on the legislative response to emergency, with the experience of the two World Wars shaping the modern response in Britain and many of its former colonies.[13] More recently, the incorporation of much of

---

[8] International Covenant on Civil and Political Rights (ICCPR), 16 December 1966, in force 23 March 1976, art 4.     [9] Gross and Ní Aoláin, *Law in Times of Crisis*, 26–30.

[10] John Ferejohn and Pasquale Pasquino, 'The Law of the Exception: A Typology of Emergency Powers', *International Journal of Constitutional Law* 2 (2004) 210 at 212–13.

[11] Gross and Ní Aoláin, *Law in Times of Crisis*, 41.

[12] AV Dicey, *Introduction to the Study of the Law of the Constitution* [1885], 8th edn (London: Macmillan, 1915), pt II, ch viii.

[13] BS Markesinis, 'The Royal Prerogative Revisited', *Cambridge Law Journal* 32 (1973) 287; Edward Philips, 'Drastic Solutions: A Comparative Study of Emergency Powers in the Commonwealth', *Denning Law Journal* 5 (1990) 57; Hilaire Barnett, *Constitutional & Administrative Law*, 6th edn (Oxford: Routledge-Cavendish, 2006).

the European Convention on Human Rights has brought Britain closer to the European model, with provisions for derogation from basic rights in times of public emergency—such as that declared two months after the September 11 attacks.[14]

The US Constitution is atypical in not providing for emergency powers at all, though this was not because the framers were unfamiliar with the concept. Alexander Hamilton wrote at length about the Roman dictator in the *Federalist Papers*; George Washington essentially functioned as a dictator appointed by Congress for seven years before returning to his farm. Yet by 1787, the view appeared to be that a strong and independent executive would remove the need for such an arrangement.[15] (Here lie, of course, the seeds of the debate during the Bush administration concerning the unitary executive and the opposition to restraints on the powers it might exercise.[16]) The possibility of exceptional circumstances requiring modification of normal constitutional processes is acknowledged in one provision that has been invoked only once: the power to suspend the writ of habeas corpus 'when in cases of rebellion or invasion the public safety may require it'.[17]

In the absence of explicit constitutional provisions, the most common means of invoking extraordinary powers is through legislation. Legislation has the benefits of remaining within the existing legal order, but risks pandering to public sentiment at a time of national crisis. It also begs the question of why existing legislation was insufficient to deal with the problem and whether swift legislative action with little debate is in fact the best response.[18] The inclusion of sunset clauses may limit the impact of such legislation, but these may be measured in years as opposed to the weeks or months of most constitutional provisions for emergency powers; the spectre of future attacks may be invoked to extend 'exceptional'

---

[14] See *A v the United Kingdom (Application no 3455/05)* (European Court of Human Rights, 19 February 2009). See also Kent Roach, 'Ordinary Laws for Emergencies and Democratic Derogation from Rights', in Victor V Ramraj (ed), *Emergencies and the Limits of Legality* (Cambridge: Cambridge University Press, 2008), 229.

[15] Ferejohn and Pasquino, 'Law of the Exception', 213–14.

[16] See Chapter four, section 1.2.

[17] US Constitution, art I, § 9. See Samuel Issacharoff and Richard H Pildes, 'Emergency Contexts Without Emergency Powers: The United States' Constitutional Approach to Rights During Wartime', *International Journal of Constitutional Law* 2 (2004) 296.

[18] Gross and Ní Aoláin, *Law in Times of Crisis*, 68–72.

provisions indefinitely. The Patriot Act, discussed in Chapter four, was passed soon after September 11 and raised all these concerns.

The empirical literature on the effectiveness of constitutional provisions concerning emergency powers is mixed. There is a general consensus among bodies such as the International Commission of Jurists and the International Law Association that constitutions should provide for emergencies, with the Paris Minimum Standards providing an example of a set of standards intended to govern the declaration and administration of a state of emergency that threatens the life of a nation.[19] Yet the application of emergency powers in practice is characterized by two apparently contradictory trends. On the one hand, it is striking how rarely emergency powers are invoked in established liberal democracies. From the Second World War to September 11, Britain, Germany, Italy, Spain, and the United States all dealt with terrorist threats at home and abroad through the adoption of normal legislation. At the same time, however, there are indications that the inclusion of provisions governing emergency powers can provide a rationalization for suspending rights on an ongoing basis, as it did in various Latin American countries in the 1980s.[20]

## 1.2.  In Theory

Emergency powers have also remained something of an embarrassment in legal theory. The rule of law is premised upon the consistent application of general rules; Carl Schmitt's signal and troubling contribution has been to argue that the existence of exceptions to those general rules challenges the very foundation of liberalism.[21]

The various theorists of emergency powers can be divided roughly into three camps: those who believe that the rule of law continues to apply even in an emergency; those who accept various models of accommodation through constitutional, legislative, or interpretive departures from

---

[19] Subrata Roy Chowdhury, *Rule of Law in a State of Emergency: The Paris Minimum Standards of Human Rights Norms in a State of Emergency* (London: Palgrave Macmillan, 1989).

[20] Linda Camp Keith and Steven C Poe, 'Are Constitutional State of Emergency Clauses Effective? An Empirical Exploration', *Human Rights Quarterly* 26 (2004) 1071.

[21] Schmitt, *Political Theology*, 13–14, 36–52; Michael Ignatieff, *The Lesser Evil: Political Ethics in an Age of Terror* (Princeton: Princeton University Press, 2004), 41–4.

the 'normal' application of the rule of law; and those who contend that emergencies may justify action outside of the rule of law. At a more abstract level, the first model might be thought of as monist in that the normative structures remain consistent; the second is dualist in that it provides for some regulated alternation between two distinct normative orders.[22] The third model does not fit neatly into such categories, though some of its proponents argue that in fact it implicitly embraces a monist position, attempting to distinguish themselves from the Schmittian position that is essentially nihilist.[23]

### 1.2.1. 'Business as Usual'

Arguments that emergencies do not warrant substantial departures from the rule of law are treated poorly by political commentators, sometimes derided as a 'business as usual model'[24] defended by 'doctrinaire civil libertarians'.[25] Not surprisingly, the position is defended most staunchly by judges and those steeped in the rule of law. In a case where the majority of the US Supreme Court sought to accommodate the Bush administration's detention of unlawful combatants, Justice Antonin Scalia wrote a vigorous dissent rejecting the majority view that the Constitution must bend to respond to terrorist threats: 'Whatever the general merits of the view that war silences law or modulates its voice, that view has no place in the interpretation and application of a Constitution designed precisely to confront war and, in a manner that accords with democratic principles, to accommodate it.'[26]

Many other judges and commentators have argued not only that constitutional structures should apply equally in the face of terrorist threats but that the same is true in times of war and of peace.[27] The 1866 decision of the US Supreme Court in which this was most forcefully articulated, *Ex parte Milligan*, proved extremely divisive—it was hailed by some as 'one of the bulwarks of American civil liberty'[28] and others as 'arrant hypocrisy'.[29]

---

[22] Ferejohn and Pasquino, 'Law of the Exception', 223–6.
[23] See, eg, Gross and Ní Aoláin, *Law in Times of Crisis*, 169–70.        [24] Ibid, 10.
[25] Richard A Posner, 'The Best Offense', *New Republic*, 2 September 2002, 28 at 30.
[26] *Hamdi v Rumsfeld*, 542 US 507, 578–9 (2004).
[27] *Ex parte Milligan*, 71 US (4 Wall) 2, 120–1 (1866).
[28] James G Randall, *The Civil War and Reconstruction* (Boston: DC Heath, 1937), 398.
[29] Edward S Corwin, *The President: Office and Powers* (New York: New York University Press, 1940), 165–6.

A leading political scientist at the time concluded: 'It is devoutly to be hoped that the decision of the Court may never be subjected to the strain of actual war. If, however, it should be, we may safely predict that it will necessarily be disregarded.'[30]

The fact that in actual war constitutional niceties may be disregarded is not, of course, an argument for abandoning them when facing the *threat* of war or unrest. There are many circumstances in which public officials may conclude that there are good reasons for disobeying the law, yet there are obvious benefits in establishing penalties to prevent them from acting on those conclusions.[31]

## 1.2.2. Accommodation

The second camp, those who allow for various models of accommodation, tend to trace their heritage to the Roman dictatorship that was embraced by both Niccolò Machiavelli and Jean-Jacques Rousseau. Machiavelli suggested that the dictatorship should be regarded as one of the institutions 'to which the greatness of Rome's vast empire was due';[32] Rousseau also approved of the model as embodying 'the general will' in a time of crisis, when 'it is clear that the people's first intention is that the State shall not perish'.[33] This approach is reflected in the widespread adoption of constitutional provisions for emergency powers, as well as the possibility of derogation from the obligations imposed by human rights treaties.

To the Victorian jurist AV Dicey, it was axiomatic to the rule of law that the response to emergency—martial law, in the English context—was an extension of, rather than an exception to, the rule of law. He allowed for the possibility of 'exceptional legislation' to enable the executive to respond to disorder, but also acknowledged that there may be times when 'for the

---

[30] John W Burgess, *Political Science and Comparative Constitutional Law* (Boston: Ginn, 1891), vol 1, 251.

[31] Larry Alexander and Frederick Schauer, 'On Extrajudicial Constitutional Interpretation', *Harvard Law Review* 110 (1997) 1359 at 1375. Cf Stephen Holmes, 'In Case of Emergency: Misunderstanding Tradeoffs in the War on Terror', *California Law Review* 97 (2009) 301.

[32] Niccolò Machiavelli, *The Discourses* [1531], translated by Leslie J Walker (London: Penguin, 1970), bk I, ch xxxiv.

[33] Jean-Jacques Rousseau, *The Social Contract* [1762], translated by GDH Cole (London: JM Dent, 1923), bk IV, ch vi.

sake of legality itself the rules of law must be broken'. In such circumstances, however, the rule of law was preserved by refusing to accept the *legality* of those acts and instead requiring the executive to seek protection in an Act of Indemnity that would shield individuals from liability and preserve the legal order by granting retrospective legality to the actions in question.[34]

In the United States, Bruce Ackerman has advocated the development of an 'emergency constitution' that would provide for effective short-term measures while drawing a line at permanent restrictions on civil liberties. His work stands in contrast to the expansive interpretation of presidential power asserted during the Bush administration.[35] In place of unlimited authority, Ackerman proposed temporal restrictions that balance the need for immediate reaction by the executive with the greater legitimacy of the legislature. After one or two weeks, emergency powers would require the support of a majority of Congress. After two months, this would lapse unless reauthorized by 60 per cent of Congress; two months later 70 per cent would be required, then 80 per cent for subsequent two month extensions. This arrangement is termed the 'supermajoritarian escalator' and suggests a novel approach to balancing the need for exceptional powers against the danger of regularizing an 'exceptional' state of affairs.[36]

## 1.2.3. Extra-Legal Measures

A third model for the exercise of power is that, *in extremis*, public officials may—or, in any event, *will* (and, perhaps, *should*)—go beyond the law in a crisis. The realist view was perhaps expressed most succinctly by Franklin Roosevelt's Attorney General during the Second World War. Describing in his memoirs the decision to send over 100,000 Japanese Americans to internment camps, he wrote that 'the Constitution has not greatly bothered any wartime President. That was a question of law, which ultimately the Supreme Court must decide. And meanwhile—probably a long meanwhile—we must get on with the war.'[37]

---

[34] Dicey, *Law of the Constitution*, pt II, ch xiii.     [35] See Chapter four, section 1.2.
[36] Bruce Ackerman, *Before the Next Attack: Preserving Civil Liberties in an Age of Terrorism* (New Haven, CT: Yale University Press, 2006), 80–3.
[37] Francis Biddle, *In Brief Authority* (Garden City, NY: Doubleday, 1962), 219.

Such pragmatism is difficult to locate within a coherent theory of limited public power. The second of John Locke's *Two Treatises of Government* is in many ways a powerful articulation of the rule of law, though he also allowed that it was essential that the executive retain the 'power to act according to discretion for the public good, without the prescription of the law, and sometimes even against it'. This prerogative power derives from the sovereign; the only recourse for those who would challenge the exercise of such power lies in an 'appeal to heaven' or, if the numbers are sufficiently great, the possibility of violent revolution.[38] In a similar vein, Oren Gross has advocated a model of 'extra-legal measures' under which public officials would be informed that they may act 'extra-legally' when they believe that such action 'is necessary for protecting the nation and the public in the face of calamity, provided that they openly and publicly acknowledge the nature of their actions.'[39] It is then up to 'the people' to decide whether to hold the actor responsible or, alternatively, to approve the act and thereby absolve the public official from the consequences that would normally follow.

All of this pragmatism tacks perilously close to Schmitt's legal nihilism. Giorgio Agamben, writing in 2003, sought to provide an alternative theory of the exception in public law. The central problem, he observed, is that the state of exception cannot be conceptualized as a special kind of law; 'rather, insofar as it is a suspension of the juridical order itself, it defines law's threshold or limit concept.' As indicated earlier, emergency powers are commonly traced back to the Roman dictatorship. Agamben argued, however, that the better foundation for these powers lies in the Roman practice of *iustitium*: far from the awarding of extraordinary powers circumscribed by law, *iustitium* denoted a period in which law itself was suspended, for example in the event of an invasion or after the death of the emperor if succession were unclear. 'From this perspective, the state of exception is not defined as a fullness of powers,...as in the dictatorial model, but as...an emptiness and standstill of the law.'[40]

---

[38] John Locke, *Two Treatises of Government* [1690] (Cambridge: Cambridge University Press, 1988), §§ 160, 168.

[39] Oren Gross, 'Chaos and Rules: Should Responses to Violent Crises Always be Constitutional?', *Yale Law Journal* 112 (2003) 1011 at 1023. Gross later expanded this into a book-length treatment written with Fionnuala Ní Aoláin: Gross and Ní Aoláin, *Law in Times of Crisis*, 11.

[40] Giorgio Agamben, *State of Exception* [2003], translated by Kevin Attell (Chicago: University of Chicago Press, 2005), 4, 48.

Though Agamben's history may be questionable and his analysis intentionally paradoxical,[41] framing the response to an emergency not as the
enhancement of laws but as a departure from law as such is a provocative
one. Certainly the post-September 11 response of the Bush administration—
characterized by secrecy and assertions of unlimited executive authority—
fits more closely with that model than the 'business as usual' or accommodation models. The secrecy points to limits in the effectiveness of
Gross's extra-legal measures model, which is premised on candour.[42] The
expansiveness of the powers asserted also undermines the claim that
endorsing violation of the law actually embraces a monist rather than
nihilist position. At the same time, however, Agamben offers no practical
framework for responding to future emergency scenarios beyond a vague
call for resistance.

### 1.2.4. Schmitt

Which brings us back to Schmitt. Schmitt argued that, in a time of crisis,
'the state remains, whereas law recedes'; yet he went far further in
concluding that the *possibility* of crisis—of chaos that would undermine
the very existence of legal order—demonstrated and required the bound-
lessness of political authority vested in the sovereign decision-maker.[43]
Schmitt traced his 'decisionism' back to Thomas Hobbes,[44] though its
forward trajectory was inevitably towards the *Führerstaat*—the state under
a *Führer*, as opposed to the *Rechtsstaat* under law—of Nazi Germany.[45]

Analogies with Nazism are to be undertaken with caution, but Schmitt's
separation of the fact of decision-making from the content of the decision
suggests clear parallels with two recent practitioners of expansive presidential authority in the United States. The first is Richard Nixon, interviewed by David Frost nearly three years after resigning from office.

---

[41] Vik Kanwar, 'Review Essay: Giorgio Agamben, *State of Exception*', *International Journal of Constitutional Law* 4 (2006) 567; Stephen Humphreys, 'Legalizing Lawlessness: On Giorgio Agamben's *State of Exception*', *European Journal of International Law* 17 (2006) 677.

[42] See also Chapter three.      [43] Schmitt, *Political Theology*, 12, 30–3.

[44] Ibid, 33, citing Thomas Hobbes, *Leviathan* [1651] (Cambridge: Cambridge University Press, 1991), ch xxvi.

[45] William E Scheuerman, *Carl Schmitt: The End of Law* (Lanham, MD: Rowman & Little-field, 1999), 123–6.

Pressed on his approval for plans to use wiretapping, burglaries, mail-opening, and infiltration to gain information about domestic opponents to the Vietnam War, Nixon defended an extreme view of presidential authority:

FROST:  So what in a sense, you're saying is that there are certain situations...
        where the President can decide that it's in the best interests of the nation
        or something, and do something illegal.
NIXON:  Well, when the President does it that means that it is not illegal.
FROST:  By definition.
NIXON:  Exactly. Exactly. If the President, for example, approves something
        because of the national security, or in this case because of a threat to
        internal peace and order of significant magnitude, then the President's
        decision in that instance is one that enables those who carry it out, to
        carry it out without violating a law. Otherwise they're in an impossible
        position.[46]

A generation later, President George W Bush was not quite so articulate in his self-asserted role as 'the decider',[47] but the clear direction of his administration and the lawyers who enabled it was towards a unitary executive with essentially unlimited powers to act against threats foreign and domestic.[48] This was, to say the least, an ironic approach to interpreting the constitution of a country founded on rebellion against monarchy, and whose political order defined the modern understanding of separation of powers.

## 2. LAW AND INTELLIGENCE

A central dilemma with respect to emergency powers is the question of timing. If a government asserts emergency powers on a long-term basis, the notion of emergencies as 'exceptional' becomes meaningless and the Schmittian analysis becomes more persuasive. Israel, Egypt, Greece, and

---

[46] 'Excerpts from Interview with Nixon About Domestic Effects of Indochina War', *New York Times*, 20 May 1977.
[47] Sheryl Gay Stolberg, 'The Decider', *New York Times*, 24 December 2006.
[48] See Chapter four, section 1.2.

Northern Ireland were governed for decades under emergency regimes.[49] The governments of Singapore and Malaysia continue to enjoy extraordinary powers of detention first invoked by colonial authorities in response to the Malayan emergency of 1948–60.[50] Singapore's Constitution includes provision for a proclamation of emergency, but as the Internal Security Act allows for detention without trial on an essentially indefinite basis it has never been invoked.[51]

These problems are particularly difficult when considering efforts to collect intelligence on a threat that has yet to materialize, especially when there is some evidence that the threat will be an ongoing one. Agamben has argued that the state of exception is becoming the new normal; that the emergency is becoming the rule. This erosion of the distinction between what he later describes as *auctoritas* and *potestas*— broadly, authority and power—suggests a collapse in the ability of law to constrain the executive and threatens the juridico-political system.[52]

Though his writing is often obscure, a public demonstration of Agamben's beliefs was the cancelling of planned lectures at New York University when he discovered that visitors to the United States would be fingerprinted and photographed upon entry. To Agamben, the policy epitomized the transformed 'biopolitical' relationship between the citizen and the state— for, as he noted, what is applied to foreigners soon comes to be applied to everyone—and crossed a threshold in the techniques of government surveillance and control by compromising the human body.[53] To many commentators and some colleagues, his comparison of such fingerprinting with the tattooing of inmates at concentration camps was paranoid and irresponsible.[54]

---

[49] Nomi Claire Lazar, *States of Emergency in Liberal Democracies* (Cambridge: Cambridge University Press, 2009).

[50] AJ Harding, 'Singapore', in AJ Harding and J Hatchard (eds), *Preventive Detention and Security Law: A Comparative Survey* (Dordrecht: Martinus Nijhoff, 1993), 193.

[51] See Michael Hor, 'Law and Terror: Singapore Stories and Malaysian Dilemmas', in Victor V Ramraj, Michael Hor, and Kent Roach (eds), *Global Anti-Terrorism Law and Policy* (Cambridge: Cambridge University Press, 2005), 273; Michael Hor, 'Terrorism and the Criminal Law: Singapore's Solution', *Singapore Journal of Legal Studies* [2002] 30.

[52] Agamben, *State of Exception*, 22, 86.

[53] Giorgio Agamben, 'Bodies Without Words: Against the Biopolitical Tatoo', *German Law Journal* 5 (2004) 168.    [54] Kanwar, 'Review Essay', 567–8.

Debates over the legal restrictions on intelligence gathering are not always rational. Within the United States, for example, provisions of the Patriot Act allowing scrutiny of library records inspired protests comparable to those concerning detention without trial.[55] In Britain, national identity card legislation was a major issue in the 2010 election, though there was little discussion of the country's extraordinary number of closed-circuit television (CCTV) cameras or the size of its DNA database.[56] For present purposes, it is helpful to separate routine expansion of surveillance technologies from exceptional actions, in particular to distinguish between non-intrusive surveillance that restricts privacy and intrusive interrogation or detention that affects liberty or due process protections.

The distinction between exceptional violation of liberties and ongoing restrictions of freedoms may strike some as artificial, yet it reflects the historical development of most modern intelligence services. Most tended to be regarded as extensions of the executive, they were highly secretive, and they operated on a legal foundation that was skeletal at best. Britain's Security Service (MI5), for example, operated for most of the second half of the twentieth century on the basis of a six-paragraph administrative directive that was itself classified.[57]

The United States was relatively unusual in having a legislative foundation for the FBI from 1908 and the CIA as early as 1947, though the National Security Agency (NSA) remained secret until the 1970s. The scandals of the 1960s and early 1970s led to greater legislative controls in the United States, but also appear to have had an influence on other countries, with Australia, New Zealand, and Canada all putting their domestic intelligence services on a legislative footing in the same period: the New Zealand Security Intelligence Service (NZSIS) Act was passed in 1969; the Australian Security Intelligence Organisation (ASIO) was first established by statute in 1956, but a Royal Commission led to major reforms adopted in 1979; the Canadian Security Intelligence Service (CSIS) was put on a legal footing in 1984. Following this practice but also driven by possible law suits under the European Convention on Human Rights, MI5 was formally established by law in 1989.

---

[55] See Chapter four, section 1.1.     [56] See Chapter five, section 4.
[57] See Chapter five, section 1, discussing the Maxwell-Fyfe Directive.

Such pressures were more acute in the case of domestic rather than foreign intelligence services. Britain's Secret Intelligence Service (MI6) and Government Communications Headquarters (GCHQ) were the subject of legislation in 1994. Australia's counterparts—the Australian Secret Intelligence Service (ASIS) and Defence Signals Directorate (DSD)—followed suit only in 2001. Canada and New Zealand lack discrete foreign intelligence services, but their signals intelligence agencies—Communications Security Establishment Canada (CSEC) and Government Communications Security Bureau (GCSB)—were also the subject of legislation adopted in 2001 and 2003 respectively.

Legal constraints on intelligence services tend to be cyclical. The turn to law has sometimes followed constitutional reforms as in Canada or South Africa, or a shift from military to civilian rule as in Argentina and South Korea. Occasionally change has been a result of legal challenges, as it was in Britain, the Netherlands, and Romania.[58] For the most part, however, reform has been driven by scandal: abuse of powers leads to legal constraints; failure to act leads to the expansion of authority and reduced oversight. In the United States, the excesses of the 1960s and early 1970s led to the enactment of new laws. Following the September 11 attacks, those laws were routinely blamed for preventing the agencies fulfilling their functions and used as a pretext for acting outside existing legislation. Towards the end of the Bush administration, growing public awareness of warrantless electronic surveillance, extraordinary rendition, and torture led to a reining in, once again, of the intelligence services.

As the next Chapter shows, the secrecy inherent in this sphere makes formal regulation difficult. Laws are important, but so are the culture and traditions of an agency.[59] Legislative oversight and judicial review must be a part of any accountability regime, but so must an independent media and active civil society. Chapter seven maps out some of the ways in which the need for legitimacy in the exercise of public powers can be balanced against the demands for effectiveness in protecting that public. For the moment, a key point to note is the general acceptance among liberal

[58] Ian Leigh, 'More Closely Watching the Spies: Three Decades of Experience', in Hans Born, Loch K Johnson, and Ian Leigh (eds), *Who's Watching the Spies: Establishing Intelligence Service Accountability* (Washington, DC: Potomac Books, 2005), 3.

[59] See also Chapter five, section 4.

democracies that intelligence services—like any other government functions—should, in theory, be subject to law and officials should be accountable for their actions. But what should happen to those people who, in Jefferson's words, comply with the higher obligation of preserving the state, rather than maintaining a 'scrupulous adherence' to those laws?[60]

## 3. THE LIMITS OF LAW

The Bush administration, responding to a horrendous attack on US soil, appears to have been drawn in two contradictory directions. On the one hand, there was a clear desire to respond vigorously, to do what was necessary, to work through the 'dark side' as Vice President Dick Cheney memorably termed it. At the same time, however, a series of credulity-stretching legal memoranda sought to apply a veneer of legitimacy to the actions taken.[61] How should these policy choices and the work of the lawyers be understood? What should be the response of the next administration?

President Barack Obama sought to distance his administration from many of the Bush White House policies. On his second day in office, he signed executive orders setting a deadline to close the detention camp at Guantánamo Bay, requiring the CIA to shut down other 'black site' holding facilities, and prohibiting torture by US personnel.[62] Yet he also ruled out investigation or prosecution of agents, and expressed little interest in looking into the actions of public officials and their lawyers.[63]

There is a wide literature on transitional justice, focusing on societies that emerge from periods of conflict in which atrocities have taken place. The possible avenues range from trials to truth commissions, conditional amnesties to vetting of public officials. Though the precise response must depend on local context, it is generally accepted that truth-telling in some form is rarely a mistake. A second generalization is that such processes typically follow a transition. In the wake of a civil war, foreign intervention, or radical constitutional change it may be possible to draw a line and

---

[60] Jefferson, 'Letter to John B Colvin'.     [61] See Chapter four.
[62] Scott Shane, Mark Mazzetti, and Helene Cooper, 'Obama Reverses Key Bush Security Policies', *New York Times*, 22 January 2009.     [63] See Chapter four, section 1.2.

attempt to deal with the past. This may not happen immediately: Spain began dealing with the legacy of Franco a generation after his death. It may not happen at all. If the cleavage is not so clear—if the transition is the gradual diminution in the perceived threat from terrorism, or a constitutionally orthodox change of government—there may be less incentive to confront the past openly. Avoiding such a confrontation is precisely the function served by emergency powers in many jurisdictions: they are premised on the assumption that normality can be restored; that the exception, *contra* Schmitt, can prove rather than destroy the rule.

Even in such cases, however, there may be incidents in which public officials went beyond the limits of the law. Leaving aside the question of society-wide evaluation of the politics of the period, the handling of such cases poses political as well as legal problems. Politically, how should discretion be exercised in the investigation and prosecution of individual offences? Legally, can the rule of law provide a mechanism to sanction its violation?

## 3.1. Ratification

Oren Gross calls for a pragmatic recognition that, facing a crisis, public officials may be required to act outside the law and should seek after the fact ratification of their 'extra-legal measures'.[64] One example that he cites is the use of illegal interrogation techniques—torture—by Israel's General Security Service (GSS) during the 1980s.[65] The Landau Commission concluded in 1987 that effective interrogation is impossible without the use of pressure, and that when non-violent psychological pressure does not achieve its purpose 'the exertion of a moderate measure of physical pressure cannot be avoided.' To guard against abuse or excess, it outlined a secret set of guidelines for interrogations (later revealed to include sleep deprivation, forceful shaking, and various forms of stress positions). This was said to be preferable—the 'truthful road of the rule of law'—to closing one's eyes to the practices.[66]

---

[64]  See section 1.2.3 in this Chapter.      [65]  Gross, 'Chaos and Rules', 1045.
[66]  'Commission of Inquiry into the Methods of Investigation of the GSS Regarding Hostile Terrorist Activities, October 1987 (Landau Commission)', *Israel Law Review* 23 (1989) 146 at 183–5.

The example is used to show the hypocrisy of legal systems that are aware of a pattern of conduct but unwilling to acknowledge it normatively. It is a plausible defence of Gross's position; the ambiguity embraced by the Landau Commission is suggestive of the preparedness of some societies to countenance extra-legal activity. But this account ignores the fact that in 1999 the Israeli Supreme Court struck down the procedures, specifically holding that detainees could not be tortured.[67] The President of the Court issued an unusual and eloquent coda to the judgment:

This is the destiny of a democracy—it does not see all means as acceptable, and the ways of its enemies are not always open before it. A democracy must sometimes fight with one arm tied behind her back. Even so, a democracy has the upper hand. The rule of law and individual liberties constitute an important aspect of her security stance. At the end of the day, they strengthen its spirit and this strength allows it to overcome difficulties.[68]

The Court left open the possibility that an individual might nevertheless claim a defence of necessity, but that is a legal concept in its own right quite different from the argument that such an official be given an opportunity to act outside the law in the hope that it might be changed or ignored.[69]

Gross might respond that this is precisely an example of his model working—the Court refused to provide the sort of de facto ratification embraced by the Landau Commission—but it highlights deep problems in the role he ascribes to ratification. The precise manner of ratification is presented as an open list of possibilities, ranging from bills of indemnity to re-election of a president who has run on a policy justifying selective use of torture. In the most concrete example given, the police officer who tortures a suspect in order to locate the ticking time-bomb may be sacked, prosecuted, sued, or impeached. For the model to be coherent, a formal choice *not* to pursue any of these avenues should be ratified by 'the people'. The clearest example of how this might happen is through legislation intended to immunize 'public officials from any potential civil or criminal liability', though the extraordinary case of *Little v Barreme* (in which the

---

[67] Gross makes a passing reference to the case but only to cite the difficult role of judges in a society like Israel: Gross, 'Chaos and Rules', 1122 n478.

[68] *Public Committee Against Torture v Israel*, 37.

[69] Necessity is discussed in section 3.2 in this Chapter.

captain of a US vessel was found guilty, lost an appeal to the Supreme Court, but was reimbursed by Congress for his fines and expenses with interest), is surely the exception that proves the rule.[70] In any event, this case is broadly consonant with Dicey's bill of attainder and thus would fall more squarely within a traditional rule of law analysis of accommodation.[71]

Political ratification is no more coherent. The fact that Americans voted President Bush back into office in 2004 cannot sensibly be understood as ratifying widely reported abuses of power, any more than the fact that they voted for the Democratic Party in 2006 and 2008 evinced a change of heart and desire for prosecutions. Much as a victorious political party is wont to claim a mandate, it is inconceivable that an election would be fought on issues defined clearly enough or won by a margin sufficient to warrant the conclusion that otherwise illegal conduct has been ratified.

Other possibilities such as prosecutorial discretion, recalcitrant juries, and executive pardons are dealt with in a couple of sentences.[72] Of these, discretion and pardons seem the most likely, though both are exercised by the executive branch that is also most likely to be the author of impugned conduct. Prosecutorial discretion in particular begs the question of what impact an explicit policy of encouraging vigilantism, on the basis that well-justified acts will be exonerated, would have on more general police investigative practices.

The extra-legal measures model seems to offer little illumination in the legal analysis of emergency measures. Due to the efforts to avoid Schmitt's 'dark shadow', the model's normative prescriptions can best be reconciled with the monist position that the law may be violated but the rule of law can survive the breach (in the case of discretionary decisions not to prosecute or to offer pardons), or the dualist position that accommodation through bills of indemnity can reassert the primacy of law after the fact. Politically, however, the model establishes dangerous incentives by underestimating the capacity of a constitutional order to deal with crises, and overestimating the ability and willingness of skittish publics to reign in officials in dangerous times.

---

[70]  Gross, 'Chaos and Rules', 1099, 1109–10; *Little v Barreme*, 6 US (2 Cranch) 170 (1804).
[71]  See section 1.2.2 in this Chapter. Cf Gross and Ní Aoláin, *Law in Times of Crisis*, 141.
[72]  Gross, 'Chaos and Rules', 1115; Gross and Ní Aoláin, *Law in Times of Crisis*, 137–9.

## 3.2. Necessity

An alternative argument, located squarely within the rule of law, is the defence of necessity. Rather than relying on the uncertainty of discretionary 'ratification' or legalization after the fact, a successful claim of necessity has the result that no wrong has been committed.[73] To be successful, a necessity defence must typically demonstrate that the harm sought to be avoided was greater than the harm caused, that there was no reasonable alternative to the action taken, and that the actor did not create the danger he or she sought to avoid. A key question is whether the honest belief of the accused is sufficient to justify the defence: in Gross's hypothetical scenario, it is highly likely that the decision whether to ratify torture or not would depend on whether the tortured person did in fact know where the bomb was located.

The American Law Institute has adopted a belief-based 'choice of evils' approach to the question in its Model Penal Code:

Conduct that the actor believes to be necessary to avoid a harm or evil to himself or to another is justifiable, provided that: (a) the harm or evil sought to be avoided by such conduct is greater than that sought to be prevented by the law defining the offense charged; and (b) neither the Code nor other law defining the offense provides exceptions or defenses dealing with the specific situation involved; and (c) a legislative purpose to exclude the justification claimed does not otherwise plainly appear.[74]

This definition of necessity was cited in the August 2002 memorandum prepared by the Department of Justice Office of Legal Counsel that purported to authorize torture outside the United States as 'especially relevant in the current circumstances'. Assuming the existence of al Qaeda sleeper cells plotting against the United States on a scale equal to or greater than the September 11 attacks, the memorandum argued that 'any harm that might occur during an interrogation would pale to insignificance compared to the harm avoided by preventing such an attack, which could take hundreds or thousands of lives.' Two factors were said to shape the contours of a necessity defence to torture: the degree of certainty that an

---

[73] AP Simester, 'Necessity, Torture, and the Rule of Law', in Ramraj (ed), *Emergencies*, 289 at 293–9.     [74] US Model Penal Code § 3.02.

individual has information needed to prevent an attack, and the likelihood and scale of that attack.[75]

This opportunistic reading of the prohibition of torture—ignoring,
among other things, explicit provisions in international treaties that the
prohibition on torture is non-derogable—adopts a logic similar to Schmitt:
one constructs an extraordinary situation in which a reasonable person
might countenance torture, and then extends this reasoning to assert that
the prohibition on torture is inherently qualified.[76] The flaw in this
approach is that the ticking time-bomb scenario is both highly seductive
and wildly implausible. Henry Shue's critique is dated but worth quoting
at length:

The proposed victim of our torture is not someone we suspect of planting the
device: he is the perpetrator. He is not some pitiful psychotic making one last
play for attention: he did plant the device. The wiring is not backwards, the
mechanism is not jammed: the device will destroy the city if not deactivated.
... The torture will not be conducted in the basement of some small-town jail
in the provinces by local thugs popping pills; the prime minister and chief justice
are being kept informed; and a priest and doctor are present. The victim will not
be raped or forced to eat excrement and will not collapse with a heart attack or
become deranged before talking; while avoiding irreparable damage, the anti-
septic pain will carefully be increased only up to the point at which the necessary
information is divulged, and the doctor will then immediately administer an
antibiotic and a tranquilizer.[77]

Even Shue concludes, however, that if the precise facts of the ticking bomb
scenario were satisfied, it would not be possible to deny the permissibility
of torture.[78] Yet the implausibility of the perfect scenario is precisely why
there is a rule against torture without the possibility of derogation.

For similar reasons, necessity as a defence in criminal law is circumscribed extremely narrowly. In the paradigmatic case of *R v Dudley and
Stephens*, two men were shipwrecked at sea for almost three weeks before

[75] Jay C Bybee, Memorandum for Alberto R Gonzales, Counsel to the President, Re
Standards of Conduct for Interrogation Under 18 USC §§ 2340–2340A (Washington, DC:
Department of Justice Office of the Legal Counsel, 1 August 2002), 39–41.

[76] Cf W Bradley Wendel, 'Legal Ethics and the Separation of Law and Morals', *Cornell Law
Review* 91 (2005) 67 at 82–4.

[77] Henry Shue, 'Torture', *Philosophy and Public Affairs* 7 (1978) 124 at 142.

[78] Ibid, 141.

killing and eating their cabin boy. Even so, they were convicted and sentenced to death:

It is not needful to point out the awful danger of admitting the principle which has been contended for. Who is to be the judge of this sort of necessity? By what measure is the comparative value of lives to be measured? Is it to be strength, or intellect, or what? It is plain that the principle leaves to him who is to profit by it to determine the necessity which will justify him in deliberately taking another's life to save his own. In this case the weakest, the youngest, the most unresisting, was chosen. Was it more necessary to kill him than one of the grown men? The answer must be 'No'—

> 'So spake the Fiend, and with necessity,
> The tyrant's plea, excused his devilish deeds.'

It is not suggested that in this particular case the deeds were 'devilish,' but it is quite plain that such a principle once admitted might be made the legal cloak for unbridled passion and atrocious crime. There is no safe path for judges to tread but to ascertain the law to the best of their ability and to declare it according to their judgment; and if in any case the law appears to be too severe on individuals, to leave it to the Sovereign to exercise that prerogative of mercy which the Constitution has intrusted to the hands fittest to dispense it.[79]

The sentence was duly commuted to six months' imprisonment by Queen Victoria.

## 3.3. Mitigation

A better view, then, may be not to absolve the wrong but to mitigate or even remove the penalty. This is not the same as ratifying the conduct—if prosecuted, an individual would still have a conviction entered against his or her name—but, in extraordinary circumstances, discretion may be exercised at the imposition of penalties. Such an approach has the virtue of reaffirming the legal norm and imposing at least nominal sanction, while recognizing that further punishment may serve no social purpose.

---

[79] *R v Dudley and Stephens* (1884) 14 QBD 273. See generally AWB Simpson, *Cannibalism and the Common Law: The Story of the Tragic Last Voyage of the Mignonette and the Strange Legal Proceedings to Which It Gave Rise* (Chicago: University of Chicago Press, 1984).

An analogy may be made with the legal status of euthanasia. Though legalized in a few jurisdictions, euthanasia is regarded generally as a grave challenge to the legal system. Arguments in favour of patient autonomy and the reality of medical practice must be weighed against the danger of eroding the bright-line rule that prohibits intentional killing. The ethical and religious response has been to qualify the intent component of this prohibition, relying on somewhat artificial doctrines such as double effect (an overdose of morphine is intended to relieve pain, rather than to kill) and act-omission (withholding food or hydration that leads to death is distinct from administering poison). The legal response, in a number of cases, has been to affirm the bright-line rule but impose no penalty.[80]

Obviously, as the demand for any such violation of an established norm increases, so the need for legal regulation of the 'exception' becomes more important. This seems to be occurring in the case of euthanasia, as medical advances have increased the discretion of doctors in making end-of-life decisions. In many jurisdictions, continued reliance on the possibility of a homicide charge is now seen as an inadequate legal response to the ethical challenges posed by euthanasia.[81] In relation to the various forms of criminal conduct contemplated in this discussion, there appears to be no such groundswell of support for a change in the law.

International law also provides some support for such an approach. In the *Corfu Channel* case, Britain claimed that an intervention in Albanian territorial waters was justified on the basis that nobody else was prepared to deal with the threat of mines planted in an international strait. The International Court of Justice (ICJ) rejected this argument in unequivocal terms, but held that a declaration of illegality was itself a sufficient remedy for the wrong.[82] Similarly, after Israel abducted the Nazi Adolf Eichmann from Argentina to face criminal charges for his role in the Holocaust, Argentina lodged a complaint with the UN Security Council. A resolution was adopted stating that the sovereignty of Argentina had been infringed and requesting that Israel make 'appropriate reparation'. Nevertheless, 'mindful' of the concern that Eichmann be brought to

---

[80] See, eg, *R v Cox* (1992) 12 BMLR 38; John Keown (ed), *Euthanasia Examined: Ethical, Clinical and Legal Perspectives* (Cambridge: Cambridge University Press, 1995).

[81] See Simon Chesterman, 'Last Rights: Euthanasia, the Sanctity of Life and the Law in the Netherlands and the Northern Territory of Australia', *International and Comparative Law Quarterly* 47 (1998) 362 and sources there cited.

[82] *Corfu Channel (United Kingdom v Albania) (Merits)* (1949) ICJ Rep 4, 35–6.

justice, the Council clearly implied that 'appropriate reparation' would not involve his physical return to Argentina.[83] The governments of Israel and Argentina subsequently issued a joint communiqué resolving to 'view as settled the incident which was caused in the wake of the action of citizens of Israel which violated the basic rights of the State of Argentina.'[84]

## 4. GREAT CASES AND BAD LAW

Thomas Jefferson's letter to John Colvin—in which he 'indulged freer views' only on the assurance that the missive would not get into the hands of 'newswriters'—is frequently quoted in the form excerpted at the beginning of this Chapter. Yet Jefferson concluded by answering many of his own questions:

It is incumbent on those only who accept of great charges, to risk themselves on great occasions, when the safety of the nation, or some of its very high interests are at stake. An officer is bound to obey orders; yet he would be a bad one who should do it in cases for which they were not intended, and which involved the most important consequences. The line of discrimination between cases may be difficult; but the good officer is bound to draw it at his own peril, and throw himself on the justice of his country and the rectitude of his motives.[85]

Efforts to subject public power to the rule of law define many of the political struggles of the past three centuries. In Britain it took a civil war, the beheading of one monarch, and the overthrow and exile of a second before the Bill of Rights Act was adopted in 1689. This provided, among other things, that it was 'illegal' for the sovereign to suspend or dispense with laws or to establish his own courts.[86] The monarchy remained powerful and institutions supporting the rule of law weak, however— judges were given security of tenure only in 1701; deprivation of trial by jury was one of the abuses cited in the American Declaration of Independence in 1776; bills of attainder were abolished only in 1870.[87]

---

[83] UN Doc S/4349 (1960); SC Res 138 (1960).

[84] Joint Communiqué of the Governments of Israel and Argentina, 3 August 1960, 36 ILR 59.     [85] Jefferson, 'Letter to John B Colvin'.

[86] An Act Declaring the Rights and Liberties of the Subject and Settling the Succession of the Crown (Bill of Rights Act) 1689 (England).

[87] See Simon Chesterman, 'An International Rule of Law?', *American Journal of Comparative Law* 56 (2008) 331.

The embrace of extra-legal—that is, illegal—measures by the United States in the aftermath of September 11 was widely criticized for the abuses that it justified as well as for the damage to US moral authority that it caused. It also offered other governments cover for a retreat from the rule of law. And, as the weeks became months and the months became years, the possibility that this 'new normal' would pay less regard to the rule of law was a troubling one.

An ongoing problem for those who would defend the rule of law is how to separate the response to a crisis from efforts to prevent one. This distinction becomes more important in subsequent chapters, separating extraordinary measures such as interrogation methods from the more general expansion of surveillance techniques. The former must be kept within the rule of law, but if actors go beyond that then the resolution must also support rather than undermine the rule of law. The latter will press at the limits of the rule of law and should be accommodated through legislation, with increasing attention not merely to the rules governing collection of intelligence but also to the governance of its use.[88]

Hard cases make bad law, as Oliver Wendell Holmes, Jr, famously warned a century ago. Justice Holmes' observation about hard cases seems especially apt here, but the context from which the cliché is typically lifted also bears examination. As Holmes noted, the hard cases are frequently the great ones:

Great cases like hard cases make bad law. For great cases are called great, not by reason of their real importance in shaping the law of the future, but because of some accident of immediate overwhelming interest which appeals to the feelings and distorts the judgment. These immediate interests exercise a kind of hydraulic pressure which makes what previously was clear seem doubtful, and before which even well settled principles of law will bend.[89]

How the current historical period will be viewed, what effects the war on terror will have on norms that were until very recently regarded as well settled, and what role lawyers and academics will play in shaping those norms depends very much on the consequences of the hydraulic pressure currently at work.

---

[88] See Chapter eight.
[89] *Northern Securities Company v United States*, 193 US 197, 400–1 (1904). Holmes, of course, was writing a dissent.

# 3

## Secrets and Lies

The subject of intelligence attracts attention out of proportion to its real importance. My theory is that this is because secrets are like sex. Most of us think that others get more than we do. Some of us cannot have enough of either. Both encourage fantasy. Both send the press into a feeding frenzy. All this distorts sensible discussion.

Sir Rodric Braithwaite, Chairman of the British Joint
Intelligence Committee[1]

Some time after the September 11 attacks, the Bush administration authorized a secret programme in which the National Security Agency (NSA) dramatically expanded its surveillance of telecommunications within the United States. Such interceptions were normally governed by the Foreign Intelligence Surveillance Act (FISA), under which a warrant could be issued if 'there is probable cause to believe that . . . the target of the electronic surveillance is a foreign power or an agent of a foreign power.' Warrants needed to be obtained in advance, but in some circumstances could be sought within 72 hours of beginning the intercept.[2] The law was passed in 1978 following a series of intelligence scandals; in the following years the court rejected only five of almost 20,000 requests for wiretaps and search warrants.[3] Under the new programme this check was removed in cases where the NSA suspected that one party to a phone conversation had links to a terrorist organization such as al Qaeda. The presidential authorization creating the programme remains classified and it appears that even congressional intelligence committees were only partially briefed

---

[1] Sir Rodric Braithwaite, 'Defending British Spies: The Uses and Abuses of Intelligence' (The Royal Institute of International Affairs, Chatham House, London, 5 December 2003).

[2] 50 USC § 1805(a)(3).

[3] Carol D Leonnig, 'Secret Court's Judges Were Warned About NSA Spy Data', *Washington Post*, 9 February 2006 (citing figures from 1979 to 2004).

on its scope. The number of telephone calls intercepted is estimated to have been in the millions.

In late 2004, *New York Times* reporters James Risen and Eric Lichtblau learned of the programme and prepared a potential front page story. White House officials contacted the newspaper to request that it withhold the story, arguing that it could jeopardize ongoing investigations and alert would-be terrorists that they were under scrutiny. Publication of the article—which later won a Pulitzer and other journalistic prizes—was delayed for more than a year.[4] The reasons for and the timing of the delay became a minor scandal, most prominently because of rumours (later substantiated) that the paper had been in a position to publish a version of the article prior to the 2004 presidential election in which President Bush was returned to office. In its official statements, the *Times* asserted that the decision to hold the story was based on a 'convincing national security argument' and assurances that a variety of legal checks satisfied everyone involved that the programme raised no legal questions. A year later, it had become clear that there were serious doubts within the administration concerning the legality of the programme and some sources advised them to publish.[5] The fact that one of the journalists was weeks away from releasing a book disclosing the same information was not mentioned, but clearly added an imperative to publish lest the paper be scooped by its own reporter.[6]

Secrecy is assumed to be central to the work of intelligence, but efforts to withhold information from public scrutiny are frequently due to political or cultural reasons rather than genuine operational concerns. At times, secrecy may actually undermine operational effectiveness: in the case of what later became known as the 'Terrorist Surveillance Program' (a name preferred by the White House over 'warrantless electronic surveillance'), so few working-level officers were authorized to know about its existence

    [4] James Risen and Eric Lichtblau, 'Bush Lets US Spy on Callers Without Courts', *New York Times*, 16 December 2005.

    [5] Paul Farhi, 'At the Times, a Scoop Deferred', *Washington Post*, 17 December 2005; Byron Calame, 'Behind the Eavesdropping Story, a Loud Silence', *New York Times*, 1 January 2006; Byron Calame, 'Eavesdropping and the Election: An Answer on the Question of Timing', *New York Times*, 13 August 2006.

    [6] James Risen, *State of War: The Secret History of the CIA and the Bush Administration* (New York: Free Press, 2006), 43–60.

that they were unable to make full use of any potential leads.[7] Secrecy may also be used precisely to avoid legal scrutiny. Only after the *Times* published its story did President Bush state, for the first time, that the programme was renewed 'approximately every 45 days';[8] only then did congressional leaders begin questioning the basis for such an authorization, culminating in the termination of the programme and the passage of new legislation in August 2007.[9]

This Chapter considers, first, the legitimate claims for secrecy in the activities of intelligence services before considering how an accountability regime can accommodate such concerns. It concludes with a discussion of the important but problematic role of the media. While the previous Chapter considered the desirability of limiting the activities of intelligence services, the focus here is on whether—given the challenges of secrecy— accountability is even possible.

## 1. NEED TO KNOW

It is generally agreed that at least three types of information relevant to intelligence services are sufficiently sensitive to justify measures guarding against their release. First, sources and methods need to be protected if they are to remain effective in the collection of information, and if similar sources are to be recruited or methods used in the future. Secondly, the identities and activities of a service's operational staff should be withheld so they can do their jobs and to ensure their safety. Thirdly, information provided in confidence by foreign governments or services must be closely held to avoid embarrassing the provider of the information and reducing the likelihood that information will be shared in future.[10] In reality, of course, spies and the governments they serve typically attempt to keep much more than this secret. Though the days of the very existence of an

---

[7] Eric Lichtblau and James Risen, 'US Wiretapping of Limited Value, Officials Report', *New York Times*, 10 July 2009.

[8] President's Radio Address, 17 December 2005.       [9] Protect America Act 2007 (US).

[10] Fred Schreier, 'The Need for Efficient and Legitimate Intelligence', in Hans Born and Marina Caparini (eds), *Democratic Control of Intelligence Services: Containing Rogue Elephants* (Aldershot: Ashgate, 2007), 25 at 36–7.

agency such as the NSA being secret appear to have passed, the amount of data that is classified has continued to grow.

The additional reasons for secrecy vary. Avoiding embarrassment may at times be in the national interest, but can also protect the careers of politicians and bureaucrats. In 1997, for example, a 93-page document was left on a reception desk at an annual meeting of South Pacific finance ministers in Cairns, Australia. Thinking it was one of the many background papers for the press, a journalist picked it up and when he looked at it more closely in his hotel was surprised to see 'AUSTEO' (Australian Eyes Only) on the top. Inside was an unusually blunt assessment, prepared for the Australian Treasurer, of the various countries and ministers represented at the meeting. In addition to economic analysis that grouped the countries in unflattering terms such as 'Melanesian Mayhem', 'Imprudent Micronesians', and 'Bottom of the Heap', it offered titillating details on the personal proclivities of the ministers—ranging from their level of corruption to their behaviour when drunk.[11] Recriminations followed.

In other circumstances, it may be prudent to avoid revealing how much—or how little—is known about a given situation. When the United States attempted to persuade the UN Security Council to authorize an invasion of Iraq in early 2003, Secretary of State Colin Powell presented a series of satellite images and radio intercepts to support the case for war. Within the intelligence community the presentation inspired two very different reactions. Some could not believe that such raw intelligence would be shared with, essentially, the entire world. Others expressed concern that after years of intrusive inspections and being the target of considerable US interest, this was the best information that was available.[12]

The handling of intelligence from foreign sources poses special problems, not least because the provenance of the information may not itself be available. As between allies that routinely share intelligence, the development of common protocols for the handling of signals intelligence and commitments to share virtually all such information suggest the manner in which these relationships are built on mutual trust.[13] At the same time,

---

[11] Terry Friel, 'Pacific Nations "Corrupt, Hopeless"', *The Australian* (Sydney), 19 July 1997; Lindsay Murdoch, 'Leaking Ship of State', *The Age* (Melbourne), 26 July 1997.
[12] See Chapter six.     [13] Cf the UKUSA relationship, discussed in Chapter one, section 1.

such a relationship can influence the domestic interpretation of freedom of information legislation. The effect was evident in a Canadian freedom of information case that, among other things, examined whether US practice should be a model for Canadian law in this area. That argument was rejected on the basis that Canada's reliance on the United States for much of its intelligence required it to be especially wary of loosening its information security laws:

[T]he United States' position is very different from our own. The United States is a net exporter of information and this exercise is supported by a massive intelligence gathering network. Canada, in contrast, is a net importer with far fewer resources. In these circumstances, it makes sense that Canada should have a greater concern about its allies' perception of the effectiveness of its ability to maintain the confidentiality of sensitive information.[14]

The Maher Arar case, discussed in Chapter eight, suggests the dangers of privileging an intelligence-sharing relationship over the critical assessment of the content being shared.

## 1.1. The Mosaic Theory

At a more general level, it is sometimes argued, certain individual pieces of information might not be sensitive, but when combined with other data may take on added significance. This 'mosaic' or compilation theory describes what many intelligence services do when putting together disparate sources to form an assessment, but as a rationale for secrecy it can justify keeping almost anything classified. It was first used in 1972 to explain a court's deference to the executive in stopping publication of a memoir by a former CIA employee:

There is a practical reason for avoidance of judicial review of secrecy classifications. The significance of one item of information may frequently depend upon knowledge of many other items of information. What may seem trivial to the uninformed, may appear of great moment to one who has a broad view of the scene and may put the questioned item of information in its proper context. The courts, of course, are ill-equipped to become sufficiently steeped in foreign

---

[14] *Ruby v Canada (Solicitor General)* (1996) 136 DLR (4th) 74, 96.

intelligence matters to serve effectively in the review of secrecy classifications in that area.[15]

The mosaic theory remains controversial because it may be employed arbitrarily or opportunistically. In the years following September 11, for example, it was used to reject Freedom of Information Act (FOIA) requests to obtain the names and location of about 700 people who had been detained after the attacks, and to exclude the public and the press from deportation hearings. In refusing to release the names of detainees, the DC Circuit Court stated, almost two years after the attacks, that releasing the names of those being held might 'give terrorist organizations a composite picture of the government investigation'.[16] In an amicus brief, the *Washington Post* had argued that this offered too much latitude to the government, and attributed to al Qaeda either extraordinary cunning, if it could garner crucial information merely from the names of detainees—or extraordinary incompetence, if it did not even know when significant people had been caught.[17] As another Circuit Court held when rejecting a similar argument, 'there seems to be no limit to the Government's argument. The Government could use its "mosaic intelligence" argument as a justification to close any public hearing completely and categorically, including criminal proceedings. The Government could operate in virtual secrecy in all matters dealing, even remotely, with "national security".'[18]

The expansive interpretation of the mosaic theory was part of a broader shift following the attacks. Under the Clinton administration, the Attorney General had announced in 1993 that responses to FOIA requests would begin with a presumption of disclosure; exemptions would be claimed only where an agency 'reasonably foresees that disclosure would be harmful to an interest protected by that exemption'.[19] In October 2001, Attorney General John Ashcroft reversed this onus, stating that the Department of Justice would defend agency decisions to withhold information 'unless

[15] *United States v Marchetti*, 466 F.2d 1309, 1318 (4th Cir, 1972).

[16] *Center for National Security Studies v US Department of Justice*, 331 F.3d 918 (DC Cir, 2003), para 38.

[17] Brief for Amicus Curiae the Washington Post et al (Washington, DC: US Court of Appeals for the District of Columbia Circuit, Nos 02–5254 & 02–5300, 2002), 24.

[18] *Detroit Free Press v Ashcroft*, 303 F.3d 681 (6th Cir, 2002), para 137.

[19] 'Attorney General Reno's FOIA Memorandum', *FOIA Update* XIV(3) (1993) 3.

they lack a sound legal basis'.[20] The result was the removal of thousands of documents from government Web sites and the classification of millions more. Though some of this secrecy may have been justified by the heightened fear of terrorist attacks, it was consistent with a broader resistance to public scrutiny that characterized much of the Bush administration.[21]

## 1.2. State Secrets

One tool that came to be used in the face of judicial scrutiny in particular was the state secrets privilege. With its origins in English common law privileges, the doctrine was officially recognized by the US Supreme Court in 1953. That case concerned efforts by the widows of three civilians killed in an Air Force crash to get accident reports on the incident. The government argued that the release of such details would threaten national security by revealing the B-29 Superfortress bomber's classified onboard equipment. Though the Court noted that the claim of privilege should not be 'lightly accepted', it nevertheless gave great deference to the government's position: if there were a reasonable danger that such reports would contain references to the secret electronic equipment, the requests for their release could be rejected. If successfully invoked, the privilege may exclude evidence or, if this goes to the heart of the case, effectively vitiate the suit or lead to its dismissal. A central difficulty is that a court must make such a determination 'without forcing a disclosure of the very thing the privilege is designed to protect'.[22]

The problems associated with such a doctrine can be shown in the subsequent history of the 1953 case. The widows' claims were settled for a cash payment, but declassification of the accident reports in 2000 did not appear to reveal any secret information—merely that the crash had been

---

[20] John Ashcroft, 'Memorandum for Heads of all Federal Departments and Agencies', *FOIA Post* 19 (2001).

[21] Geoffrey R Stone, *Perilous Times: Free Speech in Wartime from the Sedition Act of 1798 to the War on Terrorism* (New York: WW Norton, 2004), 557; David E Pozen, 'The Mosaic Theory, National Security, and the Freedom of Information Act', *Yale Law Journal* 115 (2005) 628 at 648.

[22] *United States v Reynolds*, 345 US 1, 8–11 (1953). See generally Carrie Newton Lyons, 'The State Secrets Privilege: Expanding Its Scope Through Government Misuse', *Lewis & Clark Law Review* 11 (2007) 99; Robert M Chesney, 'State Secrets and the Limits of National Security Litigation', *George Washington Law Review* 75 (2007) 1249.

caused by a fire in one engine. The daughter of one of the widows (now deceased) brought an action alleging that the misuse of classification amounted to fraud on the court. This was dismissed on the basis that 'there was no fraud because the documents, read in their historical context, could have revealed secret information about the equipment.'[23]

Though the doctrine had been used by previous administrations, it enabled the Bush administration to dismiss various lawsuits arising from post-September 11 actions, including lawsuits brought by Khaled el-Masri, a German citizen whom the CIA kidnapped and interrogated for several months on the basis of mistaken identity,[24] and Maher Arar, a Canadian citizen who was detained at JFK airport in New York and sent to Syria where he was tortured.[25]

Six months after Barack Obama took office, revelations were still emerging of programmes that had never been fully reported to Congress. President Obama did restore the FOIA presumption in favour of disclosure, yet those who believed that the new administration would abandon the secrecy of the previous administration completely were disappointed when the state secrets privilege continued to be invoked in controversial cases. In other areas, secrecy continued to be the default position. President Obama threatened to veto an intelligence authorization bill in 2009 if it allowed leaders of the intelligence committees to brief all committee members on covert actions instead of limiting such briefings to the so-called 'Gang of Eight'—the Democratic and Republican leaders of both houses and the two intelligence committees—as under existing law.[26] In June 2009, lawyers for the Obama administration opposed the release of statements by former Vice President Dick Cheney to a special prosecutor. If Cheney's remarks were published, it was argued, a future vice president might refuse to provide candid information during a criminal probe because of fears 'that it's going to get on "The Daily Show"' or be used as a political weapon.[27]

---

[23] *Herring v United States*, 424 F.3d 384, 389 (3rd Cir, 2005).
[24] *El-Masri v Tenet*, 479 F.3d 296 (4th Cir, 2007). See Chapter seven.
[25] *Arar v Ashcroft*, 532 F.3d 157 (2nd Cir, 2008). See Chapter eight.
[26] Scott Shane, 'CIA Reviewing Its Process for Briefing Congress', *New York Times*, 9 July 2009.
[27] R Jeffrey Smith, 'Judge Questions Justice Dept Effort to Keep Cheney Remarks Secret', *Washington Post*, 19 June 2009.

A policy change announced in late 2009 suggested that the bar to invoking the privilege may be raised, however. Instead of requiring only that an official determine that the disclosure of information would be harmful, it would require that an agency convince the Attorney General that disclosure would cause significant harm to 'national defence or foreign relations'.[28] An indication of change could also be seen in a new openness with respect to the funding of the 200,000 person US intelligence community, with the Director of National Intelligence disclosing that the annual budget combining civilian and military intelligence was $75 billion.[29] The budget had previously been revealed only accidentally, including when a House Appropriations Defense Subcommittee inadvertently published them in the unclassified record of its 1994 hearings, a few months after Congress had voted to keep the figures secret.[30]

## 1.3. Leaks

Public outrage may also follow the failure to protect sensitive information. In October 2007, the British tax authority lost two discs containing the personal details of 25 million Britons—almost half the population—when they were sent between offices as unrecorded internal mail. The weakly encrypted data included names, addresses, dates of birth, National Insurance numbers, and bank account details. The Chairman of Her Majesty's Revenue and Customs resigned over the scandal.[31] At the time there was speculation that the loss, which was a violation of Britain's Data Protection Act, would increase the difficulty of moves towards a national identity card system, which had been planned to extend to the entire population by 2012.[32]

---

[28] Carrie Johnson, 'Obama to Set Higher Bar For Keeping State Secrets', *Washington Post*, 23 September 2009.

[29] Walter Pincus, 'DNI Cites $75 Billion Intelligence Tab', *Washington Post*, 17 September 2009.

[30] Tim Weiner, '$28 Billion Spying Budget Is Made Public by Mistake', *New York Times*, 5 November 1994.

[31] Deborah Summers, 'Personal Details of Every Child in UK Lost by Revenue & Customs', *Guardian* (London), 20 November 2007.

[32] Identity Cards Act 2006 (UK). See Chapter five, section 4.

Secrecy may also be compromised for strategic purposes, or for more venal reasons. In March 2000, a laptop with classified material was stolen from an MI5 agent at London's Paddington Station when he put it down to purchase a ticket. A few weeks later, it was revealed that the day before the MI5 laptop was taken, an MI6 agent had lost another computer after drinking too much in a tapas bar.[33] Though little of value was said to have been compromised, there was some speculation that the story about MI6 had been leaked by MI5 due to unhappiness at the negative press it had been receiving. In the United States, CIA agent Valerie Plame Wilson's identity was leaked as part of a campaign to punish her husband for undermining the Bush administration's case for war in Iraq.[34]

Leaks of this form are common in intelligence. Indeed, they may sometimes take the form of a government programme to advance a particular agenda. In early 2002, for example, it was reported that the Pentagon was establishing an Office of Strategic Influence (OSI) in order to bolster support for the United States in foreign countries. As described by the *New York Times*, its mandate included providing 'news items, possibly even false ones, to foreign media organizations as part of a new effort to influence public sentiment and policy makers in both friendly and unfriendly countries.'[35] As commentators agonized over the choice of 'Orwellian' or 'Kafkaesque' as their preferred literary allusion, the OSI was shut down a week after its existence had become public.[36] Satirists speculated that employees might continue to turn up for work even though the office was 'closed'; in fact an Office for Support to Public Diplomacy was later created and then shut down (again) three months after the Obama administration took office amid criticism that it had violated Pentagon guidelines for 'accuracy and transparency'.[37]

---

[33] Kate Watson-Smyth, 'Another Secret Service Laptop Goes Missing as MI6 Agent Has a Drink Too Many in a Tapas Bar', *Independent* (London), 28 March 2000.

[34] Valerie Plame Wilson, *Fair Game: My Life as a Spy, My Betrayal by the White House* (New York: Simon & Schuster, 2007).

[35] James Dao and Eric Schmitt, 'Hearts and Minds: Pentagon Readies Efforts to Sway Sentiment Abroad', *New York Times*, 19 February 2002.

[36] James Der Derian, The Rise and Fall of the Office of Strategic Influence, (Info Tech War Peace, posted 5 December 2005), available at <http://www.watsoninstitute.org/infopeace/911/index.cfm?id=9>.

[37] Thom Shanker, 'Pentagon Closes Office Accused of Issuing Propaganda Under Bush', *New York Times*, 16 April 2009.

## 2. BARRIERS TO EFFECTIVE ACCOUNTABILITY

Secrecy naturally makes accountability difficult, but it is helpful to distinguish discrete ways in which it does so. In this way, it should be possible to explore precautionary measures that can safeguard necessary secrecy without compromising the broader purposes of guarding against abuses or excesses of power. In addition to punishing misdeeds, however, greater accountability can be used to encourage more effective and efficient collection and use of intelligence, a point discussed in more detail in Chapter seven.

### 2.1. Cover-Ups

Most obviously, secrecy can be used as a means of avoiding criticism or facilitating a cover-up. The destruction in 2005 of 92 videotapes of interrogations conducted by the CIA, for example, was an effort to avoid legal and political scrutiny of the harsh methods that had been used. A criminal investigation was launched into the decision to destroy the tapes, but the prospects of holding individual interrogators or those who designed the policies accountable was significantly diminished.

There are few incentives that would encourage complete openness by intelligence services, but when they engage in conduct of questionable legality there is a clear interest in remaining silent.[38] As the CIA discovered during the Cold War, silence can also enhance one's image if it encourages positive speculation about unseen triumphs: a former station chief once observed that, at the height of its powers, the CIA had a great reputation and a terrible record.[39]

Such incentives apply to individuals and agencies but also to countries. The damage to a nation that admits that it tortures may be more lasting than the harm that torture is intended to avert. Revelations of abuse of detainees in Abu Ghraib, Guantánamo Bay, and secret CIA detention

---

[38] Cf the reliance of Oren Gross's extra-legal measures model on 'candour', discussed in Chapter two, section 1.2.3.

[39] Tim Weiner, *Legacy of Ashes: The History of the CIA* (New York: Doubleday, 2007), 55.

facilities severely undermined the moral standing of the United States. Assertions that interrogations had enabled authorities to avert terror plots were difficult to substantiate and often appeared intended to deflect criticism, particularly when the 'plots' were years old and had never gone beyond the planning stages.

Once embraced, however, a culture of tolerating secrecy in pushing the limits of law can be difficult to contain. As the Church Committee found in the 1970s—part of the process that led to the adoption of FISA—the doctrine of 'plausible deniability' was developed in order to avoid attribution of illegal conduct to the United States for covert operations. Evidence before the Committee, however, clearly demonstrated that the concept, initially intended to protect the United States and its operatives from the consequences of disclosures, soon expanded to shield decisions of the President and his senior staff from public view.[40]

## 2.2. Clearance

Understanding the incentives that encourage secrecy suggests the importance of independent or external structures to oversee and review the activities of intelligence actors, though this runs into a second set of barriers to accountability: those outside a given agency or below a certain clearance level may not, as a matter of law, be allowed access to information necessary to conduct an investigation.

To be sure, such measures are sometimes invoked capriciously. Investigations of the Terrorist Surveillance Program, for example, were stopped in their tracks when the Bush administration denied security clearances to personnel from the Justice Department's Office of Professional Responsibility seeking to investigate the conduct of NSA lawyers who had approved the programme.[41] There are, of course, legitimate circumstances

---

[40] Interim Report: Alleged Assassination Plots Involving Foreign Leaders (Church Committee Interim Report) (Washington, DC: Senate Select Committee to Study Governmental Operations with Respect to Intelligence Activities, Report 94–465, 20 November 1975), 11.

[41] Scott Shane, 'With Access Denied, Justice Dept Drops Spying Investigation', *New York Times*, 11 May 2006; Richard K Betts, *Enemies of Intelligence: Knowledge and Power in American National Security* (New York: Columbia University Press, 2007), 175.

in which it is inadvisable to allow persons inexperienced with intelligence access to highly sensitive material. This has posed difficulties for judges when they are limited in their ability even to examine the basis on which information is being withheld from them.

One solution would be to reduce the amount of classified material. As indicated earlier, that does not appear to be the direction in which the United States, Britain, or most other democracies seem to be heading. An alternative would be to provide clearances for independent personnel. This suggests the third challenge to effective accountability: regulatory capture.

## 2.3. Regulatory Capture

Regulatory capture denotes the process by which a government entity intended to act in the public interest ends up acting in favour of the special interests it is intended to regulate. The theory was developed primarily by economists, suspicious of the notion that political actors would act in the 'public interest' rather than having more narrow, self-interested goals, such as job retention or re-election, self-gratification from the exercise of power, or perhaps the prospect of personal wealth after leaving office.[42] In the context of intelligence oversight, there may be reasons to suspect the economic motives of political actors in relation to some aspects of outsourcing.[43] Yet the main concerns relate to an oversight body identifying too closely with the objectives and problems of an agency, thereby losing its independence and ability to carry out its purpose effectively.[44]

Secrecy can work against accountability here also, as capture may occur when the provision of classified material encourages a regulator to see him- or herself as part of the power structure rather than as an external critic. A related problem is the credulity of some officials inexperienced in

---

[42] See, eg, Michael E Levine and Jennifer L Forrence, 'Regulatory Capture, Public Interest, and the Public Agenda: Toward a Synthesis', *Journal of Law, Economics, and Organization* 6 (1990) 167; Jean-Jacques Laffont and Jean Tirole, 'The Politics of Government Decision-Making: A Theory of Regulatory Capture', *Quarterly Journal of Economics* 106 (1991) 1089.

[43] See Chapter four.

[44] Marina Caparini, 'Controlling and Overseeing Intelligence Services in Democratic States', in Born and Caparini (eds), *Democratic Control of Intelligence Services*, 3 at 14.

the handling of intelligence: there is a tendency to confuse a stamp that says 'secret' (meaning it would be damaging to the national interest if the document were released) with a stamp meaning 'true'.

Agencies understand and sometimes manipulate these tendencies. The Terrorist Surveillance Program was authorized through a series of 45-day extensions: officials later said that each of these extensions was supported by classified threat assessments written in order to justify its continuation and known internally as the 'scary memos'.[45] A different problem is that legislators may lack the technical competence to exercise effective oversight of some activities. Speaking of the Terrorist Surveillance Program, Rush Holt, Chair of the House Permanent Select Committee on Intelligence, observed that few lawmakers were in a position to challenge assertions by the NSA: 'The people making the policy don't understand the technicalities.'[46] This can make it impossible to know what questions to ask to ensure that intelligence services are operating within their mandate.

Secrecy, then, presents real barriers to effective accountability. It may facilitate cover-ups, block investigators, or transform overseers into defenders. Chapter seven considers structural best practices in response to these and other problems, but for present purposes it is sufficient to note that there are good reasons to be wary of any structure that relies entirely on government actors. This insight is consistent with experience as most intelligence scandals—and, indeed, much intelligence reform—have been revealed and driven not by judges or legislatures but by the media.

## 3. THE FOURTH ESTATE

Meaningful accountability of intelligence services depends on a level of public debate that may be opposed by the actors in question, proscribed by official secrets acts, and constrained by the interests of elected officials. Given the difficulties of ensuring accountability through routine oversight

---

[45] Lichtblau and Risen, 'US Wiretapping of Limited Value'.
[46] James Risen and Eric Lichtblau, 'E-mail Surveillance Renews Concerns in Congress', *New York Times*, 16 June 2009.

and review, significant responsibility devolves upon the media to bring scandals to light. Such scandals may prompt investigations by organs of the state, sometimes including criminal investigations; they may also serve as a catalyst for changes in the law. Accountability in this form is opportunistic—in a metaphor discussed further in Chapter seven it corresponds to the 'fire-alarm', as opposed to the 'police-patrol', model of accountability[47]—and it relies on the quality and independence of newspapers and, to a lesser extent, other media. But it is better than nothing.

Despite the secrecy of the Bush administration, for example, much of the US 'war on terror' intelligence agenda was debated publicly, though this tended to be the result of investigative journalism or disclosures in legal action on behalf of affected individuals. There was little evidence of a willingness on the part of the executive to have arguments over legality. On the contrary, questionable conduct was asserted—at times improbably—to fall within the law. The most troubling conduct was simply denied.

## 3.1. Torture

In the case of torture, for example, the Bush administration maintained the official position that it neither used nor condoned torture. Beginning in 2001, however, it authorized interrogation techniques widely regarded as torture—at least as defined by its own Department of State in annual human rights reports on the practice of other countries.[48] The United States is a party to the Convention Against Torture and torture is prohibited under US law whether it occurs within the jurisdiction of the United States or not.[49] Nevertheless, in August 2002 the Department of Justice Office of Legal Counsel prepared a memorandum on the standards of conduct permitted under the US law implementing the Convention Against Torture. Among other things, this memorandum adopted an exceptionally narrow definition of torture, which was limited to physical pain 'equivalent in intensity to the pain accompanying serious physical

---

[47] See Chapter seven, section 1.2.

[48] Descriptions of Techniques Allegedly Authorized by the CIA (New York: Human Rights Watch, 21 November 2005).     [49] 18 USC §§ 2340, 2340A.

injury, such as organ failure, impairment of bodily function, or even death', or mental suffering that results in 'significant psychological harm of significant duration, eg, lasting for months or even years'.[50] The memorandum was one of a series of legal manoeuvres adopted in the context of the war on terror that included, among other things, attempts to limit application of the Geneva Conventions.[51]

None of this analysis was intended to be made public. Following a seminal article in the *Washington Post* in December 2002, growing allegations of mistreatment by US officials were harder to ignore,[52] but it was only after photographic evidence of abuse was leaked from the Abu Ghraib prison in April 2004 that the issue came to be publicly debated. Even then, most of the discussion was driven by the response to unauthorized leaks of information, including the August 2002 memorandum and other documents.

The legal position of the August 2002 memorandum was repudiated by the United States on 30 December 2004, though no definition of torture was provided in its place. Among other contradictory signals, the Bush administration later opposed efforts led by Senator John McCain to strengthen the legal prohibition of torture. A particular controversy continued on the question of 'waterboarding'—a technique whereby a detainee is bound to a board slanted at a decline, cellophane is placed over the face, and water is then poured to cause a physiological response similar to drowning. In March 2005, Porter Goss, then Director of the CIA, described waterboarding as a 'professional interrogation technique'.[53] In October 2006, Vice President Dick Cheney appeared to agree with the use of waterboarding, specifically for Khalid Sheikh Mohammed, concurring with the statement that a 'dunk in water' for such an individual is a 'no-brainer' if it saves American lives. White House Press Secretary Tony Snow later attempted to clarify that Cheney had not been referring to

---

[50] Jay C Bybee, Memorandum for Alberto R Gonzales, Counsel to the President, Re Standards of Conduct for Interrogation Under 18 USC §§ 2340–2340A (Washington, DC: Department of Justice Office of the Legal Counsel, 1 August 2002).

[51] See *Hamdan v Rumsfeld*, 548 US 557 (2006).

[52] Dana Priest and Barton Gellman, 'US Decries Abuse but Defends Interrogations: "Stress and Duress" Tactics Used on Terrorism Suspects Held in Secret Overseas Facilities', *Washington Post*, 26 December 2002.

[53] Mark Mazzetti, 'CIA Worker Says Message on Torture Got Her Fired', *New York Times*, 22 July 2006.

waterboarding but merely to a literal 'dunk in the water', prompting a reporter to ask 'so "dunk in the water" means what, we have a pool now at Guantánamo, and they go swimming?'[54]

## 3.2. Extraordinary Rendition

A similar dynamic was evident in the US practice of secret detention and extraordinary rendition. Following occasional reports of secret detention centres—black sites—at Bagram Air Field in Afghanistan and Guantánamo Bay's Camp Echo,[55] it was another *Washington Post* article in November 2005 that revealed the scale of the programme and growing debates within the CIA about its legality and morality.[56] At the request of senior officials, the *Post* did not publish the name of Eastern European countries— believed to be Poland and Romania—involved in the programme, but stated that sites in the programme also included Afghanistan, Guantánamo Bay, and Thailand. The reason given for the overseas location of the black sites was that it avoided US domestic law that would prohibit such secret detention, with the CIA operating on the authority of an order issued by President Bush on 17 September 2001.[57]

Secrecy was needed, however, in order not to raise legal questions in the jurisdictions concerned. When published reports in June 2003 revealed the existence of the site in Thailand, Thai officials insisted that it be closed. The CIA abandoned plans to develop its facility in Guantánamo Bay when US courts began to exercise greater authority over military detainees in the main part of the facility. The response from the CIA to the *Post* report was to request the Justice Department to open a criminal investigation to determine the source of the leak. A senior intelligence officer, Mary

[54] Press Briefing by Tony Snow, 27 October 2006. On his second day in office, President Obama signed an executive order requiring that interrogations follow the non-coercive methods provided for in the Army Field Manual. Scott Shane, Mark Mazzetti, and Helene Cooper, 'Obama Reverses Key Bush Security Policies', *New York Times*, 22 January 2009.

[55] Priest and Gellman, 'US Decries Abuse'; David Rose, 'Revealed: The Full Story of the Guantánamo Britons', *Observer* (London), 14 March 2004.

[56] Dana Priest, 'CIA Holds Terror Suspects in Secret Prisons: Debate Is Growing Within Agency About Legality and Morality of Overseas System Set Up After 9/11', *Washington Post*, 2 November 2005.

[57] David Johnston, 'CIA Tells of Bush's Directive on the Handling of Detainees', *New York Times*, 15 November 2006.

McCarthy, was later fired from the CIA, apparently in connection with the earlier story. President Bush first acknowledged the use of secret prisons in September 2006, shortly before moving 14 suspects from CIA detention to the military detention camp at Guantánamo Bay, in theory ending the programme.[58]

Estimates of the total number of detainees in black sites were about 100. A further hundred are believed to have been involved in the programme of extraordinary rendition, the transfer of untried persons to other countries for imprisonment and interrogation—including, pointedly, countries with records of abuse and torture of detainees, such as Egypt, Jordan, Morocco, Pakistan, and Uzbekistan. An official directly involved in the process described it in the following way to the *Washington Post*: 'We don't kick the [expletive] out of them. We send them to other countries so *they* can kick the [expletive] out of them.'[59] Authority for such forcible transfers is apparently outlined in a 13 March 2002 memorandum entitled 'The President's Power as Commander in Chief to Transfer Captive Terrorists to the Control and Custody of Foreign Nations'. The Bush administration refused to release or describe this memorandum, but it is referred to in the August 2002 memorandum on interrogation methods.[60]

Prominent examples of extraordinary rendition include the Arar case, discussed in Chapter eight. Another relatively well-documented case concerns Hassan Mustafa Osama Nasr, also known as Abu Omar, an Egyptian cleric abducted by the CIA from Milan in February 2003. He was taken to an American base in Aviano and then flown to Egypt, where he was taken into custody. In April 2004, he was released and telephoned his wife, informing her among other things that he had been tortured with electric shocks, had lost hearing in one ear, and could barely walk. Shortly after this call he was rearrested by Egyptian authorities and held for three more years. In June 2005, an Italian judge issued a warrant for

---

[58] Priest, 'CIA Holds Terror Suspects'; David Johnston and Carl Hulse, 'CIA Asks for Criminal Inquiry over Secret-Prison Article', *New York Times*, 9 November 2005; David S Cloud, 'Colleagues Say CIA Analyst Played by Rules', *New York Times*, 23 April 2006; Scott Shane, 'Detainees' Access to Lawyers Is Security Risk, CIA Says', *New York Times*, 5 November 2006.

[59] Priest and Gellman, 'US Decries Abuse'.

[60] Bybee, Interrogation Memorandum, 38. See Dana Priest and Dan Eggen, 'Terror Suspect Alleges Torture: Detainee Says US Sent Him to Egypt Before Guantanamo', *Washington Post*, 6 January 2005.

the arrest of 13 US citizens said to be agents or operatives of the CIA.[61] Of the 13 names, investigations by the *New York Times* indicated that 11 were probably aliases: public records showed that some names received Social Security numbers less than ten years earlier, and that some had addresses that were post office boxes in Virginia known to be used by the CIA.[62] In April 2006, shortly after the Italian general election, the outgoing Justice Minister announced that he would not seek extradition of an expanded list of two dozen CIA officers, but two high-ranking Italian intelligence officers were later arrested for alleged complicity in the kidnapping. In November 2009, an Italian judge convicted in absentia a former CIA base chief, 21 CIA operatives, and an Air Force colonel; though technically considered fugitives, there seems no prospect of them being sent to Italy and the incident did not appear to significantly harm diplomatic relations with the United States.[63]

### 3.3. Warrantless Electronic Surveillance

A third area where US government activity clearly went beyond established law is the Terrorist Surveillance Program described at the beginning of this Chapter. Administration lawyers defended the programme variously on the basis that congressional authorization was implied in the 18 September 2001 Congressional Joint Authorization for the Use of Military Force, or that the President enjoyed the inherent power to authorize such activities in his constitutional role as Commander in Chief. Legal academics largely rejected these arguments and the programme was declared unconstitutional by a district court judge, though an appeals court stayed her decision and later overturned it on the basis that the plaintiffs lacked standing to bring the suit. The Supreme Court turned down a subsequent appeal without comment.[64]

---

[61] Stephen Grey and Don van Natta, '13 with the CIA Sought by Italy in a Kidnapping', *New York Times*, 25 June 2005.

[62] Adam Liptak, 'Experts Doubt Accused CIA Operatives Will Stand Trial in Italy', *New York Times*, 27 June 2005.

[63] Peter Kiefer, 'Italian Minister Declines to Seek Extradition of CIA Operatives', *New York Times*, 13 April 2006; Ian Fisher and Elisabetta Povoledo, 'Italy's Top Spy Is Expected to Be Indicted in Abduction Case', *New York Times*, 24 October 2006; Rachel Donadio, 'Italy Convicts 23 Americans for CIA Renditions', *New York Times*, 4 November 2009.

[64] *ACLU v NSA*, 483 F Supp 2d 754 (ED Mich, 2006); *ACLU v NSA*, 493 F.3d 644 (6th Cir, 2007); *ACLU v NSA*, 128 SCt 1334 (2008). See also Unclassified Report on the President's

Once again, however, open discussion of the programme and remedies for apparent violation of the law occurred only after it was reported in a major newspaper—in this case, when the *New York Times* finally published the article it had held for over a year. Attorney General Alberto Gonzales said that the administration had 'discussions with Congress in the past— certain members of Congress—as to whether or not FISA could be amended to allow us to adequately deal with this kind of threat, and we were advised that that would be difficult, if not impossible.'[65] He later clarified that he had intended to say that it would have been difficult, if not impossible, to obtain legislation without compromising the programme. For his part, President Bush declared that leaks to the press concerning the programme were 'a shameful act'. He added that he assumed a Justice Department investigation into the leak was moving forward, though investigators do not appear to have even contacted the journalists involved.[66] In an interview on the same topic a year and a half later, Director of National Intelligence Mike McConnell gave his own alarmist assessment of the impact of debating amendments to FISA in the news media and open congressional debate: 'The fact we're doing it this way means that some Americans are going to die.'[67]

## 3.4. Public Deliberation and the Public Interest

In each of these cases—torture, extraordinary rendition, and warrantless surveillance—public deliberation on the legality of the practice clearly was never intended by the relevant officials. This is not to say that all media disclosures are in the public interest. In 1998, for example, the *Washington*

---

Surveillance Program (Washington, DC: Inspectors General of the Department of Defense, Department of Justice, Central Intelligence Agency, National Security Agency, and Office of the Director of National Intelligence, July 2009). For a spirited—if implausible—defence of the programme, see John Yoo, 'The Terrorist Surveillance Program and the Constitution', *George Mason Law Review* 14 (2007) 565 at 590.

[65] Press Briefing by Attorney General Alberto Gonzales and General Michael Hayden, Principal Deputy Director for National Intelligence, 19 December 2005.

[66] Dan Eggen, 'White House Trains Efforts on Media Leaks: Sources, Reporters Could Be Prosecuted', *Washington Post*, 5 March 2006.

[67] Chris Roberts, 'Transcript: Debate on the Foreign Intelligence Surveillance Act', *El Paso Times*, 22 August 2007.

*Times* reported that US intelligence services were able to monitor Osama bin Laden's satellite phone.[68] Soon after the story was published, bin Laden was said to have ceased using that phone and largely disappeared from view.[69] The article was denounced as a 'leak' by the 9/11 Commission, a characterization repeated by President George W Bush who said such disclosures were 'helping the enemy'; a CIA agent who ran the bin Laden desk at the time claimed that a direct causal link could be made between the publication and the September 11 attacks on the United States three years later.[70] Subsequent investigations suggested that this exaggerated the real import of the story, but it does point to the sensitivity of the subject matter.[71]

The media also needs to guard against its own form of regulatory capture. In the lead up to the 2003 Iraq war, various journalists dutifully reported on dubious intelligence that was passed to them concerning Iraqi weapons programmes; during combat, the practice of 'embedding' journalists with military units led to criticism that such journalists would be incapable of reporting objectively. A year later, the former head of media relations for the Marine Corps was candid about the armed services' interest in cultivating such relationships: 'Frankly, our job is to win the war. Part of that is information warfare. So we are going to attempt to dominate the information environment.'[72]

## 4. OPEN GOVERNMENT

In the first episode of the classic British comedy series *Yes, Minister*, Bernard, the young private secretary of an idealistic new minister, is defending a new policy proposal on open government. The permanent

---

[68] Martin Sieff, 'Terrorist Driven by Hatred for US, Israel', *Washington Times*, 21 August 1998.

[69] Daniel Benjamin and Steven Simon, *The Age of Sacred Terror* (New York: Random House, 2002), 261.

[70] 9/11 Commission Report: Final Report of the National Commission on Terrorist Attacks upon the United States (Washington, DC: US Government Printing Office, 2004), 127; George W Bush, 'Presidential News Conference', *Washington Post*, 19 December 2005; Patrick Radden Keefe, 'Cat-and-Mouse Games', *New York Review* LII(9), 26 May 2005, 41 at 41–2.

[71] Glenn Kessler, 'File the Bin Laden Phone Leak Under "Urban Myths"', *Washington Post*, 22 December 2005.

[72] Frank Rich, 'Operation Iraqi Infoganda', *New York Times*, 28 March 2004.

secretaries to the Minister, Sir Humphrey, and to the Prime Minister, Sir Arnold, attempt to explain why this is a preposterous idea:

BERNARD:　　　　But, uh, what's wrong with open government? I mean, why shouldn't the public know more about what's going on?

SIR ARNOLD:　　Are you serious?

BERNARD:　　　　Well, yes sir. It is the Minister's policy after all.

SIR ARNOLD:　　My dear boy, it's a contradiction in terms. You can be open, or you can have government.

BERNARD:　　　　But surely the citizens of a democracy have a right to know?

SIR HUMPHREY:　No, they have a right to be ignorant. Knowledge only means complicity and guilt, ignorance has a certain...dignity.[73]

As this Chapter has shown, secrecy may be required in many areas connected with effective intelligence activities. That does not explain or justify the lengths to which governments routinely go to keep their actions from public scrutiny. Addressing the difficulties that secrecy poses for accountability requires separating legitimate from questionable assertions of secrecy, but also understanding the incentives of intelligence services and the difficult environment within which they operate. In particular, it is unrealistic to put much hope in the prospect that agencies can regulate themselves, or that government will always have an interest in full disclosure.

This conclusion has important implications for the discussion of the limits of law in Chapter two, as it changes the calculus for responding to conduct that may violate the law. Among other things, it undermines the presumption that illegal conduct can be ratified through some form of candid political process. On the contrary, it suggests the need to adopt a precautionary approach that does not assume the good faith of interested officials serving as judges in their own cause.

More generally, however, the incentives linked to secrecy pose difficulties for the possibility, probability, and effectiveness of any accountability regime. As a result, much reliance has been placed on the work of investigative journalists at newspapers such as the *New York Times* and the *Washington Post*. In the absence of such journalists, few of the questionable actions discussed here would have been brought to light. Not all countries

---

[73] See Jonathan Lynn and Antony Jay, *The Complete Yes Minister* (London: British Broadcasting Corporation, 1984), 21.

have such newspapers, however, and the rise of new media often privileges derivative over original reporting. If such newspapers die or are relegated to obscurity, it is not clear what will take their place.[74]

At the same time, it is striking that public pressure for accountability is linked not merely to disclosure through authoritative sources, but to disclosure in an easily digestible and provocative form. In the case of detainee abuse, investigations by the US Army Criminal Investigation Command pre-dated public knowledge of the abuse in April 2004, but it was only after humiliating photographs of detainees were widely disseminated that serious action was taken.[75] Twelve uniformed personnel were later convicted of various charges; most were given minor sentences, but a handful of soldiers received multiple-year prison terms. Only one person above the rank of staff sergeant faced a court-martial and was cleared of any wrongdoing.[76] No investigations appear to have been conducted into any abuse that had not been photographed and published in the news media.

---

[74] Alex S Jones, *Losing the News: The Future of the News That Feeds Democracy* (Oxford: Oxford University Press, 2009).

[75] See generally Karen J Greenberg and Joshua L Dratel (eds), *The Torture Papers: The Road to Abu Ghraib* (Cambridge: Cambridge University Press, 2005); Michael Scherer and Mark Benjamin, Other Government Agencies (The Abu Ghraib Files) (Salon.com, 14 March 2006).

[76] See 'Fast Facts: Abu Ghraib Convictions, Associated Press', *Associated Press*, 27 September 2005; 'Chronology of Abu Ghraib', *Washington Post*, 17 February 2006; Eric Schmitt, 'Army Dog Handler is Convicted in Detainee Abuse at Abu Ghraib', *New York Times*, 22 March 2006; Philip Gourevitch and Errol Morris, 'Exposure: Behind the Camera at Abu Ghraib', *New Yorker*, 24 March 2008, 44 at 56.

# Part II

# Practice

# 4

## The United States and the Turn to Outsourcing

We also have to work, though, sort of the dark side, if you will. We've got to spend time in the shadows in the intelligence world. A lot of what needs to be done here will have to be done quietly, without any discussion, using sources and methods that are available to our intelligence agencies, if we're going to be successful. That's the world these folks operate in, and so it's going to be vital for us to use any means at our disposal, basically, to achieve our objective.

Vice President Dick Cheney[1]

Six days after the September 11 attacks, at a press conference held in the Pentagon, President George W Bush said that the United States was ready to defend freedom at any cost: 'We will win the war, and there will be costs.' Calling Osama bin Laden the prime suspect in the attacks he was asked whether he wanted bin Laden dead. 'I want justice,' he responded. 'There's an old poster out West that said, "Wanted, dead or alive."'[2]

Within the CIA, a small unit was already examining the possibility of taking this injunction literally. The model appears to have been the Israeli response to the Munich Olympics attack in 1972. 'It was straight out of the movies,' one former intelligence official later told the *Wall Street Journal*. 'It was like: Let's kill them all.' The programme was kept secret from Congress for almost eight years until Leon Panetta took over as Director of the CIA under a new White House in 2009. In June of that year, four months into his tenure, Panetta was briefed on the programme and

---

[1] Richard (Dick) Cheney, 'The Vice President appears on Meet the Press with Tim Russert' (Meet the Press, Camp David, 16 September 2001).

[2] Charles Babington, '"Dead or Alive": Bush Unveils Wild West Rhetoric', *Washington Post*, 17 September 2001.

immediately terminated it and informed Congress. It appears that no actual operations to assassinate alleged terrorists were launched.[3] But one of the more interesting aspects of the programme was the decision that any such operations should be undertaken by a private military and security company. A 2004 contract awarded Blackwater USA several million dollars for training and weapons. Reliance on a contractor was said to provide additional cover to the Agency in case 'something went wrong', but the move from the CIA's Counterterrorist Center also appears to have coincided with the retirement of key officials who went to work for Blackwater.[4]

The attacks of September 11 radically changed the way in which national security is perceived generally, while eroding some traditional protections long taken for granted in the United States in particular. This Chapter first considers the changes that were made to laws relating to intelligence activities following the September 11 attacks, before situating these in the context of more longstanding debates over reforming the US intelligence 'community'—a somewhat misleading term that suggests collegiality among 16 organizations that employ around 200,000 people with a budget in the order of $75 billion. Though the abuse of detainees and the erosion of civil liberties have been the subject of much debate, the Chapter then focuses on a striking trend over the past decade that may have more long-term consequences: the reliance on private contractors for an increasing portion of US intelligence.

## 1. THE DARK SIDE

The US Constitution—one of the oldest constitutions still in force—was crafted with an eye to limiting the powers of centralized authority through checks and balances. The liberties that it embraces reflect the time in which it was written, however. In the late eighteenth century, physical

---

[3] Siobhan Gorman, 'CIA Had Secret al Qaeda Plan', *Wall Street Journal*, 13 July 2009.
[4] Mark Mazzetti, 'CIA Sought Blackwater's Help to Kill Jihadists', *New York Times*, 19 August 2009; Joby Warrick and R Jeffrey Smith, 'CIA Hired Firm for Assassin Program', *Washington Post*, 20 August 2009.

surveillance consisted of following people, eavesdropping on them, or examining their property. To limit such surveillance the Fourth Amendment required that searches and seizures by government be 'reasonable'. Psychological surveillance was possible through forced testimony or torture: the Fifth and Eighth Amendments forbade compelled self-incrimination and cruel and unusual punishment. A third mode of surveillance used at the time was the record and dossier system of the European monarchies that controlled the movement of the population and the activities of 'disloyal' groups. In the United States the decision not to employ a passport or dossier system—for practical as well as political reasons—ensured a degree of freedom unusual in the industrializing world.[5]

Until the end of the following century, such provisions were seen as adequate. The development of the telephone in the 1880s and the microphone in the 1890s challenged the paradigms that had emerged and the ability of law to adapt to new technological realities. Notably, the Fourth Amendment only applies to searches and seizures, not other types of investigation. An investigative method is only considered a 'search' if it invades a 'reasonable expectation of privacy'.[6] Tapping into a telephone or using a hidden microphone is a search, for example, but observation by an undercover agent who is in the room during a conversation is not—even if that agent is transmitting the conversation.[7] Government inspection of bank records is not a search, as the customer has made such information available to the bank and its employees.[8] Similarly, installing a 'pen register' that records all numbers dialled from a telephone line is not a search—though listening to the calls would be—as customers voluntarily convey these numbers to the telephone company when using the device.[9] The more recent explosion of electronic communications in which far more data are shared with relevant companies, such as the metadata that travel with an e-mail, means that ever greater information is revealed even without opening the actual missive.

---

[5] Alan F Westin, 'Civil Liberties Issues in Public Databanks', in Alan F Westin (ed), *Information Technology in a Democracy* (Cambridge, MA: Harvard University Press, 1971), 301 at 301–2.          [6] *Katz v United States*, 389 US 347, 360 (1967).

[7] *United States v White*, 401 US 745 (1971).

[8] *United States v Miller*, 425 US 435 (1976).

[9] *Smith v Maryland*, 442 US 735 (1979). See further Stephen J Schulhofer, *The Enemy Within: Intelligence Gathering, Law Enforcement, and Civil Liberties in the Wake of September 11* (New York: Century Foundation Press, 2002), 34–6.

Some of these gaps have been filled by legislation, but the focus has typically been law enforcement; the application of constitutional and legislative protections to the growing intelligence community has not always been clear. The Right to Financial Privacy Act 1978, for example, gave customers a measure of privacy in their bank records that was more than the Supreme Court had offered under the Fourth Amendment, but included a section on 'special procedures' that exempted government agencies engaged in intelligence or counter-intelligence activities.[10] The Pen Register Act was part of the Electronic Communications Privacy Act 1986, but only requires that a law enforcement agency show that the information is relevant to an ongoing criminal investigation. The original definition of what could be collected was clearly limited to telephone numbers, but this has been broadened to include virtually all data transmitted in electronic communications except the content.[11] Intelligence agencies are exempted from the Pen Register Act if they obtain an order under the Foreign Intelligence Surveillance Act.

These legislative moves attempted to keep pace with technological change, but also coincided with the aftermath of the intelligence scandals described in Chapter one. The excesses and abuse revealed in the 1970s led to significantly greater scrutiny of US spies and these protections were intended to prevent wrongdoing and safeguard privacy. When the nation suffered the most lethal attack in its history, the view quickly formed that US vulnerability could at least in part be blamed on excessive constraints on the ability of intelligence services to collect information.

### 1.1. September 11 and the Patriot Act

The main legislative response was sweeping legislation adopted five weeks after the September 11 attacks under an unwieldy title that formed the acronym 'USA Patriot'.[12] Many provisions in the Patriot Act of 2001 merely

---

[10]  Right to Financial Privacy Act 1978 (US), § 1114(a)(1)(A); 12 USC §§ 3401–22.

[11]  18 USC §§ 3121–7.

[12]  The full title is the Uniting and Strengthening America by Providing Appropriate Tools Required to Intercept and Obstruct Terrorism Act of 2001.

corrected oversights in prior law, reduced administrative obstacles, or adjusted language to reflect new technologies. Prior law, for example, had allowed courts to authorize 'roving' wiretaps (that is, surveillance of a person rather than a particular telephone line) for domestic law enforcement, but there was no equivalent for foreign intelligence investigations. Where prosecutors had previously been required to file separate warrants in each federal district, the Patriot Act empowered federal judges to issue nationwide search warrants. Subpoenas and search warrants could be used to obtain records from telephone companies and Internet service providers; the Act extended this to cable television companies, which by then were providing similar services.[13]

But the Patriot Act also extended the search powers of law enforcement agencies and reduced restrictions on foreign intelligence gathering within the United States. Among other things, it increased the ability of the FBI and certain other government agencies to search telephone, e-mail, and financial records without a court order through the use of National Security Letters (NSLs), a form of administrative subpoena issued without judicial oversight. NSLs were first created as exceptions to legislative privacy protections in the Right to Financial Privacy Act and the Electronic Communications Privacy Act, with some expansion in the 1990s. The Patriot Act greatly broadened the circumstances in which these could be used, replacing the requirement that the information relate to an agent of a foreign power with the far looser requirement that it be relevant to an investigation to protect against international terrorism or foreign espionage.[14] These powers were supplemented by gag orders that prohibited anyone asked to give information from disclosing that the FBI had asked for it. Lawsuits led to this last provision being removed.[15]

---

[13] Patriot Act 2001 (US), § 206 (roving surveillance), §§ 216, 219, 220 (nationwide warrants), and § 211 (cable companies); Schulhofer, *The Enemy Within*, 30.

[14] Patriot Act, § 505. See also Eric Lichtblau and Mark Mazzetti, 'Military Expands Intelligence Role in US', *New York Times*, 14 January 2007; Charles Doyle, National Security Letters in Foreign Intelligence Investigations: A Glimpse of the Legal Background and Recent Amendments (Washington, DC: Congressional Research Service, 28 March 2008). The Patriot Act also broadened the general exemption from the Right to Financial Privacy Act to include agencies engaged in investigation or 'analysis' of international terrorism. Patriot Act, § 358(f)(2).

[15] Laura K Donohue, 'Anglo-American Privacy and Surveillance', *Journal of Criminal Law & Criminology* 96 (2006) 1059 at 1112.

The Patriot Act was criticized for, among other things, allowing the indefinite detention of immigrants. Where the Attorney General has reasonable grounds to believe that an alien may cause a terrorist act, that person can be detained for an unlimited series of six month periods.[16] Other restrictions on civil liberties included new 'sneak and peek' powers, also referred to as delayed-notice searches, in which law enforcement agents may surreptitiously search and photograph items without advising the owner and without leaving a copy of a warrant.[17] The Act further expanded the crime of providing material support to terrorists by including monetary instruments and expert advice or assistance within the definition of 'material support'.[18] Another provision that produced much discussion empowered the FBI to apply for an order to obtain, among other things, library records. Though these records are held by a third party and therefore not protected by the Fourth Amendment, the news prompted extraordinary protests from librarians, some of whom began shredding library records to avoid being compelled to produce them.[19]

Some of the more controversial provisions of the Patriot Act had sunset clauses that expired at the end of 2005. As discussed in Chapters two and three, however, these new powers were accompanied by other, undisclosed expansions of the powers of US intelligence services, as well as activities by specific agencies that went well beyond their authorized powers—though sometimes with tacit approval of the executive.

The consequences of these new assertions of power were both human and systemic. Some were attributable to changes in the letter of the law; others, perhaps, to the implied spirit the new laws reflected. Nearly 100 detainees died while in US custody in Iraq and Afghanistan, 34 of whom

---

[16] 8 USC § 1226a. Indefinite extensions of six months are allowed 'if the release of the alien will threaten the national security of the United States or the safety of the community or any person'.

[17] Patriot Act, § 213; Brett A Shumate, 'From "Sneak and Peek" to "Sneak and Steal": Section 213 of the USA PATRIOT Act', *Regent University Law Review* 19 (2006) 203.

[18] Patriot Act, § 805(a)(2); Jonathan D Stewart, 'Balancing the Scales of Due Process: Material Support of Terrorism and the Fifth Amendment', *Georgetown Journal of Law & Public Policy* 3 (2005) 311.

[19] Daniel J Solove, *The Digital Person: Privacy and Technology in the Information Age* (New York: New York University Press, 2004), 200–9; Dean E Murphy, 'Some Librarians Use Shredder to Show Opposition to New FBI Powers', *New York Times*, 7 April 2003; Kathryn Martin, 'The USA PATRIOT Act's Application to Library Patron Records', *Journal of Legislation* 29 (2003) 283. See generally Timothy Casey, *The USA PATRIOT Act: The Decline of Legitimacy in the Age of Terrorism* (Oxford: Oxford University Press, 2009).

were identified by the US military as victims of homicide. Of these, only 12 resulted in any form of punishment.[20] While the CIA was implicated in many deaths, only one person—a contractor—has been charged or convicted of a crime.[21] An unknown number of detainees were subjected to 'enhanced' interrogation, including the waterboarding of at least two dozen detainees; one, Khalid Sheikh Mohammed, was waterboarded 183 times.[22] A confidential report by the International Committee of the Red Cross (ICRC) concluded that the ill-treatment inflicted on detainees constituted torture.[23]

More than a thousand aliens were detained in the weeks and months after September 11 within the United States, many of them later deported. Hundreds were detained abroad in facilities at Guantánamo Bay, Bagram Air Field in Afghanistan, and various black sites. In addition to the human suffering caused by these actions, the damage to the moral standing of the United States abroad, and the possible chilling effect on political life at home, these excesses also caused operational problems in combating terrorism. When the FBI became aware of the enhanced interrogation methods being used by the CIA, for example, it ceased to participate in the interrogations, exacerbating tensions between the agencies.[24] The use of such methods as the practice of extraordinary rendition also caused rifts with traditional allies of the United States, raising legal barriers to the extradition of suspects and inhibiting the sharing of intelligence.[25]

## 1.2. Understanding the US Response

The reaction of the United States to the September 11 attacks has been described even by thoughtful commentators as 'panicked', with major legislation hastily passed in response to an undefined threat from a poorly

---

[20] Hina Shamsi, Command's Responsibility: Detainee Deaths in US Custody in Iraq and Afghanistan (New York: Human Rights First, February 2006).

[21] See section 3.1.3 in this Chapter.

[22] Scott Shane, '2 US Architects of Harsh Tactics in 9/11's Wake', *New York Times*, 12 August 2009.

[23] ICRC Report on the Treatment of Fourteen 'High Value Detainees' in CIA Custody (Washington, DC: International Committee of the Red Cross, February 2007), 26.

[24] Ali Soufan, 'My Tortured Decision', *New York Times*, 22 April 2009; A Review of the FBI's Involvement in and Observations of Detainee Interrogations in Guantanamo Bay, Afghanistan, and Iraq (Washington, DC: US Department of Justice, Office of the Inspector General, October 2009).     [25] See also Chapter eight, section 2.

understood source.[26] Friends and allies underestimated the extent to which the attacks radically changed the worldview of many Americans, but also how they exacerbated pre-existing tendencies towards unilateralism in international affairs and a unitary executive domestically. The US response was also subject to the idiosyncrasies of its political system. In deference to Second Amendment fetishists, for example, an individual listed on a terrorist watch-list could be barred from boarding an airplane but not from purchasing a firearm.[27]

Much has now been written about the Bush White House, showing how these predilections turned into policies.[28] For present purposes, two areas are of particular interest: how the challenge posed by September 11 was understood and the limited role that law played in developing the response.

The threats facing the nation were presented as requiring a 'global war on terror'—GWOT in military argot. This conceptualization framed the planet as a battlefield in which traditional rule of law restrictions might not apply, consistent with the President's Wild West rhetoric. Yet each of the words posed political and strategic problems. As was often noted, a war 'on terror' makes no sense as it essentially declares war on a tactic and is by definition unwinnable. The language of 'war' introduced two concerns: first, it suggested a military dimension to domestic counter-terrorism efforts; secondly, it implicitly defined the perpetrators of attacks on civilians as 'soldiers'. Referring to a major terrorist attack on London, Britain's chief prosecutor later rejected both implications:

London is not a battlefield. Those innocents who were murdered on July 7, 2005 were not victims of war. And the men who killed them were not, as in their vanity they claimed on their ludicrous videos, 'soldiers'. They were deluded, narcissistic inadequates. They were criminals. They were fantasists.

---

[26] Bruce Ackerman, *Before the Next Attack: Preserving Civil Liberties in an Age of Terrorism* (New Haven, CT: Yale University Press, 2006), 2; Philip B Heymann and Juliette N Kayyem, *Protecting Liberty in an Age of Terror* (Cambridge, MA: MIT Press, 2005), 5.

[27] Firearm and Explosives Background Checks Involving Terrorist Watch List Records (Washington, DC: Government Accountability Office, GAO-09-125R, 21 May 2009).

[28] See in particular James Mann, *Rise of the Vulcans: The History of Bush's War Cabinet* (New York: Viking, 2004); Jack Goldsmith, *The Terror Presidency* (New York: Norton, 2007); Jane Mayer, *The Dark Side: The Inside Story of How the War on Terror Turned Into a War on American Ideals* (New York: Doubleday, 2008).

We need to be very clear about this. On the streets of London, there is no such thing as a war on terror. The fight against terrorism on the streets of Britain is not a war. It is the prevention of crime, the enforcement of our laws and the winning of justice for those damaged by their infringement.[29]

The use of military rhetoric against an abstract noun also led to the belief on the part of some that traditional restrictions in battle might not apply. As indicated in Chapter one, the reciprocity that characterized the emergence of laws of armed conflict is lacking in a war on terror—it is noteworthy that some of those most vocal in their opposition to the abuse of detainees were the uniformed military lawyers who understood the consequences that this might have for future claims of prisoner-of-war status by US soldiers.[30]

In addition, however, the appellation 'global' may have constituted a strategic error in casting what is really more like 60 different groups scattered across the globe as part of a single unified fight. Seeing the worldwide enemy as al Qaeda or Islamist extremism in fact encouraged self-identification by disparate groups with, potentially, disaggregated interests: Lashkar-e-Taiba in Pakistan, Jemaah Islamiah in Indonesia, Abu Sayyaf in the Philippines, and so on.[31] In March 2009, the Department of Defense quietly issued a memorandum stating that the term 'global war on terror' would in future be replaced by the more anodyne phrase 'overseas contingency operations'.[32]

Lawyers often pay most attention to language and its consequences, and it is striking that the Bush White House included remarkably few of them. Neither the President, Vice President, Secretary of Defense, Secretary of State, nor the National Security Adviser was a lawyer. All of these positions during the Clinton administration were held by lawyers, with the exception of the Vice President (who had attended law school briefly). President Bill Clinton was known for reminding the lawyers who worked for him that he had previously taught constitutional law.[33]

---

[29] Sir Ken Macdonald, quoted in Lucy Bannerman, 'There Is No War on Terror in the UK, Says DPP', *The Times* (London), 24 January 2007.    [30] See Chapter one, section 2.5.

[31] George Packer, 'Knowing the Enemy: Can Social Scientists Redefine the "War on Terror"?', *New Yorker*, 18 December 2006, 60.

[32] Scott Wilson and Al Kamen, ' "Global War on Terror" Is Given New Name', *Washington Post*, 25 March 2009.    [33] Mayer, *Dark Side*, 54.

The quantity of lawyers may not, of course, lead to good decisions. The quality of what legal advice the Bush administration did receive has also been criticized, with ethical and legal investigations of Jay Bybee and John Yoo, who wrote the so-called 'torture memos'. Jack Goldsmith, former head of the Justice Department's Office of Legal Counsel, later told the Senate Judiciary Committee that the legal justifications for the National Security Agency's (NSA) programme of warrantless electronic surveillance were deeply flawed. At one White House meeting in 2004, Goldsmith's deputy, James Comey, said that 'no lawyer' would endorse Yoo's justification for the NSA programme. David Addington, legal counsel to Vice President Cheney, disagreed, saying that he was a lawyer and found it convincing. 'No *good* lawyer,' Comey is said to have replied.[34] An internal Justice Department report ultimately concluded that Bybee and Yoo had used flawed legal reasoning but were not guilty of professional misconduct.[35]

These strategic issues of how the US response to terrorism was conceived and the role that law should play in calibrating a response tended to be ignored in the post-September 11 debates over reform of the intelligence services. Those debates were made more urgent when a second scandal rocked the US intelligence community.

## 2. REFORM

Within the space of 18 months, from September 2001 to March 2003, the US intelligence community experienced two of its worst ever intelligence failures. The inability to prevent the September 11 attacks on New York and Washington, DC, has been compared to the strategic surprise of Pearl Harbor; flawed and manipulated intelligence in relation to Iraq has been blamed for the worst foreign policy decision in a generation, if not in the history of the United States.

[34] Dan Eggen, 'White House Secrecy on Wiretaps Described', *Washington Post*, 3 October 2007; Scott Shane, David Johnston, and James Risen, 'Secret US Endorsement of Severe Interrogations', *New York Times*, 4 October 2007. See now Goldsmith, *The Terror Presidency*.

[35] Eric Lichtblau and Scott Shane, 'Report Faults 2 Authors of Bush Terror Memos', *New York Times*, 19 February 2010.

Dozens of classified and unclassified reports, scores of books, and thousands of articles have since been written about these failures. Perhaps the most prominent, the 9/11 Commission Report, was a bestseller and one of very few government reports to be selected as a finalist for a National Book Award.[36] On top of a slew of works that describe the history and aftermath of each incident, various authors have set about showing how over-protection of civil liberties contributed to the vulnerability of the United States, while others argue that that vulnerability has been exploited in a sustained attack on civil liberties. There is also an expanding corpus of writing on improving the effectiveness of intelligence services, though this, too, polarizes around two ultimately contradictory positions: either agents and analysts must be liberated from bureaucracy with individual excellence encouraged, or else that bureaucracy must be strengthened to ensure that coordinated and coherent advice reaches policymakers.[37]

What is frequently lost in this burgeoning literature is the point raised by Rodric Braithwaite in the quote that opened Chapter three: how important *is* intelligence, anyway? One lesson of September 11 may be that intelligence cannot always offer up clear and actionable warnings of attacks by asymmetric forces that will push a large government into action. One lesson of Iraq is that when such a government does move into action, improved intelligence may not be able to stop it. The Silberman–Robb Commission established by President Bush to investigate intelligence failures with respect to Iraq, for example, concluded that the US intelligence community was 'dead wrong in almost all of its pre-war judgments about Iraq's weapons of mass destruction'. It also noted, however, that that same community boasts an almost perfect record of resisting external recommendations for change.[38]

The United States has undergone three major efforts at intelligence reform since it emerged as a superpower, each case marked with the passage of legislation and institutional reform.[39] The first, in the wake of

[36] 9/11 Commission Report: Final Report of the National Commission on Terrorist Attacks upon the United States (Washington, DC: US Government Printing Office, 2004).

[37] See the Introduction to this volume, section 1.

[38] The Commission on the Intelligence Capabilities of the United States Regarding Weapons of Mass Destruction (Silberman–Robb Commission Report) (Washington, DC: Laurence H Silberman and Charles S Robb, co-chairs, 31 March 2005), preface, 6.

[39] Richard K Betts, *Enemies of Intelligence: Knowledge and Power in American National Security* (New York: Columbia University Press, 2007), 3–4.

the Pearl Harbor attack, established the basic structure of its modern intelligence community after the Second World War. The second, following the Watergate scandal and during the tail end of the Vietnam War, sought to rein that community in through constraints on domestic intelligence collection and formalized oversight by Congress and a new Foreign Intelligence Surveillance Court. The third came after the September 11 attacks and saw the expansion of powers under the Patriot Act and new efforts at centralization under a Director of National Intelligence.

The barriers to reform are considerable. They include the usual obstacles posed by large bureaucracies, but also certain problems specific to the intelligence world. First, how is the mission of an intelligence service to be understood? The aims of intelligence services typically include avoiding strategic surprise, providing long-term expertise, supporting the policy process, and maintaining the secrecy of information, needs, and methods.[40] The common theme is that intelligence exists to improve the decisions of policy makers. Very different prescriptions for reform will be reached if one understands that the policy goal should be a rational weighing of costs and benefits posed by certain courses of action (or inaction), or that the goal should be preventing attacks on the homeland at any cost. A second set of questions concern how the mission of intelligence can best be achieved, in particular what legal and bureaucratic structures will improve the efficiency and effectiveness of the various agencies.

## 2.1. Prevention and the Dog that Didn't Bark

Establishing prevention of attacks as the test of an intelligence community's effectiveness is a dubious metric. Tactical surprise, such as an individual attack by an otherwise unknown terrorist group, cannot wholly be avoided. If it is not of sufficient magnitude to threaten the existence of the state or its way of life, occasional surprises can be managed.[41] It is also hard to prove when success has been achieved in avoiding surprise. As Sherlock Holmes once observed, it is difficult to establish why a dog *didn't*

---

[40] Mark M Lowenthal, *Intelligence: From Secrets to Policy*, 3rd edn (Washington, DC: CQ Press, 2006), 2–5.
[41] Richard K Betts, 'Analysis, War, and Decision: Why Intelligence Failures Are Inevitable', *World Politics* 31(1) (1978) 61.

bark on a given night.[42] Assertions by government officials that terrorist plots have been discovered and averted are now frequently greeted with suspicion. Such plots—in some cases years old and not beyond the planning stages—may be invoked opportunistically in order to justify the troubling things that governments must do in a 'war on terror'.

Prevention can also distort discussions of reform. It is tempting to focus on cases where attacks did take place and then consider whether they might have been prevented. Thomas Copeland, for example, describes five devastating attacks on the United States and looks for explanations in failures of leadership, organizational obstacles, the volume of information available, and analytical pathologies. Yet the premise that attacks on the homeland can and should be prevented at times blinds him to the dangers of unfettered national security agencies. Copeland argues, among other things, that the prospects for averting tragedy were reduced in every case as a result of legal restrictions on intelligence collection—the sort of argument that held sway in the Justice Department after September 11, where enthusiastic lawyers sought to remove *any* constraints on the power of the executive, but from which the Bush and Obama administrations gradually retreated. Elsewhere he suggests that terrorism prevention should always be the dominant focus of any US president. Though US policy might well have been improved had President Clinton not been distracted by the Monica Lewinsky scandal in 1998, it is a stretch to blame the 1993 World Trade Center attack on Clinton's focus on 'economic and social issues', the Oklahoma City bombing on 'gun control and the Oslo Peace Accords', and so on.[43] It is also telling that a book on the failure of the United States to act on what the author asserts was adequate evidence of threats to the homeland does not mention the intelligence failures that led to the 2003 invasion of Iraq.

A more plausible critique of the poor performance of US intelligence services focuses on the under-resourcing of human intelligence. This is not helped by promotion structures that favour quantity over quality of recruits. Richard Russell worked as a political-military analyst for the CIA for 17 years and offers anecdotal evidence of junior case officers who

[42] Arthur Conan Doyle, 'Silver Blaze', *Strand Magazine* 4 (1892) 645.
[43] Thomas E Copeland, *Fool Me Twice: Intelligence Failure and Mass Casualty Terrorism* (Leiden: Koninklijke Brill NV, 2007), 241.

develop second- or third-rate assets whose information is of little value but whose recruitment advances the officer's career. He describes reading a classified report on Iran and then hearing nearly identical comments from his Iranian taxi-driver on the way to the airport. Improving the quality of human intelligence requires understanding how ineffective it has been in the past, even in the days when one could meet potential contacts at a diplomatic cocktail party rather than in the tribal areas of Pakistan. His main recommendations are longer tours by CIA case officers, better use of walk-ins, more engagement with foreign intelligence services, and streamlining security vetting processes.[44]

Improving analytical capacity requires hiring real experts, with the model being a strong university faculty or perhaps a think tank with government connections such as the RAND Corporation. Russell's solution here is to hire fewer analysts on better terms, in particular bringing in more PhDs with real expertise in relevant areas. (Russell earned his PhD from the University of Virginia in 1997.) More effective use should be made of red teams or devil's advocates, encouraging individuals to express an unpopular dissenting opinion in order to allow decision-makers to consider alternative views. More generally, the CIA needs to foster a culture of education and learning.[45]

This is all well and good, but it is far from clear how any of it would solve the problems that Russell seeks to address. In his discussion of the failure of intelligence on Iraq's weapons of mass destruction (WMD) programme, he attributes the flawed assessment that Iraq had an active WMD capacity not to politicization of intelligence but rather to the insistence of senior CIA officers on definitive 'answers' that required the removal of caveats and equivocation. He denounces this as 'intellectual arrogance that permeates the CIA's managerial culture'.[46] Such *fausse naïveté* concerning the well-documented efforts to shape intelligence around policy is unpersuasive, but for his own argument the rejection of calls for 'answers' appears especially problematic. Strategic intelligence, to be useful, requires clarity and clarity entails risk of error. What Russell advocates is in fact greater

---

[44] Richard L Russell, *Sharpening Strategic Intelligence: Why the CIA Gets It Wrong and What Needs to Be Done to Get It Right* (Cambridge: Cambridge University Press, 2007), 99–102, 7–13.    [45] Ibid, 119–48.    [46] Ibid, 85.

freedom for case officers and analysts, a form of academic freedom more like the university world into which he has moved, but perhaps less likely to shape policy. As Paul Pillar—another PhD who left the CIA for academia—has written, the most remarkable thing about pre-war US intelligence on Iraq is not that it got things so wrong and misled policy-makers; rather it is that intelligence played such a small role in one of the most important foreign policy decisions in decades.[47]

## 2.2. Structures and Systems

Where Russell repeatedly decries the organizational chart approach to intelligence reform and seeks to free case officers and analysts from bureaucracy, others like Amy Zegart argue that good organizational structures matter and can have an impact on policy successes and failures that is greater than key individuals. Zegart's aim is to bring a scholarly eye not to what went wrong but *why*. A professor at UCLA's School of Public Affairs, she worked on the Clinton administration's National Security Council Staff in 1993 and spent three years at the management consultancy McKinsey & Co. Her analysis focuses on what she claims is the single most important reason for the United States' vulnerability on September 11: 'the stunning inability of US intelligence agencies to adapt to the end of the Cold War'.[48] This suggests a somewhat rosier interpretation of Cold War intelligence than Russell, but in fact many of the deficiencies Zegart identifies have their origins in the establishment of the US intelligence architecture at the end of the Second World War, something she had described in a doctoral thesis at Stanford University supervised by Condoleezza Rice, who later became National Security Adviser before being appointed Secretary of State in the Bush White House.[49]

The missed opportunities to prevent the attacks on New York and Washington, DC, are now familiar. The CIA observed an al Qaeda planning

---

[47] Paul R Pillar, 'Intelligence, Policy, and the War in Iraq', *Foreign Affairs* 85(2) (2006) 15 at 16.
[48] Amy B Zegart, *Spying Blind: The CIA, the FBI, and the Origins of 9/11* (Princeton: Princeton University Press, 2007), 3.
[49] See Amy B Zegart, *Flawed by Design: The Evolution of the CIA, JCS, and NSC* (Stanford, CA: Stanford University Press, 1999).

meeting in Kuala Lumpur in January 2000, among other things gathering information on Khalid al-Mihdhar, whom it discovered had a multiple-entry visa to the United States. Yet he was put on a State Department watch-list only on 23 August 2001—months after he had entered the country, obtained a California photo identification card, and started taking flying lessons. The FBI, for its part, failed to act on a memo from a field agent in Phoenix who warned in July 2001 that Osama bin Laden might be using US flight schools to train terrorists, and refused to seek a search warrant to investigate the computer files of Zacarias Moussaoui after he was detained. There is also the President's 6 August 2001 briefing from the CIA entitled 'Bin Laden Determined to Strike in US'.[50]

Echoing the approach of the 9/11 Commission—and the reason for the most vehement criticism of its findings—Zegart attributes blame for these failures not to individuals but to systemic and organizational problems. The three broad deficiencies she identifies are a culture that is resistant to change, perverse incentives that reward the wrong behaviour, and structural deficiencies that prevent the CIA, FBI, and other members of the US intelligence community cooperating effectively.

As she concedes, none of this is new. In the ten years before 2001, for example, at least six classified reports and a dozen major unclassified studies sought to improve the counterterrorism work of the intelligence services. Hundreds of recommendations were made, the vast majority of which resulted in no action whatsoever. The various recommendations made in the 1990s broadly concurred on four major problems confronting the intelligence community: personnel problems that fail to recruit and keep those with the most needed skills, insufficient resources for and unnecessary barriers to human intelligence activities, lack of coordination within and across agencies, and inadequate leadership by policymakers in setting intelligence priorities. Oddly, Zegart's own catalogue broadly corresponds to the first three problems but does not adequately address the last—leadership by policymakers—except where she notes that presidents have had little incentive to spend the political capital necessary to make major reforms.[51]

---

[50] Zegart, *Spying Blind*, 101–19; 9/11 Commission Report, 254–77. See also Chapter one, section 1.2.    [51] Zegart, *Spying Blind*, 57.

Organization theory is invoked to explore intelligence services' apparent failure to adapt. There are, however, significant limitations to applying theories designed for the private sector to the public sector, and in particular to the work of intelligence services where the imperative of secrecy adds a further complication. One of the insights of organization theory is that individual organizations do not adapt: *groups* of organizations do. This form of Darwinian selection is possible only when there is significant turnover—'creative destruction' far more applicable to the private sector than the public. Failure to adapt will only rarely lead to the abolition of a government entity, and there may be few other incentives to change: the US Army, for example, maintained a horse cavalry until the Second World War; until the mid-1990s, customs forms required ships entering US ports to list the number of cannons on board.[52]

Certainly, both the CIA and FBI suffer from fundamental structural problems. The CIA is at once tasked with being the lead agency for human intelligence activities outside the United States through its National Clandestine Service (previously the Directorate of Operations), and the body that undertakes all-source national security and foreign policy analysis in its Directorate of Intelligence. In many other countries these functions are performed by different agencies in a vertical relationship that passes collected information up through analysts to policymakers—rather than setting them up in a horizontal relationship that causes predictable tension between 'cowboys' and 'Ivy Leaguers'.[53] The head of the CIA was, until April 2005, also the Director of Central Intelligence (DCI): notoriously, he had responsibility for all 16 intelligence services but little power over any but his own—in particular, the DCI had no budgetary controls over those agencies located in the Defense Department that consume the lion's share of the budget. In 1998, George Tenet produced the first strategic plan for the US intelligence community since the end of the Cold War. Only a handful of agency heads ever received it; all of them ignored it.[54]

The FBI, for its part, has a far deeper identity crisis between its domestic law enforcement and intelligence responsibilities, combining functions that in many countries are located in separate organs of government. Law

---

[52] Ibid, 43–7, 50–1. See generally Joseph A Schumpeter, *Capitalism, Socialism and Democracy* [1942] (New York: Harper, 1975).
[53] Zegart, *Spying Blind*, 66–7.     [54] 9/11 Commission Report, 357.

enforcement long ago won this battle and J Edgar Hoover's 'G-men' and today's 'Feds' have long placed far greater emphasis on solving crimes than preventing terrorist attacks. The Phoenix memo, referred to earlier, was forwarded to a Portland FBI field office as it appeared pertinent to an ongoing criminal investigation—but it was never shared with the CIA despite an explicit request to do so within the document itself. Around the same time, during a period of intensifying warnings about possible terror attacks, the FBI's acting director held a conference call with all field office special-agents-in-charge in which he mentioned the heightened threat levels but recommended only that each field office have its evidence response teams ready to investigate an attack at short notice *after* it occurred.[55]

Even more mundane reforms have been difficult. FBI efforts at information technology modernization are, rightly, the subject of ridicule. Its main information system, the Automated Case Support (ACS) system, cost $67 million and was launched in 1995 with 1980s technology; it proved so unreliable that many agents simply didn't use it, preferring to keep case files in shoeboxes under their desks. Even in 2001, the ACS system was incapable of performing a data search using more than one word. One could search for the word 'flight', for example, or 'schools'—but not 'flight schools'. FBI Director Louis Freeh had his own computer removed from his office entirely because he never used it. The September 11 attacks provided new energy to the technology reform process, but in February 2005 Robert Mueller, who had taken over as Director of the FBI just a week before September 11, abandoned the new electronic case filing system Trilogy as a $170 million failure.[56]

As for relations between the CIA and the FBI, the turf battles between the two organizations are the stuff of legend. Even the limited provision for temporary secondments came to be known as the 'hostage exchange program'.[57] Information sharing was also complicated by a legal regime that appeared to create a 'wall' between the government's intelligence and law enforcement capacities, arguably to the detriment of both.[58]

---

[55] Zegart, *Spying Blind*, 156–68. On the distinction between intelligence and law enforcement, see Chapter eight, section 2.

[56] Ibid, 44, 136–9.     [57] Ibid, 79.     [58] See Chapter eight, section 2.1.

## 2.3. Politics

Eight months before the March 2003 invasion of Iraq, British Prime Minister Tony Blair met with senior foreign policy and security officials to discuss the building crisis. The classified minutes, later published by London's *Sunday Times*, show that their discussion focused more on Britain's relationship with the United States than on Iraq itself. John Scarlett, head of the Joint Intelligence Committee, began the meeting with a briefing on the state of Saddam Hussein's regime. Then came an account of meetings with Bush administration officials by Sir Richard Dearlove, head of Britain's Secret Intelligence Service (MI6), known as 'C':

C reported on his recent talks in Washington. There was a perceptible shift in attitude. Military action was now seen as inevitable. Bush wanted to remove Saddam, through military action, justified by the conjunction of terrorism and [weapons of mass destruction]. But the intelligence and facts were being fixed around the policy. The [US National Security Council] had no patience with the UN route, and no enthusiasm for publishing material on the Iraqi regime's record. There was little discussion in Washington of the aftermath after military action.[59]

The disconnect between what intelligence offers a leader and the choices he or she makes is hardly new: during the Second World War, Joseph Stalin is said to have ignored 84 separate warnings from his intelligence services of the German invasion of the Soviet Union that took place in June 1941.[60] Good intelligence will not guarantee success, but bad intelligence frequently contributes to failure.[61] The various efforts at reform seek to improve the quality of intelligence available to policymakers—or to minimize the harm that it can do. The danger, however, lies frequently in how that intelligence will be used.

---

[59] Iraq: Prime Minister's Meeting (Memorandum by David Manning; Secret and Strictly Personal—UK Eyes Only) (London: S 195 /02, 23 July 2003), available in 'The Secret Downing Street Memo', *The Sunday Times* (London), 1 May 2005.

[60] Barton Whaley, *Codeword Barbarossa* (Cambridge, MA: MIT Press, 1973).

[61] Murice R Greenberg and Richard Haass, 'Introduction', in Murice R Greenberg and Richard Haass (eds), *Making Intelligence Smarter: The Future of US Intelligence* (New York: Council on Foreign Relations, 1996), 13.

Quite apart from the ability to inform government policy, an emerging problem is the separation of much of intelligence from public institutions entirely, as a growing proportion of collection and, to some extent, analysis is conducted by private actors.

## 3. THE TURN TO OUTSOURCING

On 14 May 2007, a senior procurement executive from the Office of the Director of National Intelligence gave a presentation to an intelligence industry conference in Colorado convened by the Defense Intelligence Agency (DIA), part of the US Department of Defense. Her unclassified PowerPoint presentation, 'Procuring the Future', was posted on the DIA website, but later modified and subsequently removed. In it, she revealed that the proportion of the US intelligence budget spent on private contractors is 70 per cent. By removing the scale from a table on intelligence expenditures but not the underlying figures, she also inadvertently revealed that the amount the United States spends on such contractors is $42 billion, out of an implied total intelligence budget of $60 billion for the 2005 financial year. At its midpoint the presentation cheerily exhorted: 'We can't spy...if we can't buy!'[62]

Though it lagged behind the privatization of military services, the privatization of intelligence expanded dramatically with the growth in intelligence activities following the September 11 attacks on the United States. In a report published three days after those attacks, the Senate Select Committee on Intelligence encouraged a 'symbiotic relationship between the Intelligence Community and the private sector'.[63] In addition to dollars spent—dominated by large items such as spy satellites—this has

[62] Terri Everett, 'Procuring the Future: 21st Century IC Acquisition (PowerPoint Presentation)' (Defense Intelligence Agency, Keystone, Colorado, 14 May 2007); Tim Shorrock, The Corporate Takeover of US Intelligence (Salon.com, 1 June 2007); RJ Hillhouse, Update: DNI Inadvertently Reveals Key to Classified National Intel Budget, (The Spy Who Billed Me, posted 4 June 2007), available at <http://www.thespywhobilledme.com/the_spy_who_billed_me/2007/06/update_dni_inad.html>. A copy of the original PowerPoint presentation remains available from the Web site of the Federation of American Scientists.

[63] Senate Report on Intelligence Authorization Act for Fiscal Year 2002 (Washington, DC: Senate Select Committee on Intelligence, Report 107–63, 14 September 2001).

seen an important increase in the proportion of personnel working on contract. More than 70 per cent of the Pentagon's Counterintelligence Field Activity (CIFA) unit is staffed by contractors, known as 'green badgers', who also represent the majority of personnel in the DIA, the CIA's National Clandestine Service, and the National Counterterrorism Center. At the CIA's station in Islamabad, contractors reportedly outnumber government employees three-to-one.[64]

Controversy over government reliance on outsourcing in this area frequently coalesces around issues of cost (a contractor costs on average $250,000 per year, about double that of a government employee), 'brain-drain', and periodic allegations of self-dealing and other forms of corruption. More recently, however, the confirmation by the Director of the CIA that contractors participated in waterboarding of detainees at CIA interrogation facilities has sparked a renewed debate over what activities it is appropriate to delegate to contractors, and what activities should remain 'inherently governmental'.[65] This debate is, of course, separate from whether such activities should be carried out in the first place, a topic considered in Chapter two.

Privatization of intelligence services raises many concerns familiar to the debates over private military and security companies (PMSCs). One of the key problems posed by PMSCs is their use of potentially lethal force in an environment where accountability may be legally uncertain and practically unlikely; in some circumstances, PMSCs may also affect the strategic balance of a conflict.[66] The engagement of private actors in the *collection* of intelligence exacerbates the first set of problems: it frequently encompasses a far wider range of conduct that would normally be unlawful, with express or implied immunity from legal process, in an environment designed to avoid scrutiny. Engagement of such actors in

[64] Walter Pincus, 'Lawmakers Want More Data on Contracting Out Intelligence', *Washington Post*, 7 May 2006; Patrick Radden Keefe, 'Don't Privatize Our Spies', *New York Times*, 25 June 2007.

[65] Cf Sarah Percy, 'Morality and Regulation', in Simon Chesterman and Chia Lehnardt (eds), *From Mercenaries to Market: The Rise and Regulation of Private Military Companies* (Oxford: Oxford University Press, 2007), 11.

[66] See generally Chesterman and Lehnardt (eds), *From Mercenaries to Market*; Simon Chesterman and Angelina Fisher (eds), *Private Security, Public Order: The Outsourcing of Public Services and Its Limits* (Oxford: Oxford University Press, 2009).

*analysis* raises the second set of issues: top-level analysis is precisely intended to shape strategic policy—the more such tasks are delegated to private actors, the further they are removed from traditional account-ability structures such as judicial and parliamentary oversight, and the more influence those actors may have on the executive.

### 3.1. Collection

Contracting out hard- and software requirements is probably the biggest single item of outsourcing, but is not significantly different from other forms of government contracting. There are occasional scandals, such as the NSA's contract with Science Applications International Corporation (SAIC) to modernize its ability to sift vast amounts of electronic information with a proposed system known as 'Trailblazer'. Between 2002 and 2005, the project's $280 million budget ballooned to over $1 billion and was later described as a 'complete and abject failure'. Perhaps the most spectacular such failure was Boeing's Future Imagery Architecture, a 1999 contract with the National Reconnaissance Office (NRO) to design a new generation of spy satellites. It was finally cancelled in 2005 after approximately ten billion dollars had been spent. Nevertheless the pool of potential contractors—in particular given the requirement for security clearances—remains small. Thus when the NSA sought a replacement to the failed Trailblazer, the contractor it retained to develop the new programme ExecuteLocus was SAIC.[67]

Somewhat more sensitive than contracts for equipment and software is direct involvement in covert operations. Abraxas, for example, a company founded by CIA veterans in McLean, Virginia, devises 'covers' for overseas case officers. In Iraq, US reliance on contractors appears to have extended also to recruiting and managing human intelligence sources.[68] In 2004, Aegis Defence Services, a British company, was awarded a $300 million contract that explicitly required hiring a team of analysts with 'NATO equivalent SECRET clearance'; responsibilities included 'analysis of

[67] Keefe, 'Don't Privatize Our Spies'; Philip Taubman, 'In Death of Spy Satellite Program, Lofty Plans and Unrealistic Bids', *New York Times*, 11 November 2007.

[68] Greg Miller, 'Spy Agencies Outsourcing to Fill Key Jobs', *Los Angeles Times*, 17 September 2006; James Bamford, 'This Spy for Rent', *New York Times*, 13 June 2004.

foreign intelligence services, terrorist organizations, and their surrogates targeting [Department of Defense] personnel, resources and facilities.'[69]

The reasons given for reliance on private contractors in intelligence are similar for those given by the military: the need for swift increases in skilled personnel that had been scaled back during the 1990s, and the flexibility of such increases being temporary rather than adding permanent government employees.[70] Such hires have also been used to avoid personnel ceilings imposed by Congress; outsourcing may also enable the intelligence services to avoid congressional and other oversight of specific activities. Some of these justifications have been accepted but oversight bodies have emphasized that 'in the long term' the intelligence community must reduce its dependence on contractors, if only for reasons of cost.[71]

Privatization raises particular concerns in areas that may be construed as 'inherently governmental'. One test of this is where activities significantly affect the 'life, liberty, or property of private persons',[72] a test that would at least raise questions with respect to electronic surveillance, rendition, and interrogation.

### 3.1.1. Telecommunications Companies and Electronic Surveillance

The controversy over warrantless electronic surveillance as part of the Bush administration's 'Terrorist Surveillance Program' was discussed in Chapter three. Legislation was passed in August 2007 to provide a legal framework for surveillance,[73] but as its sunset date of 1 February 2008 approached there was a debate over whether to extend it. The two major points of contention were the appropriate levels of oversight for such powers (the 2007 Act essentially substituted internal NSA processes for the requirement of FISA warrants) and, crucially, whether to grant immunity to telecommunications companies that had helped the government

---

[69] Steve Fainaru and Alec Klein, 'In Iraq, a Private Realm of Intelligence-Gathering', *Washington Post*, 1 July 2007.

[70] Ronald P Sanders (Associate Director of National Intelligence), 'Letter to the Editor: The Value of Private Spies', *Washington Post*, 18 July 2007.

[71] Senate Report on Intelligence Authorization Act for Fiscal Year 2008 (Washington, DC: Senate Select Committee on Intelligence, Report 110–75, 31 May 2007), 11.

[72] Policy Letter 92–1: Inherently Governmental Functions (Washington, DC: Office of Federal Procurement Policy, 23 September 1992), para 5(c).

[73] Protect America Act 2007 (US).

conduct surveillance without warrants and thus potentially exposed themselves to civil liability.[74] President Bush authorized a 15 day extension and urged Congress to grant 'liability protection' to those companies:

In order to be able to discover enemy—the enemy's plans, we need the cooperation of telecommunication companies. If these companies are subjected to lawsuits that could cost them billions of dollars, they won't participate; they won't help us; they won't help protect America. Liability protection is critical to securing the private sector's cooperation with our intelligence efforts.[75]

John Ashcroft, Attorney General from 2001 to 2005, had weighed in earlier, arguing that, whatever one's view of warrantless surveillance and its legal basis, allowing litigation against cooperative telecommunications companies would be 'extraordinarily unfair'. As the by-line on his *New York Times* opinion piece noted, Ashcroft now heads a consulting firm with telecommunications companies as clients.[76]

The legislation ultimately lapsed. The following week, the Bush administration asserted that the government had 'lost intelligence information' because of the failure by Democrats in Congress to pass appropriate legislation, causing some telecommunications companies to refuse to cooperate. Hours later, the statement was retracted—apparently after the last holdout among the companies agreed to cooperate fully, even without new authorizing legislation.[77] Five months later, legislation was passed essentially granting the companies immunity as part of an overhaul of FISA.[78]

Examples of potential problems in outsourcing collection in this manner are not hard to find. As a result of an 'apparent miscommunication', an Internet provider complying with a warrant to forward e-mails from one account instead gave the FBI e-mails from every account on the domain for which it served as host. Intelligence officials refer to this as

---

[74] The number of 'contractor facilities' cleared by the National Security Agency grew from 41 in 2002 to 1,265 in 2006. Keefe, 'Don't Privatize Our Spies'.

[75] George W Bush, 'President Bush Discusses Protect America Act' (Washington, DC, 13 February 2008).

[76] John Ashcroft, 'Uncle Sam on the Line', *New York Times*, 5 November 2007.

[77] Dan Eggen and Ellen Nakashima, 'Spy Law Lapse Blamed for Lost Information; Some Telecom Firms not Cooperating for Fear of Liability, US Says', *Washington Post*, 23 February 2008; Josh Meyer, 'White House Backtracks on Lost Intelligence; Officials Acknowledge that Telecom Firms Are Furnishing All Requested Information', *Los Angeles Times*, 24 February 2008.

[78] Foreign Intelligence Surveillance Act of 1978 Amendments Act 2008 (US), § 802.

'overproduction', when third parties provide them with more information than actually required.[79] In the case of the NSA's programme, the absence of the requirement for a warrant, the secrecy of the programme, and the self-interest of companies engaging in legally questionable activity suggest little reason for confidence in oversight. Legislators only became involved after the story had become public.[80]

Such issues are not, of course, limited to the United States. In March 2008, for example, India's government threatened to ban Research In Motion's BlackBerry service unless the company facilitated decryption of communication across its network. The admission that India was incapable of breaking the BlackBerry code was unusual, but an agreement was eventually concluded allowing RIM to sell its smart-phones, presumably with some provision allowing for government interception of data.[81]

## 3.1.2. Private Aircraft and Rendition

In the case of telecommunications companies, involvement of private actors was necessary as a technical matter in order to access information. With respect to private involvement in rendition, recourse to the private sector appears to have been part of a clear effort to avoid oversight.

The CIA's use of private aircraft for moving detainees between black site detention centres is now well documented. Enterprising journalists, blogger activists, and hobbyist plane spotters combined to share information about planes that are believed to have been at the heart of the 'extraordinary rendition' programme,[82] which was originally authorized under the Clinton administration.[83] The use of proprietary or 'front' companies by the CIA is not unusual, though reliance upon private companies for

[79] Eric Lichtblau, 'Error Gave FBI Unauthorized Access to E-mail', *New York Times*, 17 February 2008.        [80] See Chapter three, section 3.3.

[81] Matt Hartley, 'RIM's Double-Edged Encryption Sword', *Globe and Mail* (Toronto), 28 May 2008; Ashwini Shrivastava, 'Govt, Blackberry Makers to Jointly Resolve Security Issues', *The Press Trust of India*, 2 October 2008; Rick Westhead, 'Indian Investment', *Toronto Star*, 17 October 2009.

[82] Stephen Grey, *Ghost Plane: The True Story of the CIA Torture Program* (New York: St Martin's Press, 2006); Jane Mayer, 'Outsourcing: The CIA's Travel Agent', *New Yorker*, 30 October 2006.

[83] Presidential Decision Directive 95: US Policy on Counterterrorism (PDD-95) (Washington, DC: White House, 21 June 1995). See also the discussion of privacy in Chapter eight, section 4.

active support rather than cover is atypical. Officials who were involved in the practice suggested this was in order to protect government officials from involvement in a legally questionable process.[84] The rendition programme became a scandal in Europe, with a report from the European Parliament leading to a resolution recommending, among other things, that 'all European countries that have not done so should initiate independent investigations into all stopovers made by civilian aircraft carried out by the CIA'.[85]

### 3.1.3. *Green Badgers and Interrogation*

A third area in which outsourcing has taken place is interrogations. In February 2008, CIA Director Michael Hayden testified before the Senate and House—appearances most memorable for his confirmation that the United States had waterboarded at least three detainees.[86] He was also asked about the use of contractors. Before the Senate Select Intelligence Committee he confirmed that the CIA continued to use 'green badgers' at its secret detention facilities.[87] In testimony before the House two days later he was asked whether contractors were involved in waterboarding al Qaeda detainees. He responded by saying, 'I'm not sure of the specifics. I'll give you a tentative answer: I believe so.'[88]

The involvement of private contractors in interrogations raises the most serious questions about accountability of persons outside government wielding extraordinary authority and discretion in an environment clearly weighted against either investigation or prosecution. As in the case of private military contractors using potentially lethal force in a conflict zone, these concerns include the dubious prospect of after the

---

[84] Dana Priest, 'Jet Is an Open Secret in Terror War', *Washington Post*, 27 December 2004.

[85] Transportation and Illegal Detention of Prisoners: European Parliament Resolution on the Alleged Use of European Countries by the CIA for the Transportation and Illegal Detention of Prisoners (P6_TA-PROV(2007)0032-(2006/2200(INI)), 2007), para 190.

[86] Scott Shane, 'CIA Chief Doubts Tactic to Interrogate Is Still Legal', *New York Times*, 8 February 2008.

[87] Annual Worldwide Threat Assessment Hearings (Washington, DC: Senate Select Committee on Intelligence, 5 February 2008), 26 (referring to 'greenbaggers', presumably a transcription error).

[88] Annual Worldwide Threat Assessment Hearings (Washington, DC: House Permanent Select Committee on Intelligence, 7 February 2008), 26.

fact accountability, but also the absence of standardized levels of training or a defined command structure.

Both sets of concerns were proven justified after revelations that detainees had been abused at the Abu Ghraib prison in Iraq, discussed in Chapter three. No charges have been laid against contractors, despite repeated allegations that they participated in abuse. The companies Titan and CACI provided interpreters and interrogators to the US military respectively; the commanding officer at the prison, Brigadier General Janis Karpinski (later demoted to colonel), claimed in an interview with a Spanish newspaper that she had seen a letter signed by Secretary of Defense Donald Rumsfeld allowing civilian contractors to use techniques such as sleep deprivation during interrogation.[89] A class action against Titan and CACI under the Alien Tort Claims Act was lodged in 2004 and is ongoing in the US District Court for the Southern District of California. The case against Titan was dismissed as its linguists were found to have been 'fully integrated into the military units to which they were assigned and that they performed their duties under the direct command and exclusive operational control of military personnel.' As CACI interrogators were subject to a 'dual chain of command', with significant independent authority retained by CACI supervisors, the case against it was allowed to continue.[90]

There appears to be only one case of a contractor being convicted of a crime in the United States connected with interrogations during the 'war on terror'. David Passaro, a contractor working for the CIA, was convicted of misdemeanour assault and felony assault with a dangerous weapon charges for his connection with the torture and beating to death of Abdul Wali in Afghanistan in June 2003. In February 2007, Passaro was sentenced to eight years and four months in prison. His background is testimony to the danger of contracting out such interrogations: both his previous wives have alleged that he was abusive at home, and he had been fired from the police force after being arrested for beating a man in a parking lot brawl.[91]

---

[89] 'Rumsfeld Okayed Abuses Says Former US Army General', *Reuters*, 25 November 2006.

[90] *Ibrahim v Titan*, 556 F Supp 2d 1, 28–30 (DC, 2007).

[91] James Dao, 'A Man of Violence, or Just "110 Percent" Gung-Ho?', *New York Times*, 19 June 2004. See also EL Gaston, 'Mercenarism 2.0? The Rise of the Modern Private Security Industry and Its Implications for International Humanitarian Law Enforcement', *Harvard International Law Journal* 49 (2008) 221 at 229.

Soon after the Passaro story broke a 'Detainee Abuse Task Force' was established, but does not appear to have brought any charges against contractors.[92]

## 3.2. Analysis

The involvement of contractors in analysis raises somewhat different questions from their involvement in collection of intelligence. A company's analytical work is less likely to be linked to abusive behaviour or the type of activities typically discussed in the context of private military contractor accountability. Nevertheless, through its participation in and influencing of high-level decisions about national security, the consequences are troubling if they indicate a removal of such decisions from democratically accountable structures.[93]

For the most part, problems in this area have tended to be at the level of personnel, notably the drain encouraged by significantly higher salaries in the private sector. A practice known as 'bidding back' sees officials leaving for industry and then being brought back in the capacity of consultant at a higher salary. Some estimate that as many as two-thirds of the Department of Homeland Security's senior personnel and experts have left for industry in recent years.[94] A 2006 report by the Office of the Director of National Intelligence noted that the intelligence community increasingly finds itself in competition with its contractors:

Confronted by arbitrary staffing ceilings and uncertain funding, components are left with no choice but to use contractors for work that may be borderline 'inherently governmental'—only to find that to do that work, those same contractors recruit our own employees, already cleared and trained at government expense, and then 'lease' them back to us at considerably greater expense.[95]

---

[92] Susan Burke, 'Accountability for Corporate Complicity in Torture', *Gonzaga Journal of International Law* 10 (2006) 81 at 85; Corporate Accountability in the "War on Terror" (New York: Amnesty International USA, 2007).

[93] A separate concern would be the potential for misuse of personal data. See the discussion concerning CCTV in Chapter five, section 3.1.

[94] Keefe, 'Don't Privatize Our Spies'; Bamford, 'This Spy for Rent'.

[95] The US Intelligence Community's Five Year Strategic Human Capital Plan (An Annex to the US National Intelligence Strategy) (Washington, DC: Office of the Director of National Intelligence (ODNI), 22 June 2006), 6.

From 1 June 2007, the CIA began to bar contractors from hiring former agency employees and then offering their services back to the CIA within the first year and a half of retirement.[96]

As indicated earlier, a second general concern is the cost of retaining contractors. In May 2007, the Senate Select Committee on Intelligence criticized the intelligence services' 'increasing reliance on contractors'.[97] The CIA subsequently announced that it would reduce the number of contractors by ten per cent.[98]

In addition to individual contractors, firms such as Booz Allen Hamilton have established themselves as consultants to the intelligence community. Booz Allen currently employs a former CIA director (R James Woolsey), a former executive director of the President's Foreign Intelligence Advisory Board (Joan Dempsey), and a former director of the National Reconnaissance Office (Keith Hall). Mike McConnell headed the NSA and then went to Booz Allen in 1996 as a Senior Vice President working on intelligence and national security issues; in 2007, President Bush appointed him as Director of National Intelligence.[99] Dedicated human resources personnel handle job applicants with security clearances.

Though there are occasional breathless accounts of contractor involvement in high-level analytical documents such as the President's Daily Brief,[100] it is enough to note that even the perception of a conflict of interest should raise questions about the involvement of the corporate sector in the analytical functions of the intelligence services. It might be argued that this is little different from the influence of wealth on US politics more generally, though the secrecy, incentive structures, and potentially abusive powers of the intelligence community warrant special care in regularizing the participation of private actors.

---

[96] Walter Pincus and Stephen Barr, 'CIA Plans Cutbacks, Limits on Contractor Staffing', *Washington Post*, 11 June 2007.

[97] Senate Report on Intelligence Authorization Act for Fiscal Year 2008, 11.

[98] Keefe, 'Don't Privatize Our Spies'; Mark Tarallo, 'Hayden Wants Fewer CIA Contractors', *Federal Computer Week*, 25 June 2007.

[99] Tim Shorrock, The Spy Who Came In from the Boardroom (Salon.com, 8 January 2007).

[100] See, eg, RJ Hillhouse, Corporate Content and the President's Daily Brief, (The Spy Who Billed Me, posted 23 July 2007), available at <http://www.thespywhobilledme.com/the_spy_who_billed_me/2007/07/corporate-conte.html>.

### 3.3. Accountability

Oversight and review of intelligence services is always difficult given the secrecy necessary for many of their activities to be carried out effectively. In the case of privatization of these services within the US intelligence community, however, secrecy appears to have compounded ignorance.

In May 2007—the same month as the 'We can't spy...if we can't buy!' presentation—the House Permanent Select Committee on Intelligence reported that the leaders of the US intelligence community

do not have an adequate understanding of the size and composition of the contractor work force, a consistent and well-articulated method for assessing contractor performance, or strategies for managing a combined staff-contractor workforce. In addition, the Committee is concerned that the Intelligence Community does not have a clear definition of what functions are 'inherently governmental' and, as a result, whether there are contractors performing inherently governmental functions.[101]

Legislators subsequently called for the Department of Defense to compile a database of all intelligence-related contracts, and for a Government Accountability Office investigation of contractors in Iraq.[102]

Reports have been commissioned before. In fact, only one month before the House report a year-long examination of outsourcing by US intelligence services was held up by the Director of National Intelligence, and then reclassified as a national secret.[103] The secrecy was justified on the basis that the United States does not reveal the cost and size of its intelligence operations, though recent disclosures on that topic by senior officials belie this explanation.

Such information as does exist about the involvement of contractors often remains classified. Much is available to the contractors themselves,

---

[101] House of Representatives Report on Intelligence Authorization Act for Fiscal Year 2008 (Washington, DC: Permanent Select Committee on Intelligence, Report 110–131, 7 May 2007), 42. Cf Conference Report on Intelligence Authorization Act for Fiscal Year 2008 (Washington, DC: House of Representatives, Report 110–478, 6 December 2007), 68.

[102] Walter Pincus, 'Defense Agency Proposes Outsourcing More Spying', *Washington Post*, 19 August 2007; Fainaru and Klein, 'In Iraq, a Private Realm of Intelligence-Gathering'.

[103] Scott Shane, 'Government Keeps a Secret After Studying Spy Agencies', *New York Times*, 26 April 2007; RJ Hillhouse, 'Who Runs the CIA? Outsiders for Hire', *Washington Post*, 8 July 2007.

however, who are able to lobby members of Congress using that information. SAIC, for example, spent well over a million dollars in each of the past ten years on lobbying; in that period it was awarded between one and three billion dollars in government contracts annually. Earmarks, in which members of Congress add provisions to legislation directing funds to specific projects, have long been tacitly accepted in the intelligence sector but rarely made public. In some cases a list of the amounts of projects might be made available, but redacting the names of companies.[104] In November 2007, Congress broke with tradition by releasing information about $80 million worth of earmarks included in a defence appropriations bill.[105]

As is frequently the case, this new found transparency was driven by scandal. The previous year Randy 'Duke' Cunningham, a Republican Congressman from California, had been sentenced to eight years in prison for accepting $2 million in bribes from MZM, a defence contractor. Cunningham had used his position on the House appropriations and intelligence committees to win MZM tens of millions of dollars' worth of contracts with the CIA and the Pentagon's CIFA office. In a related case, Kyle 'Dusty' Foggo, a former executive director of the CIA (its third-ranking official), was indicted for conspiring with former MZM CEO Brent Wilkes (who inexplicably lacked a folksy nickname) to direct contracts to the company.[106]

In addition to undermining effective oversight either by formal or informal means, such as media scrutiny, access to secrets creates the possibility of abuse of those secrets. In 2006, the Boeing Corporation, a major defence contractor, agreed to a $565 million civil settlement arising from its use of sensitive bid information to win rocket launch contracts. The information had been provided by an engineer formerly employed by a competitor for the contracts, who had moved to the Department of Defense.[107]

---

[104] Shorrock, Corporate Takeover.
[105] Roxana Tiron, 'Congress Discloses Intel Earmarks for First Time', *The Hill*, 24 November 2007. See Conference Report on Making Appropriations for the Department of Defense for the Fiscal Year Ending September 30, 2008, and for Other Purposes (Washington, DC: House of Representatives, Report 110–434, 6 November 2007), 378–9.
[106] Shorrock, Corporate Takeover.
[107] Semiannual Report to the Congress, April 1, 2006–September 30, 2006 (Washington, DC: Inspector General, United States Department of Defense, 2006), 55.

The abuse of sensitive information is suggestive of the potential conflict of interest on the part of private actors engaged in intelligence activities. Discussions of this issue frequently paint a somewhat idealized picture of the patriotism and competence of full-time government employees, but there are reasonable grounds to be wary of inserting a profit motive into intelligence activities. The former head of the CIA's clandestine service has been quoted as saying that 'There's a commercial side to it that I frankly don't like...I would much prefer to see staff case officers who are in the chain of command and making a day-in and day-out conscious decision as civil servants in the intelligence business.'[108]

It is also arguable that the freedom to outsource alters the incentives of the intelligence services themselves. John Gannon, a former CIA Deputy Director for Intelligence and now head of BAE Systems' Global Analysis Group, has noted that this freedom offers flexibility but also avoids the need to justify a full-time employee and allocate responsibility, thereby breeding duplication and inhibiting collaboration. In the 1980s, 'what we discovered was that having smaller numbers forced collaboration, and collaboration was a good thing. As soon as you start throwing money at the intelligence community, not only does it lead to more contractors, it also leads to individual units thinking "We want to get one of our own."'[109] This in turn makes it harder to contain costs.

It is possible, of course, that a profit motive may encourage *better* behaviour through the operation of a kind of market. There is evidence that this may be happening gradually in the context of PMSCs, particularly through professionalization of the industry and the creation of industry associations such as the British Association of Private Security Companies and the International Peace Operations Association. The move is largely being driven by self-interest as some actors seek to establish themselves as 'legitimate' and thereby raise the costs of entry for competitors while enabling the charging of higher fees for similar services.[110]

Markets can indeed be an effective form of regulation, but they operate best where there is competition, an expectation of repeat encounters, and

---

[108]   Miller, 'Spy Agencies Outsourcing' (quoting James Pavitt).

[109]   Sebastian Abbot, 'The Outsourcing of US Intelligence Analysis', *News21*, 28 July 2006 (quoting John Gannon).

[110]   Simon Chesterman and Chia Lehnardt, 'Conclusion: From Mercenaries to Market', in Chesterman and Lehnardt (eds), *From Mercenaries to Market*, 251 at 254–5.

a free flow of information. It is far from clear that these qualities apply to the commercial military sector; there is even more reason to be wary of embracing such a philosophy in the realm of intelligence.

Competition is severely restricted by the requirement that intelligence contractors meet security clearances. The process of granting new clearances is famously inefficient while the government frequently needs to hire people quickly.[111] The 'market' thus tends to be dominated by former military and civilian officials who already have such clearances, exacerbating the 'brain drain' cited earlier and creating predictable monopoly-type problems.

Though this arrangement has led to some established relationships with a select group of firms, in respect of individuals being retained to collect human intelligence—especially interrogators and interpreters—the need to get personnel on the ground and results back home has negated considerations of repeat encounters. As in the case of PMSCs, the assumption that such activities are atypical reduces the incentive to use any leverage that does exist to require adequate training or oversight.[112]

Finally, and most obviously, the secrecy necessary for certain intelligence operations undermines the possibility of information flowing freely. In some circumstances there may be collusion in avoiding oversight, as when activities—such as rendition—are outsourced precisely for this reason. More generally, the movement of a limited number of individuals between the government and private intelligence worlds may encourage a form of regulatory capture if government employees are nominally tasked with overseeing former colleagues and future employers.[113]

### 3.4. 'Inherently Governmental' Functions

The simplest way of containing many of these problems would be to forbid certain activities from being delegated or outsourced to private actors at all. Intelligence services have a chequered history of abuse, but their legitimate activities tend to be justified in established democracies by reference

---

[111] Lawrence Wright, 'The Spymaster', *New Yorker*, 21 January 2008, 42.
[112] See, eg, Martha Minow, 'Outsourcing Power: How Privatizing Military Efforts Challenges Accountability, Professionalism, and Democracy', *Boston College Law Review* 46 (2005) 989 at 1005–16.     [113] See Chapter three, section 2.3.

to their grounding in the rule of law—a relatively recent requirement in some countries—and the existence of an accountability chain to democratic institutions.[114]

In the United States, this question is framed in the language of 'inherently governmental' functions, which are presumed to be carried out by government employees only. Debates concerning public functions in the United States frequently emphasize not the need to maintain certain functions in public hands but rather to justify passing them to the government in the first place; the definition of 'inherently governmental' has thus emerged not as a sphere to be protected, but as an exception to the more general push to privatization. Legislation adopted by Congress in 1998 as part of a larger privatization effort required government agencies to identify inherently governmental functions in order to enable cost comparisons between private bids and public budgets for everything else. An inherently governmental function was defined as a 'function that is so intimately related to the public interest as to require performance by Federal Government employees.'[115]

The Government Accountability Office (GAO) noted in a 2002 report that there had been some uncertainty about how to apply this broad definition, but argued that it was 'clear that government workers need to perform certain warfighting, judicial, enforcement, regulatory, and policy-making functions... Certain other capabilities,... such as those directly linked to national security, also must be retained in-house to help ensure effective mission execution.'[116] Uncertainties about the limits continue, however, and the Department of Defense in particular has failed to adopt or apply a clear interpretation.[117]

The executive has adopted various guidelines seeking to define what is meant by the term. The 1983 version of an Office of Management and Budget (OMB) circular stated that 'Certain functions are inherently

[114] See generally Hans Born and Marina Caparini (eds), *Democratic Control of Intelligence Services: Containing Rogue Elephants* (Aldershot: Ashgate, 2007).

[115] 31 USC § 501 note.

[116] Commercial Activities Panel: Improving the Sourcing Decisions of the Federal Government (Washington, DC: US General Accounting Office (GAO), GAO-02-847T, 27 September 2002), 21.

[117] Steven L Schooner, 'Contractor Atrocities at Abu Ghraib: Compromised Accountability in a Streamlined, Outsourced Government', *Stanford Law and Policy Review* 16 (2005) 549 at 554–7.

Governmental in nature, being so intimately related to the public interest as to mandate performance only by Federal employees.' The definition was said to include 'those activities which require either the exercise of discretion in applying Government authority or the use of value judgment in making decisions for the Government' and embraced 'direction of intelligence and counter-intelligence operations'.[118] A 1992 'Policy Letter' from the Office of Federal Procurement Policy essentially repeated the same text, but also included 'the interpretation and execution of the laws of the United States so as to . . . significantly affect the life, liberty, or property of private persons'.[119] The illustrative list of examples provided in an appendix included the 'direction *and control* of intelligence and counter-intelligence operations'.[120]

A 2003 revision kept the general definition in place, but opened up significant loopholes by allowing for activities to be performed by contractors 'where the contractor does not have the authority to decide on the course of action, but is tasked to develop options or implement a course of action, with agency oversight'. The revision also dropped any reference to intelligence or counter-intelligence operations. Another aspect of the Circular worthy of note is the ability of the Defense Department to 'determine if this circular applies to the Department of Defense during times of a declared war or military mobilization'.[121] It is not clear whether this provision has been implemented.

In the absence of strong political direction, there is little prospect of intelligence services adopting a robust definition of 'inherently governmental' functions. In any case, the significance of this limitation is diminished by the ability to outsource even inherently governmental functions in so far as they may be construed merely as implementing policy with some form of oversight.

---

[118] OMB Circular No A-76: Performance of Commercial Activities (superseded) (Washington, DC: White House Office of Management and Budget, 1983), paras (b), (e).

[119] Policy Letter 92–1, para 5(c).

[120] Ibid, Appendix A, para 8 (emphasis added). Cf OMB Circular No A-76: Performance of Commercial Activities (Revised 1999) (superseded) (Washington, DC: White House Office of Management and Budget, 1999).

[121] OMB Circular No A-76 (Revised): Performance of Commercial Activities (Washington, DC: White House Office of Management and Budget, 29 May 2003), Attachment A: Inventory Process, para B(1)(a)–(c), 5(h).

With respect to the activities considered in this Chapter, electronic surveillance by telecommunications companies may be an acceptable or necessary delegation of the implementation of government policy, though in some circumstances it might have fallen foul of the broader 'control' of intelligence operations test included in the 1992 Policy Letter. Rendition might also be construed as mere implementation of government policy, though it may violate other laws—notably including those of the territories through which CIA transport planes have passed.[122] There would, however, seem to be some prospect for agreement at the political level that interrogation of detainees falls 'squarely within the definition of an inherently governmental activity'.[123] Analysis by private contractors is somewhat trickier: clearly if it amounted to direction or the exercise of government discretion this would cross the line, but in most circumstances it would be easy to construe the work as merely 'developing options'.

Uncertainty in this area appears to be intentional and thus exacerbates the accountability challenges posed by secrecy and problematic incentives. At the very least, the responsibility to determine what is and is not 'inherently governmental' should itself be an inherently governmental task.

## 4. BACK TO THE LIGHT?

'Americans will always do the right thing,' Winston Churchill once observed, 'after they've exhausted all the alternatives.' In the wake of the repudiation of torture, renewed vigilance on the part of the judiciary, and the falling of scales from the eyes of the American public, there is some reason to hope that the cliché will be borne out.

Difficulties remain. On the second full day of his presidency in January 2009, Barack Obama issued executive orders to close the detention facility at Guantánamo Bay, end the CIA's secret prison programme, and renounce

---

[122] See Monica Hakimi, 'The Council of Europe Addresses CIA Rendition and Detention Program', *American Journal of International Law* 101 (2007) 442.

[123] Dianne Feinstein, Letter to the Honorable Michael B Mukasey, Attorney General of the United States (6 February 2008); Gorman, 'CIA Likely Let Contractors Perform Waterboarding'.

torture.[124] Yet the closure of Guantánamo presented the question of where detainees could be held or how they could be tried: some were released, others transferred to detention in third countries, while many remain in a legal limbo. The closure of secret prisons has not halted the growth of the detention facility at Bagram Air Field outside Kabul, which is less visible and attracts less criticism than its counterpart in Cuba. The renunciation of torture was accompanied by agonized debate over the extent to which past actions should be the subject of investigation.

The surveillance powers of the state have, to some extent, been regularized, though anecdotal evidence continues to emerge that rules are routinely disregarded. One trend that shows little sign of abating is the reliance upon private actors. Indeed, under the Obama administration there was a significant increase in the use of unmanned drones for targeting alleged terrorists in the Afghanistan-Pakistan border region. These drones, technically under the control of the CIA, are maintained by Xe Services—the corporate reincarnation of Blackwater.[125]

Reliance on the private sector is, to some extent, inevitable. Procuring hardware and software from the private sector and engaging in electronic surveillance through the cooperation of telecommunications companies may be the only way to carry out such functions effectively. More troubling are those circumstances in which outsourcing has been undertaken to avoid oversight, as in the case of rendition, where it places the life or liberty of persons in the hands of private actors, as in the case of interrogation, or where it renders the formulation of national security policy susceptible to actual or apparent influence.

Consideration of these issues has tended to focus on overblown costs, drains on government personnel, and episodic outrage at scandals in the form of corruption or, more recently, abuse. Addressing the problems raised by privatization of intelligence services requires engagement with the structural bars to accountability; accepting the necessary secrecy of much—but not all—of these activities requires a corresponding limitation on their further removal from public scrutiny. Understanding the

[124] Scott Shane, Mark Mazzetti, and Helene Cooper, 'Obama Reverses Key Bush Security Policies', *New York Times*, 22 January 2009.
[125] Simon Chesterman, 'Blackwater and the Limits to Outsourcing Security', *International Herald Tribune*, 13 November 2009.

incentives also suggests the need for wariness in embracing a market regulatory approach to the problem. Clarity could most effectively be achieved by a transparent definition of what functions should be 'inherently governmental', though this requires political capital that is unlikely to be spent in the absence of scandal.

Such a scandal in the form of Blackwater's activities in Iraq—in particular the killing of 17 civilians in Baghdad in September 2007—pushed the United States and Iraq to revisit the accountability of private military companies. Despite revelations that contractors employed by the US government appear to have engaged in torture, in the form of waterboarding, this was insufficient to start a major debate on the topic. Instead, reforms—if any—seem most likely to come because each of those torturers cost the US taxpayer double the salary of a Federal employee.

# 5

# Britain and the Turn to Law

The members of the Service are, in the eye of the law, ordinary citizens with no powers greater than anyone else. They have no special powers of arrest such as the police have. No special powers of search are given to them. They cannot enter premises without the consent of the householder, even though they suspect a spy is there...They have, in short, no executive powers. They have managed very well without them. We would rather have it so, than have anything in the nature of a 'secret police'.

Lord Denning[1]

In the mid-1970s, James Malone was an antique dealer living in Dorking, an historic market town in Surrey, England. He began receiving mail that had been opened and resealed with identical tape and suspected that his phone was being tapped. It transpired that he had been the target of a police investigation and in 1977 he was charged with receiving stolen goods. Two trials ended with hung juries and a third attempt at prosecution was abandoned. During the first trial, however, a police officer under cross-examination read from a notebook what appeared to be extracts of telephone conversations. This departure from police practice at the time—which was never to reveal the use of wiretapping—led to a countersuit by Malone challenging the lawfulness of the intercept. That case was dismissed as the judge concluded that there was no law prohibiting such wiretapping in England, but he added that the potential for abuse made this a subject that 'cries out for legislation'.[2]

---

[1] Lord Denning, Report on the Profumo Affair (London: HMSO, Cmnd 2152, 1963), para 273.   [2] Malone v Metropolitan Police Commissioner [1979] Ch 344, 380–1.

Malone pursued his complaint to the European Court of Human Rights, which allows an individual right of petition to challenge violations of the European Convention on Human Rights. The Convention includes a right to privacy, which is not to be interfered with except 'in accordance with the law' and as necessary in a democratic society in pursuit of national security, public safety, for the prevention of crime, and other defined aims.[3] It became clear that the British guidelines for granting wiretaps were vague to the point of obscurity. The Court held that the law did not indicate with reasonable clarity the extent of discretion conferred on the public authorities, and that 'it would be contrary to the rule of law for the legal discretion granted to the executive to be expressed in terms of an unfettered power.'[4]

Malone won his case and a measure of damages, but the more lasting result was the passage of the Interception of Communications Act 1985. This was the first in a series of statutes that brought the British intelligence services and their powers onto a legislative footing. For the better part of four decades, the Security Service (better known as MI5) operated on the basis of a six-paragraph administrative directive until legislation was passed in 1989. The British government only officially acknowledged even the existence of the Secret Intelligence Service (known as MI6) in 1992— well after the release of the sixteenth James Bond film popularizing the exploits of its most famous fictional agent.

This turn to law has been discussed in general terms in Chapter two.[5] Here the focus will be the impact that the formalization of the intelligence services and their powers have had in Britain. As the quote from Lord Denning indicates, Britain long adopted the legal fiction—manifestly false in practice if not in theory—that the representatives of its intelligence services were merely 'ordinary citizens'. In fact they exercised considerable power and the moves to establish a legal foundation for those powers and appropriate checks and balances in the past two decades are, as the European Court held, demanded by the rule of law. At the same time, however, Britain demonstrates some of the problems attendant to

---

[3] [European] Convention for the Protection of Human Rights and Fundamental Freedoms, done at Rome, 4 November 1950, in force 3 September 1953, art 8.

[4] *Malone v the United Kingdom* (1984) 7 EHRR 14, paras 68, 79.

[5] See Chapter two, section 2.

establishing such a legal regime. These include the question of how the mandate of intelligence services should be defined, as well as the possibility that powers granted by law may be exercised by a far wider range of actors than when a key check was the need to keep those powers and actors secret. Finally, Britain is of interest in showing the limitations of law in regulating socially-pervasive technologies, such as the closed-circuit television (CCTV) cameras that are ubiquitous in London and other cities large and small. The belated effort to regulate CCTV suggests lessons for other new technologies such as biometric identification and DNA databases.

## 1. 'ORDINARY CITIZENS'

The *Malone* case highlighted a key difference between the US and British approaches to intelligence. The United States, somewhat unusually for the English-speaking world, put its intelligence services on a statutory basis very soon after the Second World War. This was consistent with the strict separation of executive and legislative powers under the US Constitution, which are vested in the distinct institutions of the President and Congress. In Britain and the rest of the Commonwealth, by contrast, the intelligence services traced their origins and powers—like all military matters—to the royal prerogative.[6] The protections against abuse of those powers were similarly distinct: in the United States the written Constitution and its Bill of Rights could be used to strike down legislation; in Britain the lack of a written constitution and the recognition of few formal rights meant that liberties (such as privacy) were traditionally protected only through the *absence* of legislation.[7]

---

[6] Laurence Lustgarten and Ian Leigh, *In from the Cold: National Security and Parliamentary Democracy* (Oxford: Clarendon Press, 1994), 374. See Chapter two, section 1.1. Cf arguments during the Bush administration concerning the powers of the unitary executive discussed in Chapter four, section 1.2.

[7] Specific statutes did protect certain rights, such as the Data Protection Act 1984 (UK). Case law had also provided limited protections to home life. See Basil Markesinis et al, 'Concerns and Ideas About the Developing English Law of Privacy (and How Knowledge of Foreign Law Might Be of Help)', *American Journal of Comparative Law* 52 (2004) 133.

The military origins of the Security Service and the Secret Intelligence Service live on in their colloquial names MI5 and MI6: Military Intelligence, Sections 5 and 6—administrative divisions dating back to the First World War, but not in active use since the 1920s. (Section 1, dealing with codes and ciphers, ultimately became what is now Government Communications Headquarters, or GCHQ.)[8] MI5 effectively reported to the Prime Minister until 1952, when responsibility was transferred to the Home Secretary. The shift was intended to bring MI5 under some measure of ministerial responsibility as the previous arrangement had allowed its Director-General virtual autonomy. Sir David Maxwell-Fyfe, the Home Secretary at the time, wrote up a six-paragraph directive addressed to the Director-General that provided the contours of the governance, mandate, and powers of MI5 for the next four decades.[9]

The governance structure was that the Director-General would be 'personally' responsible to the Home Secretary, though MI5 itself remained part of the Defence Forces. The directive also maintained the 'well-established convention' that ministers would not concern themselves with the detailed information obtained by the Security Service in particular cases, 'but are furnished with such information only as may be necessary for the determination of any issue on which guidance is sought'. The mandate was framed broadly as 'the Defence of the Realm as a whole' from internal and external espionage and sabotage, but also against the actions of persons and organizations 'which may be judged to be subversive to the State'. At the same time, the directive emphasized the need to keep MI5 free of any political bias or influence, and that no investigations should be undertaken on behalf of a government department unless an important public interest bearing on the 'Defence of the Realm' was at stake. The agency's powers were not defined, but a further caveat enjoined the Director-General to 'take special care to see that the work of the Security Service is strictly limited to what is necessary for the purposes of their task.'[10]

In addition to the breadth of the discretion it conferred, the Maxwell-Fyfe Directive lacked any legal mechanisms to deal with complaints about

---

[8] See Chapter one, section 1.      [9] Lustgarten and Leigh, *In from the Cold*, 375.
[10] Maxwell-Fyfe Directive (issued by the UK Home Secretary, Sir David Maxwell-Fyfe, to the Director-General MI5, 1952), reprinted in Lustgarten and Leigh, *In from the Cold*, 517.

abuses and violations of rights. It was also a mere administrative directive that could be changed without reference to Parliament, establishing no formal limits or controls.[11] Following the *Malone* decision—which dealt with the surveillance powers of the police rather than the intelligence services as such—it was clear that these deficiencies would be open to challenge before the European Courts.

## 2. THE RULE OF LAW

In practice, of course, members of the intelligence services exercised powers far beyond those of 'ordinary citizens'. As Peter Wright, a former Assistant Director of MI5, put it in his scandalous and self-aggrandizing memoir *Spycatcher*: 'we bugged and burgled our way across London at the State's behest, while pompous bowler-hatted civil servants in Whitehall pretended to look the other way.'[12] Ironically, the use of telephone intercepts appears to have been subject to more thorough controls than other activities, though it was wiretapping in the *Malone* case that provided the impetus for change.[13]

As indicated in Chapter two, scandal is frequently the driving force for change in the legal regime governing intelligence. Britain is relatively unusual in that the most important change in the century since its modern intelligence services were established appears to have been inspired by the desire to *avoid* legal action. There had been criticism since the 1960s of the uncertain legal basis on which the intelligence services acted and the absence of protections against abuse. Moves by former colonies such as Australia, New Zealand, and Canada to put their services on a legislative footing also influenced debate in Britain.[14] Other factors included the unwanted attention GCHQ had received because of a labour dispute in

---

[11] Ian Leigh, 'Accountability of Security and Intelligence in the United Kingdom', in Hans Born, Loch K Johnson, and Ian Leigh (eds), *Who's Watching the Spies: Establishing Intelligence Service Accountability* (Washington, DC: Potomac Books, 2005), 79 at 79–80.

[12] Peter Wright, *Spycatcher: The Candid Autobiography of a Senior Intelligence Officer* (New York: Viking, 1987), 54.

[13] Ibid, 46. See generally Christopher M Andrew, *The Defence of the Realm: The Authorised History of MI5* (London: Allen Lane, 2009).      [14] See Chapter two, section 2.

the mid-1980s, and the futile efforts to suppress the publication of *Spycatcher*—which, predictably, boosted sales and undermined the British government's credibility. Nevertheless, it appears to have been the threat of further human rights challenges in the European system that led to the surprise passage of the Security Service Act 1989 and, five years later, the Intelligence Services Act 1994.[15]

Though the *Malone* case did not directly involve the intelligence services, it set the benchmark for the exercise of surveillance powers and the need for them to be grounded in law. In fact the interception of telecommunications, which had historically been assumed to be consistent with the common law (which recognized no right to privacy), had already been the subject of legislation. Prior to 1969, the Post Office was a part of the government and the Postmaster General was an officer of state. As a matter of policy, it was the practice at least from 1937 only to allow intercepts on the authority of the Home Secretary; any dispute between the Home Secretary and the Postmaster General was, presumably, resolved as a political matter within the cabinet.[16] In 1969, however, the Post Office was established as a public corporation no longer under ministerial control. Language was included in the Post Office Act to preserve the same powers of interception, but framed in delightfully circumlocutory language:

A requirement to do what is necessary to inform designated persons holding office under the Crown concerning matters and things transmitted or in course of transmission by means of postal or telecommunication services provided by the Post Office may be laid on the Post Office for the like purposes and in the like manner as, at the passing of this Act, a requirement may be laid on the Post-master General to do what is necessary to inform such persons concerning matters and things transmitted or in course of transmission by means of such services provided by him.[17]

The effect was that the Home Secretary could continue to authorize wiretaps, but the indirection and vagueness with which this power was to be exercised is evident.

The need for any interference with the right to privacy to be 'in accordance with the law' is understood under the European Convention as

---

[15]  Leigh, 'Accountability of Security and Intelligence', 80.
[16]  *Malone v Metropolitan Police Commissioner*, 369–70.
[17]  Post Office Act 1969 (UK), s 80.

embracing two requirements. First, the law must be accessible: a citizen must be able to know the legal rules applicable to a given case. Secondly, those rules must be formulated with sufficient precision to enable him or her to foresee the consequences that any given action may entail.[18] The Court in *Malone* accepted that it was not appropriate to require that individuals should be able to foresee when the authorities were likely to intercept their own communications, but held that the law must nevertheless be sufficiently clear to give them an indication of when the authorities were empowered to resort to such secret and potentially abusive powers.[19]

In the case of interception of telecommunications, the legislation passed after the *Malone* decision made it a criminal offence to intercept post or telecommunications without a warrant issued by the Home Secretary and established a tribunal to hear complaints if unlawful interception was suspected. The Act also prohibited the introduction of evidence of wiretapping in legal proceedings—presumably to avoid the type of mistake that had led to James Malone's troublesome lawsuit in the first place.[20] The legislation covering MI5 and MI6 was significantly broader, establishing their authority in legislation and under ministerial control, setting out their mandate and powers, and taking the first steps towards an accountability framework that included remedies for abuse of those powers. Though there was some criticism of the approach taken, the legislation succeeded in placating the European Convention organs, which dropped two pending cases concerning MI5 shortly after the Security Service Act came into force.[21]

## 2.1. Authority and Governance

The Security Service Act essentially preserved the constitutional framework of the Maxwell-Fyfe Directive: MI5 continued to operate under a Director-General who reported to the Home Secretary and, as necessary,

---

[18] *Sunday Times v United Kingdom* (1979) 2 EHRR 245, para 49.
[19] *Malone v UK*, para 68.      [20] Interception of Communications Act 1985 (UK).
[21] *Hewitt and Harman v United Kingdom* (Committee of Ministers, 13 December 1990) Resolution DH (90) 36. But see *PG and JH v the United Kingdom (Application no 44787/98)* (European Court of Human Rights, 25 September 2001), in which the European Court found a violation of article 8 in a case involving conduct that the British government conceded was unlawful.

to the Prime Minister.[22] It remained, therefore, under ministerial rather than parliamentary control. The budget for the agencies continued to be adopted in a 'secret vote' as part of a global figure without breakdown or explanation of the details; ministers continued the convention of refusing to answer questions in parliament that concerned the agencies or touched on national security.[23]

This changed somewhat when the Intelligence Services Act was passed. As with its counterpart, MI6 was to continue operations broadly on the same basis as it had been, operating under a Chief—traditionally known as 'C'—who reported to the Foreign Secretary and, as necessary, to the Prime Minister. Similarly, GCHQ continued under a Director who also reported to the Foreign Secretary. The Act provided for the creation of a new parliamentary committee (the Intelligence and Security Committee), which would examine the budget, administration, and policies of all three services.[24]

Such arrangements are broadly consistent with the situation in other Commonwealth countries, where heads of agencies report to the various ministers or equivalent. The directors of their US counterparts enjoy considerably more independence: they are appointed by the President and subject to confirmation of the Senate. Appointments therefore tend to be more politically driven. In the case of the FBI, a ten year term limit was imposed by Congress through legislation passed towards the end of J Edgar Hoover's half century at the helm.[25]

## 2.2. Mandate

Both statutes sought to articulate the mandates of the agencies. Eschewing the language of defence of the realm, the Security Service Act provided that the functions of MI5 are, first, 'the protection of national security', in particular against threats from espionage, terrorism, sabotage, the activities of agents of foreign powers, and actions intended to overthrow or undermine parliamentary democracy. In addition, MI5 is tasked with

[22] Security Service Act 1989 (UK), ss 1–2.
[23] Lustgarten and Leigh, *In from the Cold*, 441–50.
[24] Intelligence Services Act 1994 (UK), ss 2, 4, 10.
[25] See also Chapter seven, section 2.1.

safeguarding the country's 'economic well-being' against threats posed by 'the actions or intentions' of persons outside the country.[26] The Intelligence Services Act was even more general, providing that the powers of MI6 and GCHQ are exercisable 'only': (*a*) in the interests of national security, with particular reference to the defence and foreign policies of the government; (*b*) in the interests of the country's economic well-being; or (*c*) in support of the prevention or detection of serious crime.[27]

A mandate serves at least two important purposes for an intelligence agency. First, and most obviously, it sets boundaries on the information that the agency may collect and the people or activities it may target. Given the history of many intelligence services and their tendency to show an excessive interest in domestic political protest and dissent, it is appropriate to put in place checks against activities that might lead to abuse or stifle political discourse. These boundaries may or may not be subject to external enforcement, but can be important factors shaping the behaviour of the officials in question. As Laurence Lustgarten and Ian Leigh concluded in their 1994 study of the security services of Britain, Canada, and Australia: 'security officials are bureaucrats'. Though it would be unwise to rely on bureaucratic structures entirely, a clear and limited mandate shapes the internal rules and procedures of the bureaucracy; it influences the organizational culture and thus serves as a potent force for compliance.[28] Secondly, however, a mandate can provide a degree of protection for the agency itself. There are obvious temptations for politicians to use the considerable powers of the intelligence services to political ends. A well-crafted mandate can provide some insulation from these pressures.

In both areas, the British legislation represented a departure from best practice. On the establishment of boundaries, it is noteworthy that the British legislation governing MI5 offers an inclusive list of what is meant by the broad term 'national security', whereas the comparable Australian and Canadian statutes provide exhaustive definitions of 'security'. The Australian Security Intelligence Organisation (ASIO) had previously operated on the basis of a 'Charter' issued by the Prime Minister with

[26] Security Service Act, s 1(2), (3).
[27] Intelligence Services Act (UK), s 1(2). GCHQ's mandate uses almost identical language but its ability to act in the interests of Britain's economic well-being is limited to the actions or intentions of persons outside the country. Intelligence Services Act (UK), s 3(2).
[28] Lustgarten and Leigh, *In from the Cold*, 411.

many similarities to the Maxwell-Fyfe Directive before legislation was first adopted in 1956.[29] This and subsequent statutes defined security as including, among other things, protection against 'subversion'—a notoriously elastic term that plausibly covers a range of legitimate political activities. A Royal Commission later recommended that it be abandoned in favour of more specific reference to 'politically motivated violence'. The legislation was also amended to provide that the powers granted to ASIO should not limit the right of persons to engage in 'lawful advocacy, protest, or dissent' and that the exercise of these rights should not, in themselves, be regarded as falling within the mandate of the agency.[30] The latter amendment tracked language in a Canadian law passed two years earlier, which prevents the Canadian Security Intelligence Service (CSIS) investigating lawful advocacy, protest, or dissent unless carried on in conjunction with one of the listed threats, which pointedly excluded subversion.[31]

On the insulation from political interference, the Maxwell-Fyfe Directive, for all its other deficiencies, may have been clearer in its provision authorizing, or perhaps requiring, non-compliance with a request unless the Director-General was satisfied that an important public interest bearing on the Defence of the Realm was at stake. It also required the Director-General to ensure that MI5 was 'kept absolutely free from any political bias or influence', whereas the 1989 legislation confined this prohibition to 'action to further the interests of any political party'.[32] Australia's legislation went further in providing that the Director-General of ASIO cannot be overridden by the Minister concerning the nature of advice given by the agency; on the collection and sharing of intelligence on a particular individual the Director-General can be overridden, but

[29] Charter of the Australian Security Intelligence Organisation (A Directive from the Prime Minister to the Director-General of Security) (Canberra: Office of the Prime Minister, 1950); Australian Security Intelligence Organisation (ASIO) Act 1956 (Australia).

[30] Australian Security Intelligence Organisation (ASIO) Act 1979 (Australia), s 4; Australian Security Intelligence Organisation Amendment Act 1986 (Australia), ss 3, 9. See also Royal Commission on Australia's Security and Intelligence Agencies, Report on the Australian Security Intelligence Organisation (Canberra: AGPS, 1984); Greg Carne, 'Thawing the Big Chill: Reform, Rhetoric, and Regression in the Security Intelligence Mandate', *Monash University Law Review* 22 (1996) 379; Jenny Hocking, *Terror Laws: ASIO, Counter-Terrorism, and the Threat to Democracy* (Sydney: UNSW Press, 2004), 34–8.

[31] Canadian Security Intelligence Service (CSIS) Act 1984 (Canada), s 2.

[32] Lustgarten and Leigh, *In from the Cold*, 377–8; Security Service Act, s 2(2)(b); Intelligence Services Act (UK), s 2(2)(b).

written instructions to that effect must be copied to the Inspector-General of Intelligence and Security and the Prime Minister.[33] Interestingly, Canada considered and rejected similar language because it reduced the direct political responsibility of the Minister. Instead the CSIS Act provides that the head of the agency operates under the 'direction of the Minister'.[34]

The question of whether intelligence services need to be protected from undue influence depends, then, on whether that concern ranks higher than the danger that the service itself will act inappropriately, or that the political leadership will use that insulation to ensure the deniability of controversial activities.[35]

## 2.3. Powers

Lord Denning's comment that the members of the Security Service were 'ordinary citizens' was, at least technically, true. Before 1989, they enjoyed no special legal powers and their transgressions of the laws applicable to other 'ordinary citizens' were either not detected by the police or not prosecuted through the use of discretion.[36] The extent of those transgressions was, presumably, constrained by the injunction in the Maxwell-Fyfe Directive that the Service's work should be 'strictly limited to what is necessary'.

The Security Service Act replaced this—or, more realistically, supplemented it—with a system whereby the Home Secretary may issue a warrant authorizing 'entry on or interference with property'. Such a warrant confers immunity from criminal or civil liability for the action concerned.[37] The provision bears similarities to Australian and Canadian counterparts but is somewhat broader. The comparable Australian provision is more specific about the purposes for which warrants may be authorized and the types of information that may be collected; warrants are also limited to 90 days rather than six months under the British legislation.[38] The Canadian

---

[33] ASIO Act, s8.
[34] CSIS Act, s 6(1); Philip Rosen, The Canadian Security Intelligence Service (Ottawa: Library of Parliament, Research Branch, 84–27E, 24 January 2000).
[35] See Chapter three, section 2.1.
[36] Laurence Lustgarten and Ian Leigh, 'The Security Service Act 1989', *Modern Law Review* 52 (1989) 801 at 823.     [37] Security Service Act, s 3.     [38] ASIO Act, s 25.

legislation is also more detailed and requires that warrants be issued by a Federal Court judge; at the same time it extends the duration of warrants to one year except for those enabling the investigation of the most general category of threat to the security of Canada, in which cases the maximum duration is 60 days.[39]

The powers of foreign intelligence services tend to be considerably broader. As a general rule, actions in a foreign country are not subject to liability in one's own country. The Intelligence Services Act went further in providing that the Foreign Secretary can authorize action outside of Britain that would otherwise subject a person to criminal or civil liability. The Act is unclear as to what may be authorized, but among other things it requires the Foreign Secretary to be satisfied that the action is necessary for the proper discharge of a function of MI6 and that the nature and likely consequences will be 'reasonable'. With only slight exaggeration, this might be thought of as the statutory basis for James Bond's 'licence to kill'—though it requires renewal every six months.[40] The Australian Intelligence Services Act offers still broader protection to staff and agents of the Australian intelligence agencies from civil or criminal liability for any act outside the country if it was done 'in the proper performance of a function of the agency'. This is limited by the requirement for ministerial authorization of collection activities involving an Australian person, but such authorizations are not required for other activities abroad.[41]

## 2.4. Remedies

Before the passage of legislation in the 1980s, there were essentially no remedies available to citizens alleging abuse of powers by the intelligence services. In the first place, the absence of a right to privacy meant that much conduct was not, in fact, unlawful. Though the law did require a minimum degree of suspicion before a person or property could be seized, this did not apply to other conduct to gather information. In any event, there was little judicial willingness to investigate wrongdoing in the absence of significant public outcry.[42]

---

[39] CSIS Act, ss 21–8.          [40] Intelligence Services Act (UK), s 7.
[41] Intelligence Services Act 2001 (Australia), ss 8(1), 14(1).
[42] Lustgarten and Leigh, 'The Security Service Act 1989', 829.

With respect to MI5, the 1989 legislation established a Security Service Commissioner to review the exercise of the powers granted to the Service and a Tribunal to investigate complaints. The Security Service Tribunal was empowered to investigate whether a person had been the subject of 'inquiries' and, if so, whether the Service had reasonable grounds for instigating them. If the Tribunal concluded that there were no such reasonable grounds, it could order that inquiries be terminated, records destroyed, and compensation paid—though the complainant would merely get a notification as to whether or not a determination had been made in his or her favour. No reasons would be given, though a report would be made to the Home Secretary and the Commissioner.[43]

These provisions were modelled on the Interception of Communications Act and essentially reprised in the Intelligence Services Act, which also established a Commissioner and a Tribunal. By that time, neither of the two earlier tribunals had ever upheld a complaint. All three tribunals maintained their 'perfect' record until the regime was replaced in 2000.[44]

The impetus for change followed the adoption of more far-reaching legislation incorporating much of the European Convention on Human Rights into domestic law. The Human Rights Act 1998 prohibited any public authority from acting in a manner incompatible with the Convention unless legislation left it no other choice. The Act also required that legislation be interpreted as far as possible in a manner consistent with the Convention, allowing for a declaration of incompatibility to be made if there is a divergence.[45] Among other things, when most of the Act came into force in October 2000, it introduced for the first time a right to privacy in Britain. In preparation for this, the Regulation of Investigatory Powers Act (RIPA) had been passed three months earlier, entering into force eight days before the Human Rights Act.

RIPA created new judicial and administrative oversight provisions. An Intelligence Services Commissioner and an Interception of Communications Commissioner replaced the previous commissioners and will be

---

[43] Security Service Act, Schedule 1.

[44] It should be noted, however, that the vast majority of complaints appear to have been from persons not under surveillance at all.

[45] Human Rights Act 1998 (UK), ss 3–4, 6. The law remains in force until Parliament acts to remove the incompatibility.

discussed briefly in Chapter seven.[46] In terms of remedies, the Investigatory Powers Tribunal replaced the three earlier tribunals and enjoyed a significantly wider mandate to investigate claims under the earlier legislation as well as the Human Rights Act. The first determination in favour of any complainant was made in 2005, though the only public explanation was that the conduct complained of 'was not authorized in accordance with the relevant provisions' of RIPA. Compensation was awarded to the (unidentified) joint complainants, and the records in question destroyed.[47] Two further complaints were upheld in 2008,[48] making a total of three out of around 800 complaints upheld in the Tribunal's first eight years.

At the same time, however, RIPA also significantly *expanded* the state's powers. In addition to regulating communications intercepts and allowing for roving wiretaps, it also provided a statutory basis for surveillance and covert human intelligence sources—the use of undercover officers, informants, and so on. Perhaps most importantly, it significantly expanded the number of agencies authorized to use these powers. When the Act was passed in 2000, nine agencies were allowed to acquire communications data: the three intelligence services, designated police forces, HM Customs and Excise, and the Ministry of Defence. By 2006, this figure had grown to nearly 800 agencies, including 475 local authorities.[49] RIPA thus allows MI5, MI6, and GCHQ to gather intelligence in the interests of national security, but it also empowered, among other things, local authorities to authorize directed surveillance and employ covert human intelligence to protect public health or to assess or collect money owed to a government department.[50] From 2003, the powers of local authorities were restricted to preventing crime and disorder, though some appeared to be continuing to assert broader powers.[51] By 2009, the Chief Surveillance Commissioner (an office previously established under the Police Act but with additional powers under RIPA) reported that law enforcement agencies were granting

---

[46] See Chapter seven, section 2.2.

[47] Report of the Interception of Communications Commissioner for 2005–2006 (London: House of Commons, HC 315, 2007), para 39.

[48] Report of the Interception of Communications Commissioner for 2008 (London: House of Commons, HC 901, 2009), para 6.5.

[49] Report of the Interception of Communications Commissioner for 2005–2006, para 8.

[50] Regulation of Investigatory Powers Act (RIPA) 2000 (UK), ss 28–9.

[51] Annual Report of the Chief Surveillance Commissioner to the Prime Minister and to Scottish Ministers for 2008–2009 (London: House of Commons, HC 704, 2009), para 5.5.

16,000 directed surveillance authorizations annually, with a further 10,000 approved by other public authorities.[52]

## 3. THE SURVEILLANCE SOCIETY

Interestingly, these legislative upheavals barely affected the technology that has come to symbolize Britain's approach to surveillance: closed-circuit television (CCTV). There are estimated to be more than four million cameras in public spaces in Britain, around one for every 14 citizens and by far the highest concentration of such cameras in the world.[53]

Though the use of photographic images in crime control dates back almost to the invention of the camera, the history of CCTV as a technology of surveillance really began with the commercial availability of the video recorder in the 1960s. The early growth in Britain, as elsewhere, was largely confined to the retail sector, with occasional experiments in using CCTV for security on underground railway stations, to monitor traffic flow, or to capture images of groups such as political demonstrators and football hooligans. The first large-scale public system was erected in Bournemouth in 1985 at the time of the annual conference of the Conservative Party. The year before, the Irish Republican Army (IRA) had bombed the conference hotel in an attempt to assassinate Prime Minister Margaret Thatcher. She was not injured but five others were killed; security at the Bournemouth conference became a high priority. The experience proved atypical, however, and the slow diffusion of CCTV continued in shops and train stations. By 1991, only ten British cities had open street systems in operation, mostly small-scale and locally-funded.[54]

---

[52] Ibid, paras 4.7–4.8.

[53] A Report on the Surveillance Society (London: For the Information Commissioner by the Surveillance Studies Network, September 2006), 19. Cf Benjamin J Goold, *CCTV and Policing: Public Area Surveillance and Police Practices in Britain* (Oxford: Oxford University Press, 2004), 1–2. The accuracy of this estimate is disputed, but the lowest serious estimates are 1.5 million cameras, though this number does not include cameras in smaller retail stores.

[54] Clive Norris and Gary Armstrong, *The Maximum Surveillance Society: The Rise of CCTV* (Oxford: Berg, 1999); Clive Norris, Mike McCahill, and David Wood, 'The Growth of CCTV: A Global Perspective on the International Diffusion of Video Surveillance in Publicly Accessible Space', *Surveillance & Society* 2 (2004) 110.

The turning point was the 1993 abduction and murder of the toddler James Bulger by a pair of ten-year-old boys. A still from the grainy CCTV image, showing him being led by the hand from a Liverpool shopping centre, was broadcast around the nation and published on the front of every newspaper. In the debate over youth crime that followed, Home Secretary Michael Howard announced a 'city challenge competition' and £2 million of government funding for open-street CCTV systems. Given the overwhelming demand, three further challenges awarded a total of £85 million for the capital funding of CCTV. By the mid-1990s, CCTV accounted for three-quarters of the government's crime prevention budget.[55]

Debates over whether CCTV 'works' in preventing or solving crime continue, but to some extent those debates miss the point. As with the Bulger case, the most important factor appears to be the symbolic value of showing that *something* is being done.[56] Many commentators have puzzled over the British tolerance for surveillance. As a population, Britons are generally protective of their privacy at home, though unlike their counterparts across the Atlantic that privacy long lacked legal protection.[57] It is sometimes suggested that the economic dislocations experienced in the 1980s exacerbated fear of crime in urban centres, and that the threat of terrorism from the IRA increased the public perception of threats posed in public spaces. Periodic successes—such as the Bulger case, the 1999 London Nail Bomber, and the '7/7' London bombings of 7 July 2005—also serve to erode any significant opposition. In what was probably intended to be a reassuring statement, the head of an industry association has said that people see the cameras as 'a kind of benevolent father, rather than as Big Brother'.[58] Most of the accounts of the use of CCTV in Britain tend to conclude with the helpless observation that, given the sunk costs in erecting the cameras and

---

[55] DJ Smith, *The Sleep of Reason: The James Bulger Case* (London: Century, 1994); Norris, McCahill, and Wood, 'Growth of CCTV', 112. This trend continued: from 1999–2003 a further £170 million was made available to local authorities to install CCTV cameras. National CCTV Strategy (London: Home Office, October 2007), 7.

[56] Norris, McCahill, and Wood, 'Growth of CCTV', 123. See Martin Gill and Angela Spriggs, Assessing the Impact of CCTV (London: Home Office, Home Office Research Study 292, 2005).          [57] See Chapter four, section 1.

[58] Brendan O'Neill, 'Watching You Watching Me', *New Statesman*, 2 October 2006.

in the absence of a radical political shift, any reduction in CCTV usage is highly unlikely.

In fact, CCTV is becoming more widespread and more sophisticated. Already the term 'closed-circuit' is misleading as it suggests that images are available only to a limited number of monitors on a circuit that is literally closed. Surveillance systems increasingly use networked digital cameras capable of storing data; a growing number are also available to a wider range of viewers. Footage from CCTV is routinely broadcast in televised programmes about crime, and in some cases 'CCTV' is streamed live to the Internet. In October 2009, the company 'Internet Eyes' announced that it would begin a service streaming real-time CCTV images to subscribers who earn points and cash rewards by identifying suspicious behaviour.[59]

The increase in observers may be less significant than the ability of new software to analyse footage automatically. Automatic number plate recognition (ANPR) has allowed licence plate numbers to be read automatically since the late-1970s; beginning around 2005, a single camera could record the plates of all cars on a busy highway even at night. ANPR is today used to administer the London congestion charge, tracking every vehicle going into or out of central London. Facial recognition systems have been in use for more than a decade with ever-improving accuracy; many governments now require digital storage of passport photographs to facilitate the technology. Gait analysis and other biometric identifiers are also in development. In addition to identification of persons and vehicles, video analytics makes it possible to flag suspicious conduct, reducing the need for continuous human monitoring. Intelligent Pedestrian Surveillance was first trialled on the London underground in 2003, initially focusing on loitering and potentially suicidal behaviour on station platforms. Similar technology now allows CCTV to detect perimeter intrusions and unattended packages, as well as 'street crime or deviation from social norms'.[60] Digitization thus makes it easier to store data indefinitely and to search them intelligently. A report by Britain's Royal Academy of Engineering speculates

[59] Jon Henley, 'Spot a Crime in Progress on CCTV. Win a Prize!', *Guardian* (London), 7 October 2009.

[60] Chris Gomersall, 'A Closer Look at Video Analytics', *GIT Security + Management*, November–December 2007, 36 at 36 (Gomersall is the CEO of IPSOTEK, a video analytics company). See also Jenny Hogan, 'Your Every Move Will Be Analysed', *New Scientist*, 12 July 2003, 4.

about being able to 'Google space-time'—to pinpoint the location of a given individual at a specific time and date.[61]

### 3.1.  CCTV and Privacy

As indicated earlier, a right to privacy was only incorporated into British law in 2000, well after the government had committed significant resources to CCTV as part of its crime prevention strategy. Most CCTV systems are not covered by RIPA as they are typically overt and not targeted for a specific operation or investigation, though of course the images captured may be used later for a variety of purposes.[62] The most important regulation, then, initially came under the Data Protection Act 1998. Though it does not mention the word privacy, the Act regulates the use of personal data in accordance with the 1995 European Data Protection Directive.[63] The Act requires that anyone controlling personal information must comply with eight principles. These require that data must be fairly and lawfully processed for lawful purposes; the data must be relevant and not excessive for those purposes, accurate and up to date, kept securely and for no longer than necessary, not transferred outside the European Economic Area unless there is adequate protection, and handled in accordance with the rights of data subjects (including, among other things, the right of access to data).[64]

In addition to more limited exceptions, notably concerning the investigation of crime, a broad exception allows the Minister to certify that certain personal data, which may be described generally and prospectively, should be exempted from the principles for reasons of national security. An affected person can appeal to the National Security Appeals Panel of the Information Tribunal, which has broad powers of judicial review and can quash a certificate if the Minister did not have 'reasonable grounds' for issuing it.[65] It is unclear how any such person would become

---

[61] Dilemmas of Privacy and Surveillance: Challenges of Technological Change (London: Royal Academy of Engineering, March 2007), 7.

[62] RIPA, s 26; Surveillance Commissioner Annual Report 2008–09, para 5.8(d).

[63] Directive 95/46/EC of the European Parliament and of the Council of 24 October 1995 on the protection of individuals with regard to the processing of personal data and on the free movement of such data.          [64] Data Protection Act 1998 (UK), Schedule 1.

[65] Ibid, s 28. The Information Tribunal replaced the Data Protection Tribunal in 2000.

aware of the existence of a certificate, however. Of the seven appeals that have been published, all but one related to suspicions that MI5 was controlling personal data but had refused to confirm or deny it. Five of the appeals were dismissed, but one led to the quashing of a certificate that specified the reason and circumstances in which personal data were acquired, rather than the consequences for national security if they were released or their existence acknowledged.[66] The last case was an attempt by Privacy International to challenge the use of CCTV in central London, but was dismissed on a technicality.[67]

In any event, the English courts have adopted a narrow definition of personal data that means that many CCTV systems are not covered by the Data Protection Act at all. The Act defines personal data as data 'which relate to a living individual who can be identified' either from those data or the combination of those data and other information likely to come into the data controller's possession.[68] Academic commentary had assumed that the main point of contention would be over the meaning of 'identified', but in a 2003 case concerning an investigation by the Financial Services Authority, the Court of Appeal focused on the term 'relate to' and held that the Act did not protect all information that merely mentioned a person's name. Instead, personal data had to be relevant to the data subject as distinct from mere transactions in which he or she may have been involved. This included information that was 'biographical in a significant sense' or in which the information had the data subject as its 'focus'.[69] The case was understandable on its facts as the complainant appears to have sought the information not so much to protect his own privacy as to use the information requested as part of ongoing litigation with Barclays Bank 'as a proxy for third party discovery'.[70] But the implications of the ruling were far wider.

Although the case did not mention CCTV, the restrictive interpretation of personal data was initially interpreted as meaning that unless CCTV was being used to target an individual—that is, depending on the capacities of

---

[66] *Norman Baker MP v Secretary of State for the Home Department* (Information Tribunal (National Security Appeals), 1 October 2001).
[67] *Privacy International v Secretary of State for the Home Department* (Information Tribunal (National Security Appeals), 9 June 2009).     [68] Data Protection Act, s 1(1).
[69] *Durant v Financial Services Authority* [2003] EWCA Civ 1746, para 28.
[70] Ibid, para 31.

the system and intent of the operator—captured images that happened to include an individual would not be regarded as personal data for the purposes of the Act. The Information Commissioner issued a guidance note stating that most small businesses using CCTV, for example, were now outside the Data Protection Act entirely.[71] A revised Code of Practice issued in 2008 adopted a broader interpretation that would cover 'most' CCTV if it is directed at viewing or recording the activities of individuals.[72]

For many privacy advocates, the emphasis on regulating CCTV through ensuring that it is not covert and restricting its focused targeting of individuals fails to address the underlying concerns about privacy. It assumes that the problem lies in the occasional abuse of data rather than on the extent to which the *potential* use might force a large number of people to change their behaviour. In this respect, even dummy cameras—a cheap alternative to CCTV sometimes used to deter crime—may also have privacy implications. Furthermore the notion that one consents to the use of CCTV by entering an area where that fact is prominently displayed presumes that alternatives are possible. If there is no way to leave one's house, take public transport, or enter a workplace without having one's image recorded, then the notion of consent is artificial.[73]

The European Court of Human Rights has not ruled on the privacy implications of CCTV generally, but has challenged the use of footage. Late one evening in August 1995, Geoff Peck was captured on camera in Essex wielding a knife, apparently in preparation for suicide. A CCTV operator alerted police who went to the scene. The police quickly determined that he was a threat to no one but himself, detained him on mental health grounds, and ultimately chose not to charge him with an offence. Some of the footage was later aired on national television, however, and a still image—clearly identifiable as Peck—was used in a public relations exercise to demonstrate the effectiveness of CCTV. Having unsuccessfully

---

[71] Steven Lorber, 'Data Protection and Subject Access Requests', *Industrial Law Journal* 33(2) (2004) 179 at 183–4; Susan Singleton, *Tolley's Data Protection Handbook*, 4th edn (London: LexisNexis, 2006), 15–28; Rosemary Jay, *Data Protection: Law and Practice*, 3rd edn (London: Sweet & Maxwell, 2007), 134–6.

[72] CCTV Code of Practice (Revised Edition) (London: Information Commissioner's Office, 2008), 5.

[73] Marianne L Gras, 'The Legal Regulation of CCTV in Europe', *Surveillance & Society* 2 (2004) 216 at 225–6. See also Chapter nine, section 2.

pursued all domestic avenues, Peck went to the European Court of Human Rights in Strasbourg.

The Court held that photographic monitoring of an individual in a public place does not, as such, violate the right to privacy. Nevertheless, the recording of the data and the systematic or permanent nature of the record may give rise to such considerations.[74] In this case, Peck had not complained of the recording itself but the use to which it had been put, leading to him being recognized by family, friends, neighbours, and colleagues. The broadcast of his image without obtaining his consent or masking his identity was held to be a disproportionate violation of his private life, when compared with the intended end of advertising CCTV and its benefits.[75]

## 3.2. CCTV in the United States

In the United States, these questions have tended to be addressed through the reasonable expectation of privacy test and there appears to be no constitutional barrier to public surveillance.[76] The Supreme Court has held, for example, that a person driving on a public road has no reasonable expectation of privacy in his or her movements from one place to another.[77] There is also an implicit assumption of the risk of surveillance by a person being in public. Challenging CCTV generally would require moving away from these doctrines. One possibility would be to emphasize the 'reasonableness' component of the Fourth Amendment to ensure that the intrusiveness of CCTV and other surveillance systems is proportionate to the ends being served, implemented through court-determined minimal guidelines.[78] This is an intriguing argument, but is regarded as unlikely given the increasing use of CCTV in public and commercial spaces, and a

---

[74] *Peck v the United Kingdom* (2003) 36 EHRR 41, para 59.

[75] Ibid, paras 62–3, 87. Cf *Bartnicki v Vopper*, 532 US 514 (2001), in which the US Supreme Court protected on First Amendment grounds a radio commentator who broadcast a conversation recorded illegally by an unidentified third party.

[76] See also Chapter four, section 1.      [77] *United States v Knotts*, 460 US 276, 281 (1983).

[78] Christopher Slobogin, *Privacy at Risk: The New Government Surveillance and the Fourth Amendment* (Chicago: University of Chicago Press, 2007), 90–118. See the list of cases in Christopher Slobogin, 'Public Privacy: Camera Surveillance of Public Places and the Right to Anonymity', *Mississippi Law Journal* 72 (2002) 213 at 236 n106.

string of lower-court cases holding that surveillance by public cameras is not a search within the meaning of the Fourth Amendment.[79]

As in Britain, CCTV spread first in the retail sector but is now quickly moving to wider use in policing and homeland security. The first deployment by police appears to have been two pairs of cameras installed in Hoboken, New Jersey in 1966 and Mt Vernon, New York in 1971; both were soon dismantled as they were seen as expensive and ineffective.[80] Today, elaborate systems are operating in Manhattan, Washington, DC, and a growing number of other US cities. Since 2003, Chicago has deployed one of the most sophisticated networked systems, linking 1,500 cameras placed by police to thousands more installed by public and private operators in trains, buses, public housing projects, schools, businesses, and elsewhere. Funded in significant part through homeland security grants, Operation Virtual Shield integrates the cameras with the emergency calling system and automatically feeds nearby video to the screen of an emergency services dispatcher after a 911 call. Mayor Richard Daley has said that he hopes to have a camera on every street corner by 2016, but appears to have abandoned plans to require every business open more than 12 hours a day to install indoor and outdoor cameras.[81] More recently, New York City announced the Lower Manhattan Security Initiative, based on London's experience and including many of the same features as its 'Ring of Steel'.

### 3.3. CCTV in Canada

Canada provides an interesting counterpoint to the British and US examples. Unlike Britain, laws protecting privacy were in place well before technological advances made video surveillance more effective and efficient.

---

[79] Peter P Swire, 'Proportionality for High-Tech Searches', *Ohio State Journal of Criminal Law* 6 (2009) 751 at 755.

[80] Robert R Belair and Charles D Bock, 'Police Use of Remote Camera Systems for Surveillance of Public Streets', *Columbia Human Rights Law Review* 4 (1972) 143; Jennifer Mulhern Granholm, 'Video Surveillance on Public Streets: The Constitutionality of Invisible Citizen Searches', *University of Detroit Law Review* 64 (1987) 687. Another early deployment was in Olean, NY, around the same time.

[81] Fran Spielman, 'Eyes Everywhere: City Wants Businesses, Residents to Share Surveillance Video', *Chicago Sun Times*, 24 July 2008; William M Bulkeley, 'Chicago's Camera Network Is Everywhere', *Wall Street Journal*, 17 November 2009.

Unlike the United States, those laws were interpreted expansively and internalized by government authorities and the larger public. This combination appears to have slowed the diffusion of cameras in public spaces, at least temporarily.

The Canadian Charter of Rights and Freedoms, which came into force in 1982, established constitutional protections against 'unreasonable search or seizure'. Comparable to US jurisprudence on the Fourth Amendment, this has been interpreted on the basis of the reasonableness of an individual's expectation of privacy, as well as the reasonableness of the search.[82] The Privacy Act 1985 regulates the collection, use, and disclosure of information by federal authorities; other relevant legislation is the Personal Information Protection and Electronic Documents Act (PIPEDA) 2000, which serves some purposes comparable to the British Data Protection Act and was similarly inspired by the European Data Protection Directive. Unlike Britain and the United States, Canada for some time resisted a default acceptance of the spread of CCTV. A Supreme Court decision in 1990 stated that 'to permit unrestricted video surveillance by agents of the state would seriously diminish the degree of privacy we can reasonably expect to enjoy in a free society'.[83]

The issue has also been pressed by a series of activist Privacy Commissioners, one of whom proposed the four-prong test adopted in 2004. In determining whether surveillance is reasonable, it should be established that the measure fulfils a specific need, that the measure will be effective in meeting the need, that the loss of privacy is proportionate to the gained benefit, and that there is no less intrusive method to achieve the goals.[84] In addition to formulating general guidelines, the office has taken on specific campaigns. Among other things, it played a role in Google modifying the roll-out of its 'Street View' feature, which includes images of streets and initially included identifiable individuals and vehicles. Google subsequently undertook to blur faces and licence plates, and to delete the original images permanently after one year.

In preparation for the 2010 Winter Olympics, however, Canada announced plans to install around 1,000 CCTV cameras in Vancouver.

---

[82] *R v Kang-Brown* [2008] 1 SCR 456, paras 138–48.
[83] *R v Wong* [1990] 3 SCR 36, 47.
[84] *Eastmond v Canadian Pacific Railway* [2004] FC 852, para 127.

The report justifying the deployment of the cameras used the word 'temporary' 19 times, but there was early speculation that a control room was designed to be permanent and that cameras were unlikely to be sold after the Games concluded.[85] One test of Canada's possible divergence from Britain and the United States was whether, after the Olympics, those cameras were dismantled. (Early indications suggested that most had been.) Greece installed some 2,000 cameras for the 2004 Athens Olympics but many were subsequently dismantled or vandalized; a judge ordered that the remainder could be used in future only for monitoring traffic. Three years later the police were fined for using the cameras to monitor student protests. Security for the 2008 Beijing Olympics was accompanied by the deployment of 300,000 cameras around the Chinese capital. In preparation for the 2012 London Olympics, Britain was reported to be studying the Chinese model carefully.[86]

## 4. BIG BROTHER IS A BUREAUCRAT

The US Supreme Court, in the case that found that movements on a public road are not private, considered and rejected the argument that improvements in technology would lead to more extensive and intrusive surveillance. Writing in 1983, the Court held that, if such dragnet-type law enforcement practices should eventually occur, 'there will be time enough then to determine whether different constitutional principles may be applicable.'[87]

The notion that courts will have a leisurely opportunity to consider the implications of new surveillance technologies and their use now seems quaint. As this Chapter has shown, it is right and proper that intelligence services should be established by laws that determine their mandate and powers, and provide remedies for when these are exceeded. Such laws are important not only in limiting possible abuse of authority, but also in

---

[85] Mark Hasiuk, 'City Admits Surveillance Cameras Here to Stay in Vancouver', *Vancouver Courier*, 7 April 2009.

[86] 'Beijing to Reactivate Olympic Security Plan for Anniversary', *South China Morning Post*, 24 August 2009; David Leppard, 'Spy Bugs May Be Deployed for 2012', *Sunday Times* (London), 7 June 2009.        [87] *United States v Knotts*, 284.

protecting the agencies themselves from their political masters. At the same time, however, the importance of the turn to law should not be overstated.

If it essentially means the formalization of existing practices, as it did with the moves to put MI5 and MI6 on a statutory basis, there may be minimal impact on those practices. Indeed, if not written carefully, legislation may in fact *reduce* protections and widen powers when compared to the discreet practices of a 'secret' agency. In Britain, this may be seen in the far wider use of surveillance methods not just by the intelligence services and police but hundreds of local authorities. A notorious recent case saw council officials in Dorset obtain telephone records and secretly follow Jenny Paton for three weeks, logging movements of the 'female and three children' in their 'target vehicle'. The surveillance was justified by suspicions—later proven unfounded—that the woman had falsified her address to get her daughter into a nearby school.[88]

Alternatively, if the turn to law comes well after the spread of a new technology, such as CCTV, it may be too late to affect its deployment or use. The spread of CCTV in Britain was, at least in part, facilitated by the absence of meaningful privacy protections. Moves to use biometric identification and build DNA databases will be the next frontier in these debates.[89] Already, however, Britain has one of the largest DNA databases in the world—including samples of around one tenth of the population—and police routinely collect DNA samples from individuals who are arrested but not charged or subsequently acquitted.[90]

Laws matter. Intelligence officials are, in the end, bureaucrats in the sense of being members of a large organization that is intended to operate

---

[88] Sarah Lyall, 'Britons Weary of Surveillance in Minor Cases', *New York Times*, 24 October 2009; Nicola Woolcock, 'Mother Sues Council for Spying on Her Family Home', *The Times* (London), 6 November 2009.

[89] Lisa Madelon Campbell, 'Rising Governmental Use of Biometric Technology: An Analysis of the United States Visitor and Immigrant Status Indicator Technology Program', *Canadian Journal of Law and Technology* 4 (2005) 99.

[90] Criminal Justice Act 2003 (UK), s 10; *R v Chief Constable of South Yorkshire Police (ex parte LS and Marper)* [2004] UKHL 39. In December 2008, the European Court of Human Rights held that the retention of DNA and other samples from mere suspects was a disproportionate interference with the right to respect for private life. *S and Marper v the United Kingdom (Application nos 30562/04 and 30566/04)* (European Court of Human Rights, 4 December 2008). In early 2010 there were proposals to modify the law to allow such samples to be held for six years and then destroyed.

in accordance with a set of rules. But the laws adopted may be less important than the culture of an organization and the political climate within which it operates. Good laws can support that culture and protect it from the vagaries of politics. Bad laws can hollow out the culture and lay it bare to the winds of political fortune.

Or they may be irrelevant to the larger issues at stake. In the 2010 general election, Britain's Conservative Party campaigned on a platform of scrapping plans for an identity card that would be linked to a National Identity Register. For the country with the highest concentration of CCTV cameras in the world, which records every car entering and leaving its capital city, and which stores DNA from a growing proportion of its population, this would appear to be a fairly modest issue on which to draw the line.

# 6

## 'The United Nations Has No Intelligence'

The United Nations has no intelligence.

Boutros Boutros-Ghali[1]

Six weeks before the United States and Britain, together with Australia
and Poland, commenced military operations against Iraq in March 2003,
US Secretary of State Colin Powell addressed the UN Security Council to
make the case for an invasion. Weapons inspectors had been on the ground
in Iraq for almost three months and found no evidence of a 'smoking gun'
that might have served as a trigger for war. Senior figures from the Bush
administration continued to assert, however, that there was no doubt that
Saddam Hussein's regime continued to manufacture weapons of mass
destruction in violation of UN resolutions. Powell's presentation was
intended to explain that certainty, drawing upon an impressive array of
satellite images, radio intercepts, and first-hand accounts. 'My colleagues,'
Powell said, 'every statement I make today is backed up by sources, solid
sources. These are not assertions. What we are giving you are facts and
conclusions based on solid intelligence.'[2] Though he did not speak during
the meeting, the Director of the CIA, George Tenet, sat behind Powell for
the entire 80-minute presentation—an apparent effort to dispel percep-
tions of discord in the US intelligence and defence communities about the
threat posed by Iraq, but also underlining the unprecedented nature of
this public display of the fruits of US espionage.

The failure to substantiate most of the claims made by Powell before the
Council prompted little reflection as to what significance this episode

---

[1] Georgie Anne Geyer, 'Limited Tools for Complex Tasks', *Dallas Morning News*, 28
September 1993.
[2] 'Powell's Address, Presenting "Deeply Troubling" Evidence on Iraq', *New York Times*,
6 February 2003.

might have for the United Nations and other institutions of collective
security. The speech was used by critics of the Bush administration as
evidence of its alleged bad faith in the negotiations on alternatives to war;
within the United States, a Senate committee issued a scathing report on
the US intelligence community's pre-war assessments of Iraq's military
capabilities.[3] When attention did turn to the United Nations, the emphasis
tended to be on the larger questions of the organization's 'relevance',
prompting the Secretary-General to create a high-level panel to rethink
the mechanisms of collective security in a world dominated by US power
and defined by its concerns.[4]

What these various accounts overlook is the more basic question of
whether collective security is even possible when the evaluation of current
threats and the calibration of responses turn on the use of national intelligence that, by its nature, cannot be shared openly. In this sense, Iraq is
merely the most prominent example of a tension that runs through much
of the current counter-terrorism and counter-proliferation agenda. Differences of policy on Iran's nuclear programme or the Korean peninsula, for
example, depend in large part on diverging intelligence assessments of
Iran and North Korea's capacities and intentions. Since the basis of these
assessments will not be discussed freely, they may as well be, to borrow
Powell's phrase, 'assertions'. Similarly, the tools available to address even
agreed threats depend increasingly on intelligence findings, ranging from
targeted financial sanctions to extraordinary rendition of suspects and
pre-emptive military action. Despite this increased practice, there has
been no serious attempt to reconcile the fact that multilateral action is
pursued on the basis of unilateral determinations.

The issue is important to those who believe that multilateral responses
to emerging threats are inherently more legitimate than and therefore
preferable to unilateral action. But it is also relevant to those who are wary
of entrusting a nation's security to an international organization: debates
over whether the United States should share intelligence with and through
the United Nations, for example, have arisen in many administrations

---

[3] See Report on the US Intelligence Community's Prewar Intelligence Assessments on Iraq
(Washington, DC: US Senate Select Committee on Intelligence, S Rpt 108–301, 7 July 2004), 14.
[4] See A More Secure World: Our Shared Responsibility (Report of the High-Level Panel on
Threats, Challenges, and Change), UN Doc A/59/565 (2004).

and been won on every occasion by those who showed that it was in the US interest to do so. The question is no longer whether intelligence should be shared, but rather how and with what protections to guard against errors and abuse.

This Chapter first describes the context of intelligence sharing before considering five areas in which it has been used—with varying degrees of controversy—within the UN system: peacekeeping, justifying the use of force, weapons inspections, targeted financial sanctions, and international criminal prosecution. Of particular interest is the use of national intelligence in an international forum. Such usage naturally challenges the ability of intelligence agencies to maintain appropriate secrecy. The use of intelligence in bodies like the United Nations has also exposed it to new forms of legal scrutiny as it expands from serving the traditional function of threat assessment to being treated as a form of evidence.

## 1. SHARED SECRETS

Intelligence services tend to regard their relationship with peers in other countries in terms of concentric rings. A first tier includes those countries with which an established relationship is built on history, trust, and common protocols for the handling of information. The closest such relationships derive from formal intelligence alliances established during the Second World War, notably the relationship between the United States and Britain, later expanded to include Australia, Canada, and New Zealand.[5] A second tier embraces trusted governments with common interests. For the United States this might include other NATO allies such as France (intelligence relationships are always more robust than their political counterparts), while for a country like Australia, it might mean Japan or Singapore. Specific interests at times encourage unusual candour, such as the intelligence shared between nuclear powers that may exceed their sharing of such intelligence with non-nuclear allies. Beyond this is less a tier of relationships than a series of opportunistic exchanges. It is

---

[5] See Chapter one, section 1.

revealing that those who cannot keep a secret are often lumped in with those from whom secrets must be kept.

The reasons for intelligence sharing vary, but typically involve an exchange of information, analysis, or resources. The 'quid' may be access to a particular country, translation and analytical assistance, or the use of strategically important territory; the 'quo' might take the form of sharing the fruits of this labour, training, or the supply of related equipment. Intelligence may sometimes be treated as a kind of foreign assistance; its withdrawal may be used as a kind of punishment.[6] For the majority of countries, the most important partner in any such relationship is the United States. Despite having the largest intelligence budget of any country, even the United States relies on some assistance from countries such as Britain in relation to the Near and Middle East, Australia in relation to South-East Asia, and a series of countries that support its global signals intelligence reach. A specific agency may be given the formal role of coordinating external intelligence relations, usually the national human intelligence service—the CIA;[7] Britain's Secret Intelligence Service (MI6);[8] the Australian Secret Intelligence Service (ASIS);[9] and so on.

The sharing of intelligence through international organizations—on display most prominently in the lead-up to the Iraq war—has a long but murky history. The United Nations was originally regarded more as a source of intelligence than a potential recipient of its products. During the 1945 conference in San Francisco that drafted the UN Charter, the US Army's Signal Security Agency, the precursor to the NSA, was obtaining intercepts on at least 43 of the original 45 nations in attendance.[10] Any proposals to enhance the capacity of international organizations to use

---

[6] The United States, for example, curtailed intelligence sharing after New Zealand refused to allow nuclear-armed or powered vessels into its ports. Duncan H Cameron, 'Don't Give New Zealand the ANZUS Heave-Ho', *Wall Street Journal*, 29 July 1986. The relationship was quietly restored soon afterwards. Around 2003, Canada suffered similar exclusion from limited intelligence following its stance on the Iraq war. See also Dale F Eickelman, 'Intelligence in an Arab Gulf State', in Roy Godson (ed), *Comparing Foreign Intelligence: The US, the USSR, the UK, and the Third World* (Washington, DC: Pergamon-Brassey's, 1988), 89.

[7] 50 USC § 403–4a(f) (under the direction of the Director of National Intelligence).

[8] Intelligence Services Act 1994 (UK), s 1.

[9] Intelligence Services Act 2001 (Australia), s 6(1)(d).

[10] Stephen Schlesinger, *Act of Creation: The Founding of the United Nations* (Boulder, CO: Westview, 2003), 93–4.

intelligence must therefore be tempered by the reality that most states' participation in such organizations is geared more towards gathering intelligence than sharing it.

Ever since the United Nations deployed peacekeepers into conflict zones, however, it has been necessary to have a deep understanding of the theatre of operations and parties to a conflict. Yet intelligence was long regarded as a 'dirty word' as the 1984 *Peacekeeper's Handbook* put it; 'military information' was the preferred euphemism.[11] The Capstone Doctrine, intended to provide a strategic framework for UN Peacekeeping adopted in January 2008, at times appears to have undergone a word processor-assisted scrubbing. It refers variously to 'information gathering', 'information sharing', 'information management protocols', 'operational information', and 'analysis of all-sources of information', but scrupulously avoids the word 'intelligence'.[12]

The prospect of the United Nations or any other international organization developing an independent intelligence collection capacity is remote. Member states are, understandably, wary of authorizing a body to spy on them; the United Nations itself has been reluctant to assume functions that might undermine its actual or perceived impartiality. At the same time, however, this position reflects a larger anomaly in the status of intelligence under international law as an activity commonly denounced but almost universally practised: empowering an international organization to engage in espionage or other intelligence activities might give the lie to this example of diplomatic doublethink.[13]

Where intelligence activity of any kind is authorized, it tends to be within narrowly defined parameters. On occasion, this has led to absurd results. From August 1988, for example, the United Nations had an observer group in place to monitor the suspension of hostilities between Iran and Iraq. Beginning in July 1990, these observers had noted the movement of large numbers of Iraqi units to the south, in the direction of the border with Kuwait. As the troops had not moved east, towards Iran, the

[11] International Peace Academy, *Peacekeeper's Handbook* (New York: Pergamon Press, 1984), 39, 59–62, 120–1. See also Carl von Horn, *Soldiering for Peace*, 1st American edn (New York: David McKay, 1967), 222.

[12] UN Peacekeeping Operations: Principles and Guidelines (Capstone Doctrine) (New York: UN Department of Peacekeeping Operations and Department of Field Support, 2008).

[13] See Chapter one, section 2.

observers were prevented from making an official report—and appear not even to have issued an informal report prior to Iraq's invasion of Kuwait the following month.[14]

## 2. INTELLIGENCE AND COLLECTIVE SECURITY

In the early years of the United Nations there appears to have been little consideration at all of intelligence as such. Swift paralysis by the Cold War and limited operational activities meant that intelligence was, for the most part, confined to espionage by and against the various governments represented in the UN organs, and against the host nation in particular.[15] The Korean War (1950–53), though fought under UN auspices, was a United States affair, while the Suez crisis of 1956 indicated precisely the poverty of independent UN analysis—though this was by design of the French and British, who also deceived the United States. Secretary-General Dag Hammarskjöld actively rejected proposals to establish a permanent UN intelligence agency in 1960, in part because of his conviction that the United Nations must have 'clean hands'.[16]

It was only when the United Nations undertook its first major field operation in the Congo beginning in 1960 that questions of intelligence had to be confronted directly. Intelligence was only a small part of the debate over the Congo operation, a conflict that split the Security Council, almost bankrupted the United Nations, and ensured that force was not used on a comparable scale for decades.[17] For the next quarter of a century, peacekeeping was limited to small observation or goodwill missions, most of them monitoring post-conflict situations.

'Military information' thus continued to feature in subsequent peace-keeping operations, but there was little discussion of any form of UN intelligence capacity for the remainder of the Cold War. In 1978, the

---

[14] Cees Wiebes, *Intelligence and the War in Bosnia, 1992–1995* (Münster: LIT Verlag, 2003), 25–6.    [15] Schlesinger, *Act of Creation*, 93–4.

[16] Connor Cruise O'Brien, *To Katanga and Back* (New York: Simon & Schuster, 1962), 76; Brian Urquhart, *Hammarskjöld* (New York: Knopf, 1972), 159–60.

[17] Trevor Findlay, *The Use of Force in UN Peace Operations* (Oxford: SIPRI & Oxford University Press, 2002), 51–86.

French government proposed the creation of an International Satellite Monitoring Agency that could monitor disarmament agreements and international crises.[18] A group of experts appointed by the Secretary-General reported on the feasibility of such a body in 1981, envisaging an agency that might eventually operate independently, with its own satellites and receiving stations, but that would begin with facilities for processing and interpreting data acquired from other sources.[19] A General Assembly resolution was passed and the Secretary-General produced his own report. Without support from either the United States or the Soviet Union, however, the project was doomed.[20] Writing in 1985, former director of the CIA Stansfield Turner said that his own opposition to the agency while in office had been a mistake: the paramount concern of protecting US technical collection capacities had overwhelmed the potential benefits of such an agency to prevent wars ignited by misunderstanding or miscalculation, and to aid developing countries in more effective use of resources.[21] Such concerns also proved short-sighted—even more sophisticated imagery was commercially available from around 1986.[22]

In 1987, Secretary-General Javier Pérez de Cuéllar established an 18-member Office for Research and the Collection of Information (ORCI). Though the United States, together with Britain and France, had pushed for the creation of the office to save money and remove the preparation of a daily press-summary from the Political Information News Service, which was seen as a Soviet redoubt, nine conservative US senators opposed the creation of ORCI on the basis that the new office itself might provide a cover for Soviet spying in the United States. Undeterred by the fact that

[18] Memorandum submitted on 24 February 1978 to the Preparatory Committee for the Special Session of the General Assembly Devoted to Disarmament; Address by His Excellency Mr Valery Giscard d'Estaing, President of the French Republic, UN Doc A/S-10/PV.3 (1978); GA Res S-10/2 (1978), para 125(d).

[19] Report of the Secretary-General: The Implications of Establishing an International Satellite Monitoring Agency, UN Doc A/AC.206/14 (1981).

[20] GA Res 37/78K (1982); Report of the Secretary-General on the Proposal for the Establishment of an International Satellite Monitoring Agency, UN Doc A/38/404 (1983).

[21] Admiral Stansfield Turner, *Secrecy and Democracy: The CIA in Transition* (Boston: Houghton Mifflin, 1985), 280–2.

[22] Michael R Hoversten, 'US National Security and Government Regulation of Commercial Remote Sensing from Outer Space', *Air Force Law Review* 50 (2001) 25. See also Chapter one, section 2.2.

the office was run by Sierra Leonean James Jonah and essentially limited to summarizing newspaper reports and other openly available material, a bill to block US funds for the office was introduced.[23] Cooler heads prevailed, but the tactic of legislating to limit the capacity of the United Nations to use intelligence returned during a period of genuine activism in the 1990s.

This activism, beginning with the expulsion of Iraq from Kuwait and ending with the failure to intervene in Rwanda in 1994, commenced with the disbanding of ORCI as a separate body in 1992. (A second period of activism, which saw the number of peacekeepers grow from a low of 12,000 in mid-1999 to almost 110,000 deployed in September 2008, began with a failed attempt to establish a new information and strategic analysis secretariat as part of a package of reform proposals tabled in 2000.[24]) Even in the most active periods of the United Nations, then, profound ambivalence about it possessing either a collection or analytical capacity manifested in a rejection of the former and fragmentation of the latter. Halting progress was made on systemic analytical capacities during the consolidation of the Department of Political Affairs in 1992, but real change in how the United Nations handled intelligence was seen only, once again, in the conduct of its peacekeeping operations.[25]

## 2.1. Peacekeeping

In the period 1990 to 1993, the United Nations doubled the number of peacekeeping missions, increasing the number of troops deployed in the field by a factor of five. The complexity of these operations also increased, with the United Nations taking on ambiguous responsibilities in the former Yugoslavia and Somalia far removed from the traditional peacekeeping role of monitoring a ceasefire between standing armies. With size

[23] 'Nine Senators Try to Block Funds for UN Office Asked by US', *New York Times*, 16 April 1987; Lewis H Diuguid, 'Soviets Are Changing Their Obstructionist Ways at UN', *Washington Post*, 24 July 1988; 'A UN Office Looks to Prevent Wars', *New York Times*, 16 April 1989.

[24] See section 2.1 in this Chapter.

[25] Leonard Doyle, 'Washington Opposes Spy Role for UN', *Independent* (London), 20 April 1992; Mark Curtis, *The Great Deception: Anglo-American Power and World Order* (London: Pluto Press, 1998), 200–1.

and difficulty came risk: more peacekeepers were killed in 1993 than in the entire preceding decade.

In April of the same year, a Situation Centre was created in the Department of Peacekeeping Operations to provide a continuous link between senior staff members at UN Headquarters, field missions, humanitarian organizations, and member states through their diplomatic missions in New York. In addition to monitoring specific operations, it drew upon reports and open source information to provide daily situation reports on all peacekeeping and some political and humanitarian missions. An Information and Research Unit was added in September 1993, beginning with a single intelligence officer seconded from the United States and soon joined by representatives of Britain, France, and Russia, typically drawn from the intelligence branches of their respective militaries.[26] The United States later provided a computer system that linked the Situation Centre with databases operated by countries using the same system; essentially the United States and one or two other NATO countries.[27] The system was designed to avoid interoperability problems encountered during Operation Desert Storm, which drove Iraq from Kuwait in 1991. Its use at the United Nations was originally proposed to support US participation in operations in Somalia from 1993—the troubled operation that began the US withdrawal from UN peace operations.[28]

This level of cooperation took place in a period of unusual enthusiasm for the United Nations at senior levels of the US government. President George HW Bush, who in 1990 heralded a 'new world order', included within this vision a United Nations that was able to back up its words with action.[29] The Clinton administration inherited this policy and initially proposed to develop a Presidential Decision Directive (PDD) on multilateral peacekeeping operations that would have included a forward-leaning

[26] Robert E Rehbein, Informing the Blue Helmets: The United States, UN Peacekeeping Operations, and the Role of Intelligence (Kingston, ON: Centre for International Relations, Queen's University, 1996), 30.

[27] Hugh Smith, 'Intelligence and UN Peacekeeping', Survival 36(3) (1994) 174 at 184; Rehbein, Informing the Blue Helmets, 30–2.

[28] See Mats R Berdal, 'Fateful Encounter: The United States and UN Peacekeeping', Survival 36(1) (1994) 34 at 46; David Ramsbotham, 'Analysis and Assessment for Peacekeeping Operations', Intelligence and National Security 10(4) (1995) 162.

[29] George HW Bush, 'Address Before a Joint Session of the Congress on the Persian Gulf Crisis and the Federal Budget Deficit' (Washington, DC, 11 September 1990).

US policy on participation in peacekeeping, including provision of intel-ligence.[30] The death of 18 US soldiers in Somalia in October 1993 saw any such enthusiasm evaporate; what became PDD 25 was released at the height of the genocide in Rwanda and widely interpreted as a manifesto for inaction.[31]

The Somalia debacle and suspicions that it might have been connected to intelligence leaks from the UN mission had led to a minor rebellion in Congress, with legislation proposed in November 1993 and January 1994 that would have substantially curtailed intelligence sharing with the United Nations. The discovery of large quantities of classified US docu-ments and imagery in open cabinets at a deserted UN office in Mogadishu was greeted with apoplexy: a series of amendments and entire bills were proposed that would have made sharing US intelligence with the United Nations virtually impossible.[32]

What is interesting about these legislative manoeuvres is that none of them was pursued with particular vigour. In part this was due to the threat of a presidential veto, but other reasons were illustrated in hearings by a House intelligence committee concerning a provision that would have required the President and the Secretary-General to conclude a written agreement before any US intelligence could be provided to the United Nations. Unclassified testimony sketched out the regime in place for selec-tive transfer of intelligence to the United Nations, normally through representatives of the Joint Staff (J2), one of whom would be based in the US Mission to the United Nations, with a second based in the UN Situa-tion Centre. At the same time, a UN Support Desk in the US National Military Joint Intelligence Center provided UN partners with sanitized intelligence on a daily and ad hoc basis. The regime enabled the United States to use intelligence selectively in support of its foreign policy as and when it was helpful to do so, without requiring the provision of other intelligence or the revelation of sources and methods.[33]

---

[30] Jeffrey R Smith and Julia Preston, 'United States Plans Wider Role in UN Peace Keeping', *Washington Post*, 18 June 1993.

[31] See, eg, 'Trotting to the Rescue', *Economist* (London), 25 June 1994.

[32] R Jeffrey Smith and Julia Preston, 'US Probes Security for Somalia Files; Secret Docu-ments Left Unprotected by UN', *Washington Post*, 12 March 1995.

[33] Permanent Select Committee on Intelligence, Intelligence Support to the United Nations (Open Session) (Washington, DC: United States Congress, House of Representatives, One

Selectivity in shared intelligence is a recurring problem, with numerous UN staff suspecting—accurately—that intelligence is provided to them in support of national policy and frequently in order to manipulate the United Nations. A former military adviser to the Secretary-General cites the crisis in Eastern Zaïre in the mid-1990s as an example: one permanent member in favour of intervention provided intelligence showing large numbers of displaced persons in wretched conditions; a second permanent member opposing intervention offered intelligence suggesting a far smaller number of people subsisting in more reasonable conditions. It was, he concluded, a 'shameful exhibition'.[34]

Both the Situation Centre and its analytical unit were staffed by 'gratis military officers', on loan from member states from Australia to Zimbabwe but disproportionately drawn from Western countries. This led to considerable suspicion on the part of developing countries and protests under the auspices of the Non-Aligned Movement. By the late 1990s, it had become a politically contentious issue and the United Nations began phasing out the practice in the period 1998–99, taking with it the Information and Research Unit.[35] This reduction in UN military expertise coincided with a resurgence of peace operations, as the United Nations assumed civilian responsibilities in Kosovo and temporary sovereign responsibilities for East Timor in the same year. A major review of UN peace operations was commissioned for the following year, its first meeting coinciding with the near collapse of a third mission in Sierra Leone as a result of poor planning, under-equipped and badly trained personnel, inadequate communication, weak to the point of mutinous command and control, and determined local spoilers.[36]

The Report of the Panel on UN Peace Operations, known as the Brahimi Report after the panel's Algerian chairman, was established in part to

Hundred Fourth Congress, first session, CIS 96 H431-1, 19 January 1995), 12 (statement by Toby T Gati, Assistant Secretary of State for Intelligence and Research).

[34] FE van Kappen, 'Strategische inlichtingen en de Verenigde Naties', *Militaire Spectator* 170(11) (2001), in Wiebes, *Intelligence and Bosnia*, 31.

[35] GA Res 51/243 (1997); 'UN: Fifth Committee Approves Draft Texts on Financing and Support Staff for Peacekeeping', *M2 Presswire*, 29 June 1998; William J Durch et al, The Brahimi Report and the Future of UN Peace Operations (Washington, DC: Henry L Stimson Center, 2003), 38.

[36] David M Malone and Ramesh Thakur, 'UN Peacekeeping: Lessons Learned?', *Global Governance* 7(1) (2001) 11.

justify the expansion of the UN Department of Peacekeeping Operations and compensate for the lost gratis personnel. At the same time, it touched on intelligence issues in two ways. First, at the insistence of some of the members of the panel with military backgrounds, the report stated that UN peace operations 'should be afforded the field intelligence and other capabilities needed to mount a defence against violent challengers.' Though not elaborated upon, this view reflected the emerging wisdom that the traditional aversion to collecting and using intelligence in peace operations was untenable.[37]

Secondly, however, the panel noted that the United Nations lacked a professional system for managing knowledge about conflict situations—gathering it, analysing it, and distributing it. To remedy the deficit, the panel proposed the creation of an Information and Strategic Analysis Secretariat (EISAS). The new body was to be formed by consolidating the Department of Peacekeeping Operations Situation Centre and the handful of policy planning units scattered across the organization, with the addition of a small team of military analysts.[38]

From the moment EISAS was referred to as a 'CIA for the UN', it was dead as a policy. Some states expressed concern about the United Nations being seen as involved in the business of espionage, but the real concern appeared to be the potential for an early warning capability to conflict with sovereignty. Following so soon after unusually blunt statements by the Secretary-General on the topic of humanitarian intervention in September 1999,[39] the defenders of a strict principle of non-interference found a receptive audience. The Secretary-General stressed that EISAS 'should not, in any way, be confused with the creation of an "intelligence-gathering capacity" in the Secretariat', but would merely serve as a vehicle

---

[37] Report of the Panel on United Nations Peace Operations (Brahimi Report), UN Doc A/55/305-S/2000/809 (2000), para 51. See, eg, Comprehensive Report on Lessons Learned from United Nations Assistance Mission for Rwanda (UNAMIR) (New York: UN Department of Peacekeeping Operations Lessons Learned Unit, December 1996), 4.

[38] Brahimi Report, paras 65–75. The initial 'E' denotes yet another acronym: the Executive Committee on Peace and Security, which was established in 1997 as 'the highest policy devel opment and management instrument within the UN Secretariat on critical, cross-cutting issues of peace and security': Comprehensive Review of the Whole Question of Peacekeeping Operations in All Their Aspects, UN Doc A/C.5/55/46/Add.1 (2001), para 3.2.

[39] See generally Kofi A Annan, *The Question of Intervention: Statements by the Secretary-General* (New York: UN Department of Public Information, 1999).

to ensure more effective use of information that already exists.[40] In an effort to save at least the idea of system-wide policy analysis, he later proposed a unit half the size and without media monitoring responsibilities, but even this failed to generate any traction.[41]

The lack of formal capacity has encouraged ad hoc responses. The Information and Research Unit has been replaced by informal links with military advisers from a handful of member states, supplemented as needed by states with particular expertise or capacity in a specific crisis area. Such ad hockery is replicated in procedures adopted in the field: in the absence of standard protocols for classification of information, they may be invented on the fly. Predictable problems follow, as when the ad hoc label 'UN-classified' is misread by military personnel as 'unclassified'.

Modest advances have been made through the introduction of Joint Mission Analysis Centres (JMACs) which are intended to provide 'integrated analysis of all-sources of information to assess medium- and long-term threats to the mandate and to support [mission leadership team] decision-making.'[42] A driving force in this area has been mission security, especially following the bombing of the UN compound in Baghdad in August 2003 and subsequent attacks on UN staff—leading to concerns that the security agenda may be subordinating the other goals of the United Nations.[43]

Intelligence functions in peacekeeping have been driven by the exigencies of the situation, notably focusing on force protection and effective implementation of the mandate. The key check on such activities has been the extent to which the mandate authorizes a departure from the default respect for sovereignty. Toleration of intelligence activities in practice has

---

[40] Report of the Secretary-General on the Implementation of the Report of the Panel on United Nations Peace Operations, UN Doc A/55/502 (2000), para 45.

[41] Implementation of the Recommendations of the Special Committee on Peacekeeping Operations and the Panel on United Nations Peace Operations, UN Doc A/55/977 (2001), paras 301–7. See generally Owen Philip Lefkon, 'Culture Shock: Obstacles to Bringing Conflict Prevention Under the Wing of UN Development...and Vice Versa', *New York University Journal of International Law and Politics* 35 (2003) 671 at 711–15.

[42] UN Department of Peacekeeping Operations and Department of Field Support, Capstone Doctrine, 71.

[43] See Philip Shetler-Jones, 'Intelligence in Integrated UN Peacekeeping Missions: The Joint Mission Analysis Centre', *International Peacekeeping* 15(4) (2008) 517. Operations under other bodies, such as the European and African Unions, are sometimes more open in their approach to intelligence but are beyond the scope of this Chapter.

not been matched by acceptance in theory, however, with the result that such activities are often inefficient, inconsistent, or ineffective. The predisposition in the United Nations against intelligence originally extended even to avoiding encrypted transmissions. Though this is no longer official policy, it may still lead to perverse results. At one point in the Bosnian conflict, Scandinavian soldiers in the UN Protection Force (UNPROFOR) were monitoring the impact of mortar fire from Serb units outside a besieged Muslim town and duly reporting to UN force headquarters the location of the hits. Unknown to them, the Serb forces were listening to UN radio communications and using this information to improve the accuracy of their strikes.[44]

## 2.2. Justifying the Use of Force

It is important to distinguish between two legal frameworks within which intelligence might be introduced in the UN Security Council to justify the use of force: as the basis of an *ex ante* determination that a threat to international peace and security requires enforcement action under Chapter VII, or as an *ex post facto* explanation of the exercise of the right of self-defence under Article 51 of the Charter. The Charter does not offer a complete definition of self-defence, providing instead in Article 51 that the Charter does not impair the 'inherent right of individual or collective self-defence if an armed attack occurs.'[45] With respect to Security Council action, the only formal requirement to invoke the enforcement powers of Chapter VII of the Charter is a determination that a 'threat to the peace' exists and that non-forcible measures would be inadequate.[46] In neither case is there an indication of what evidence, if any, must be adduced in order to justify a claim of self-defence or recourse to Chapter VII. Thus, when the United States in 2003 presented evidence of Iraq's alleged violations of past Council resolutions, there were no procedures to evaluate the veracity and accuracy of that evidence or, indeed, to make any independent findings of fact.

---

[44] A Walter Dorn, 'The Cloak and the Blue Beret: Limitations on Intelligence in UN Peacekeeping', *International Journal of Intelligence and Counterintelligence* 12(4) (1999) 414 at 416.
[45] UN Charter, art 51. Any such action is to be 'immediately reported' to the Council.
[46] UN Charter, arts 39, 42.

These problems are not new to the United Nations. In the area of self-defence, the emergence of nuclear weapons led to sustained debate as to whether the requirement for an armed attack to occur should be taken literally. 'Anticipatory self-defence' became a controversial sub-theme in the literature, which often cites Israel's actions in the Six-Day War of 1967 and its destruction of Iraq's Osirak nuclear reactor in 1981. The normative impact of either case is debatable, however. The 1967 war provoked mixed views in the General Assembly;[47] the Osirak incident, which successfully derailed Iraq's nuclear programme for some years, is viewed positively today but was unanimously condemned at the time by the Security Council as a clear violation of the Charter.[48] Other incidents are occasionally discussed by commentators, but states themselves have generally been careful to avoid articulating a right of self-defence that might encompass the first use of force—even if they have been unable or unwilling to rule it out completely.[49]

One year after the September 11 attacks, the United States released a National Security Strategy that justified and elaborated a doctrine of pre-emptive intervention. The document recognized the new strategic reality in which non-state actors were an increasing threat to countries like the United States and not susceptible to deterrence. Raising the spectre of a terrorist or rogue state attack using weapons of mass destruction, it stated that the United States would act pre-emptively to 'forestall or prevent such hostile acts by our adversaries'[50] The document sparked vigorous debate about the limits of such a policy, particularly when combined with the stated aim of dissuading potential adversaries from hoping to equal the power of the United States and when followed so swiftly by the US-led invasion of Iraq—though the formal basis for that war was enforcement of Security Council resolutions. The rhetoric from the White House toned down significantly over the following years, though this has not removed the need for greater consideration of the circumstances in which

[47] Bruno Simma (ed), *The Charter of the United Nations: A Commentary*, 2nd edn (Oxford: Oxford University Press, 2002), 803–4.         [48] SC Res 487 (1981), para 1.

[49] Thomas M Franck, *Recourse to Force: State Action Against Threats and Armed Attacks*, Hersch Lauterpacht Memorial Lectures (Cambridge: Cambridge University Press, 2002), 97–108.

[50] The National Security Strategy of the United States of America (Washington, DC: President of the United States, September 2002), 15.

self-defence might legitimately be invoked against a non-state actor or a state manifestly unable to be deterred.

In 2004, the UN High-Level Panel on Threats, Challenges, and Change attempted to address this problem by drawing a line between the issue of pre-emptive action and an even more radical doctrine of preventive war. Where the former was broadly consonant with earlier arguments for a right of anticipatory self-defence, the latter was a direct challenge to the prohibition on the use of force itself. The Panel concluded that a state may take military action 'as long as the threatened attack is *imminent*, no other means would deflect it and the action is proportionate.' This glossed over the many legal questions concerning anticipatory self-defence, but was intended to discredit the larger evil of a right of preventive war: if good arguments can be made for preventive military action, with good evidence to support them, the Panel concluded, these should be put to the Security Council, which can authorize such action if it so chooses.[51]

But is the Council in a position to assess such evidence and make such decisions? The history of Council decision-making when authorizing military action does not inspire confidence: it has been characterized by considerable flexibility of interpretation, tempered mainly by the need for a pre-existing offer of a state or group of states to lead any such action.[52] There have been attempts to make Council decision-making more rigorous, including efforts to limit the veto power of the five permanent members, but these are likely to remain the most politicized of all questions raised in the United Nations.[53]

An alternative approach would be to improve the analytical capacity of the UN Secretariat, enabling it to advise the Council, or to develop some kind of fact-finding capacity that could report independently on a

[51] High-Level Panel Report, paras 188, 190. The Panel continued: 'If it does not so choose, there will be, by definition, time to pursue other strategies, including persuasion, negotiation, deterrence and containment—and to visit again the military option.'

[52] See generally Simon Chesterman, *Just War or Just Peace? Humanitarian Intervention and International Law*, Oxford Monographs in International Law (Oxford: Oxford University Press, 2001).

[53] Cf International Commission on Intervention and State Sovereignty, The Responsibility to Protect (Ottawa: International Development Research Centre, December 2001); High-Level Panel Report, para 207; In Larger Freedom: Towards Development, Security, and Human Rights for All (Report of the Secretary General), UN Doc A/59/2005 (2005), para 126.

developing situation. Member states have historically been wary of giving the United Nations an independent voice, sticking to a general divide between governance and management responsibilities: governance remains the province of the member states, while management falls to the Secretariat. This theory has never been quite so neat in practice. The best example of the ambiguity that frequently results is the role of the UN Secretary-General: in theory the chief administrative officer of the United Nations, the incumbent also functions as the chief diplomat of the United Nations. The sole power given to the Secretary-General in the Charter is that of bringing to the attention of the Security Council any matter that, in his or her opinion, threatens international peace and security. Common sense would suggest that the Secretary-General's opinion should ideally be an informed one; common sense rarely determines the structure of international organizations, however.[54]

It is possible, then, that the Council's consideration of the threat posed by Iraq in late 2002 and early 2003 was as effective as could be expected. The provision of intelligence by the United States was an attempt to use the Council as a forum for decision-making as well as a vehicle for advancing a foreign policy agenda. Indeed, one reason the US was prepared to share so much intelligence was that—whatever the outcome of discussion in the Council—the human and technical sources of that intelligence were not going to remain in place much longer.

Yet it remains striking that the three countries most active in the initial hostilities themselves had different assessments of Iraq's actual weapons of mass destruction capacity. Drawing upon similar but more limited material available to the United States and Britain, for example, Australian assessments of Iraq's weapons of mass destruction were more cautious and, as it happened, closer to the facts. This was true on the issues of sourcing uranium from Niger, mobile biological weapon production capabilities, the threat posed by smallpox, Iraq's ability to deliver chemical and biological weapons via unmanned aerial vehicles, and links between al Qaeda, Iraq, and the September 11 terrorist strikes in the United States.[55]

---

[54] UN Charter, arts 97, 99. See generally Simon Chesterman (ed), *Secretary or General? The UN Secretary-General in World Politics* (Cambridge: Cambridge University Press, 2007).

[55] Report of the Inquiry into Australian Intelligence Agencies (Flood Report) (Canberra: Australian Government, 22 July 2004), 27–8.

A multilateral approach to intelligence sharing might not get beyond using a body such as the United Nations as a forum, but even that—if done effectively—would mark a significant advance on current practice.

## 2.3. Weapons Inspections

Whereas peacekeeping operations established a clear and justified *demand* for the collection of intelligence, the use of intelligence in the context of weapons inspections is frequently driven by *supply*. Controversies over abuse of intelligence in the lead-up to the Iraq war have complicated the use of intelligence in future weapons inspections regimes—indeed, the concern today is not that intelligence will, again, be used to lead a credulous population into war but that even good intelligence will be ignored. The willingness of member states to *share* intelligence is determined by their national interest but also by the ability of the recipient to handle that intelligence effectively; the policy consequences that flow from the *use* of that intelligence are largely determined by the national interest of the members of the international organization concerned. As in the case of peacekeeping, greater accountability would be achieved by allowing greater independence on the part of bodies such as the International Atomic Energy Agency (IAEA), or specially created entities such as those deployed in Iraq, to collect and analyse intelligence themselves, though there is no political will to do so.

Prior to Colin Powell's February 2003 presentation, there had been much talk of an 'Adlai Stevenson moment', referring to the tense scene in the Security Council in October 1962 when the US Ambassador to the United Nations confronted his Soviet counterpart on its deployment of missiles in Cuba. 'Do you, Ambassador Zorin, deny that the USSR has placed and is placing medium- and intermediate-range missiles and sites in Cuba?' Stevenson had asked in one of the more dramatic moments played out in the United Nations. 'Don't wait for the translation! Yes or no?' 'I am not in an American courtroom, sir,' Zorin replied, 'and I do not wish to answer a question put to me in the manner in which a prosecutor does—' 'You are in the courtroom of world opinion right now,' Stevenson interrupted, 'and you can answer yes or no. You have denied that they exist, and I want to know whether I have understood you correctly. I am prepared to wait for my answer until hell freezes over, if that's your decision. And I am also prepared to present the evidence in this room.' Zorin did not respond. In a *coup de théâtre* Stevenson then produced poster-sized photographs of the missile sites taken by US spy planes.[56]

This exchange highlights the problem Powell confronted four decades later and a key dilemma in the use of intelligence in bodies such as the United Nations. Powell was presenting intelligence on Iraq that was intended to demonstrate Saddam Hussein's non-compliance with previous Security Council resolutions. His audience heard, however—and was intended to hear—evidence.[57] This was perhaps necessary given the various audiences to whom Powell was speaking: the members of the Council, the US public, world opinion more generally. But it meant that the onus of proof subtly shifted from Iraq being required to account for the dismantling of its weapons to the United States asserting that such weapons were in fact in Iraq's possession. Lacking evidence as compelling as Stevenson's, Powell persuaded only those who were already convinced.

The fact that US and British intelligence was essentially wrong on the central question of Iraq's weapons programmes naturally dominates consideration of this issue—though it bears repeating that chief UN weapons inspector Hans Blix also believed that Iraq retained prohibited weapons.[58] This section examines the somewhat different question of how comparable intelligence might be used in bodies such as the Security Council in future. Ambassador Zorin was correct, of course, that the Council is not a courtroom; it lacks the legitimacy and the procedures necessary to establish guilt or innocence. Nonetheless, as Stevenson replied, it may function as a chamber in the court of world opinion. In such circumstances, the limitations of intelligence as a form of risk assessment intended to guide action may conflict with the desire of policymakers to use intelligence to justify rather than inform their decisions.

---

[56] See generally Robert F Kennedy, *Thirteen Days: A Memoir of the Cuban Missile Crisis* (New York: WW Norton, 1969); Robert A Divine (ed), *The Cuban Missile Crisis* (Chicago: Quadrangle Books, 1971).

[57] On the distinction between intelligence and law enforcement in the domestic context, see Chapter eight, section 2.        [58] Hans Blix, *Disarming Iraq* (New York: Pantheon, 2004).

### 2.3.1. Containing Iraq (1991–2002)

Prior to the 2003 war, Iraq had represented a highly unusual case of intrusive inspections in the context of the series of measures adopted by the UN Security Council after the expulsion of Iraq from Kuwait in 1991. Nevertheless, the lessons learned from the two inspection missions—UNSCOM and UNMOVIC—bear directly on the larger question of what role the United Nations and other organizations can and should play in counter-proliferation activities in the future. Given the controversies over the 2003 war, there is a danger that these lessons are being ignored.

Security Council resolution 687 (1991), which provided the ceasefire terms at the end of Operation Desert Storm, established a 'Special Commission' (UNSCOM) to implement the destruction of Iraq's chemical and biological weapons programmes; the IAEA was to play a similar role in relation to Iraq's nuclear programme.[59] A subsequent resolution encouraged states to provide UNSCOM with 'the maximum assistance, in cash and in kind' in fulfilling its mandate—support that was understood at the time to include intelligence.[60]

The nature of intelligence cooperation with UNSCOM can be considered in three discrete areas. First, in the area of technical collection, UNSCOM had access to imagery from high-altitude U-2 planes from the United States. US satellite imagery was also provided, though at times with reduced detail in order to protect sources and methods. Video cameras and other unmanned sensors were installed at sensitive dual-use sites, transmitting information to the Baghdad Monitoring and Verification Centre. The German government provided helicopters with ground penetrating radar. Signals intelligence was supported by Britain, which provided sensitive communication scanners to monitor Iraqi military communications.[61] The Baghdad office also employed counter-intelligence measures to guard against Iraqi espionage, supplemented by unorthodox tactics such as running air conditioners as loud as possible and using a large whiteboard instead of speaking.[62] These measures were unlikely to

---

[59] SC Res 687 (1991), para 9.      [60] SC Res 699 (1991), para 4.
[61] Dorn, 'The Cloak and the Blue Beret', 437–8.
[62] Scott Ritter, *Endgame: Solving the Iraq Problem—Once and for All* (New York: Simon & Schuster, 1999), 25.

be effective against surveillance by those states providing the hardware and, in some cases, the personnel for UNSCOM's operations.

The most important revelations, however, came from a second area: human intelligence. Though UNSCOM was not running spies as such, high-level defections encouraged far greater disclosure by Iraqis than anything discovered through technical collection. One defector, Hussein Kamel, had directed Iraq's Military Industrial Commission and was one of Saddam Hussein's sons-in-law. Cooperation with UNSCOM was not the purpose of his defection—it is assumed that he was attempting to gain international support for a *coup*—but his disclosures to UNSCOM, Western intelligence services, and the media about Iraq's deception of the inspectors prompted a flood of new documents from Iraq, 1.5 million of which were 'discovered' on a chicken farm belonging to Kamel south-east of Baghdad. Failure to disclose the documents was explained by Iraq as due to Kamel's own 'illegal' conduct, and accompanied by new pledges of cooperation with the inspectors. (Six months later, Kamel and his brother, also married to one of Saddam Hussein's daughters, had been fully debriefed and were becoming an embarrassment to their hosts in the Jordanian royal court. A move to more humble accommodation and the homesickness of the two women appear to have persuaded them to take seriously the offer of a complete pardon. The couples duly returned to Iraq and within 24 hours the Kamel brothers were divorced and executed.) [63]

A third aspect of UNSCOM's intelligence activities was the creation of an analytical capacity. From its inception in 1991, UNSCOM depended heavily on both US information and analysis. In August that year it created an Information Assessment Unit to analyse and store imagery and inspection reports, as well as to liaise with nations providing information to UNSCOM. The first four staff members were, not coincidentally, from Canada, Australia, France, and the United States. [64] UNSCOM's first Executive Chairman, Rolf Ekéus, cited the unit as part of a response to Iraqi challenges that UNSCOM employed CIA agents. Naturally inspectors received briefings from various services, he acknowledged, but such information was then evaluated by the Information Assessment Unit: 'Sometimes it's

[63]  Ibid, 47–8; Dorn, 'The Cloak and the Blue Beret', 439.

[64]  Chantal de Jonge Oudraat, 'UNSCOM: Between Iraq and a Hard Place', *European Journal of International Law* 13 (2002) 139 at 150; Wiebes, *Intelligence and Bosnia*, 23.

impressive, sometimes it's useless.'[65] It later became clear, however, that UNSCOM's relations with intelligence services went beyond the mere provision of information. Such accusations dogged Ekéus' successor, Australian diplomat Richard Butler, whom Scott Ritter, a former inspector, later accused of putting US interests ahead of the UN's.[66] Writing in the *New Yorker*, Seymour Hersh detailed efforts by the CIA to use UNSCOM to collect information about Iraq that was unrelated to inspections. From April 1998, Hersh wrote, the CIA took control of a recently enhanced information system that had been penetrating Iraqi efforts to conceal its weapons programme but now was focused on monitoring Saddam Hussein himself.[67]

The relationship between UNSCOM and member states providing intelligence was always going to be fraught. As indicated earlier, intelligence is rarely shared on an altruistic basis; at the very least interests must be seen to be aligned. In addition to the United States, UNSCOM's relationship with Israel's military intelligence service, Aman, raised eyebrows—U-2 imagery sent to Israel for assistance in analysis could easily be used for other purposes, such as future espionage or military operations.[68]

By the time the UN Monitoring Verification and Inspection Commission (UNMOVIC) commenced inspections in Iraq, the process could not have been more politicized. The role of intelligence providers was also being discussed more openly. Briefing the Council on 19 December 2002, UNMOVIC Executive Chairman Hans Blix noted that sites to be inspected in Iraq following the return of inspectors included not only those that had been declared by Iraq or inspected in the past, but also 'any new sites which may become known through procurement information, interviews, defectors, open sources, intelligence or overhead imagery.'[69] In February 2003, as the prospects for avoiding war diminished, Blix responded to Colin Powell's briefing of the Security Council. 'We are fully aware that many governmental intelligence organizations are convinced and assert that proscribed weapons, items and programmes continue to exist,' he

[65] Judy Aita, 'UN Expects to Resume Weapons Inspections in Iraq', *United States Information Agency*, 19 January 1993.    [66] Ritter, *Endgame*, 196.

[67] Seymour M Hersh, 'Saddam's Best Friend', *New Yorker*, 5 April 1999.

[68] Dorn, 'The Cloak and the Blue Beret', 440.

[69] Hans Blix, Briefing of the Security Council: Inspections in Iraq and a Preliminary Assessment of Iraq's Weapons Declaration (New York: UNMOVIC, 19 December 2002).

observed. Governments, of course, had access to sources of information that were not available to inspectors.[70]

The inspections regime in Iraq was exceptional in both its intrusiveness and its explicit reliance on intelligence provided by the services of interested states. Larger lessons are, therefore, to be drawn with caution. UNSCOM and UNMOVIC are, arguably, a warning to the United Nations against relying upon the intelligence services of member states and thereby being tainted with accusations of collusion.[71] They are also examples of both a precedent for and the effectiveness of an analytical capacity in a UN operation handling intelligence. In part it was the ad hoc and contingent nature of cooperation with intelligence services that appears to have undermined the inspectors' independence; if one is dependent on the United States for imagery, Israel for analysis, Britain for communications intercepts, and so on, it is not a strong bargaining position from which to insist that this assistance should come without conditions.

The question of whether such activities are appropriate for the United Nations will remain linked to the troubled question of Iraq policy for some time to come. It is possible that intrusive inspections will be used again in the context of disarmament—Iran and North Korea are plausible candidates—but for the time being the Security Council has focused its attention on more general obligations in the area of counter-proliferation. In April 2004, following the revelations of nuclear smuggling by Pakistani scientist AQ Khan, the Council passed resolution 1540 (2004), requiring all states to criminalize proliferation of weapons of mass destruction to non-state actors and impose effective domestic controls over such weapons and their means of delivery.[72] This suggested a slightly different role for the Council, more akin to that which it was playing in the area of counter-terrorism.

## 2.3.2. Other Arms Control Regimes

Members of arms control and non-proliferation agreements have a clear shared interest in verifying the implementation of such agreements.

---

[70] Hans Blix, Briefing of the Security Council: An Update on Inspections (New York: UNMOVIC, 14 February 2003).

[71] See, eg, Christopher Hitchens, 'Weapons of Mass Distraction', *Vanity Fair*, March 1999, 92.

[72] SC Res 1540 (2004), paras 1–3.

Intelligence has long formed a part of this process, but in an unusual way: a number of such agreements—prominently the Anti-Ballistic Missile Treaty and the Strategic Arms Limitation Talks (SALT I) Agreement of 1972—rather than encouraging sharing instead merely prohibit interference with intelligence efforts ('national technical means') aimed at verifying compliance.[73] Unilateral verification still remains the most important check on compliance, but the establishment of comprehensive regimes in the area of nuclear proliferation has begun to change this.

Originally established in 1957 as an 'atoms for peace' organization, the IAEA promotes the peaceful use of nuclear technology and verifies that it is not being used for military purposes. This dual role has led to predictable conflicts and occasional calls for the division of the agency into two entities. The Nuclear Non-Proliferation Treaty, signed a decade after the IAEA was created, segregated the world into nuclear and non-nuclear states, requiring those without nuclear weapons to accept 'safeguards' negotiated with the IAEA to prevent the diversion of nuclear energy from peaceful uses.[74] Formally, the administration of these safeguards consists of verifying information provided by the state in question; in practice, there is considerable reliance on information provided by other states.[75]

The IAEA lacks a collection capacity as such, but employs experts who are able to assess information in their possession. This works when states provide information but is least effective against those with the most to hide. By the mid-1990s, the rules governing inspection and verification had come to be seen as inadequate and the IAEA developed a more stringent Model Additional Protocol, though only one-third of states party to the Non-Proliferation Treaty (NPT) have ratified it.[76] In 2004, the UN High-Level Panel on Threats, Challenges, and Change recommended that the IAEA Board of Governors should recognize the Model Additional Protocol as a new basic standard for IAEA safeguards.[77]

---

[73] See Chapter one, section 2.4.

[74] Treaty on the Non-Proliferation of Nuclear Weapons, done at Washington, London, and Moscow, 1 July 1968, in force 5 March 1970, art 3.

[75] Statute of the International Atomic Energy Agency, done at New York, 23 October 1956, in force 29 July 1957, arts III, VIII.

[76] Model Protocol Additional to the Agreement(s) Between State(s) and the Agency for the Application of Safeguards (Vienna: International Atomic Energy Agency, INFCIRC/540, 1997). See Laura Rockwood, 'The IAEA's Strengthened Safeguards System', *Journal of Conflict and Security Law* 7(1) (2002) 123.     [77] High-Level Panel Report, para 129.

The role of third states in providing information is explicitly provided for in the IAEA Statute, article VIII of which states that each member should 'make available such information as would, in the judgement of the member, be helpful to the Agency'. The IAEA itself is to 'assemble and make available in accessible form' all such information, but there is no evidence that this requirement is taken literally. On the contrary, there are occasional suggestions of the importance of intelligence provided by third states in the verification process. In the case of Iran, for example, the IAEA's Board of Governors passed a resolution in 2003 calling for 'urgent, full and close co-operation' by third states in clarifying outstanding questions on Iran's nuclear programme and later 'noting with appreciation' that it had 'received some information from other states that may be helpful'.[78] In May 2008, the Director General noted that, as part of its investigation of alleged military dimensions to its nuclear programme, the IAEA had presented Iran with

information, which was provided to the Agency by several Member States, appears to have been derived from multiple sources over different periods of time, is detailed in content, and appears to be generally consistent. The Agency received much of this information only in electronic form and was not authorized to provide copies to Iran.[79]

One of the reasons the IAEA can be relatively open about such activity is that its role in handling confidential information is long-standing. The IAEA Statute prohibits staff disclosing 'any industrial secret or other confidential information'.[80] The Model Additional Protocol goes further, requiring the agency to maintain 'a stringent regime to ensure effective protection against disclosure of commercial, technological and industrial secrets and other confidential information', which includes protocols for the handling of confidential information, conditions of staff employment

---

[78] IAEA Board of Governors, Implementation of the NPT Safeguards Agreement in the Islamic Republic of Iran, Resolution adopted by the Board (GOV/2003/81, 26 November 2003), para 6; IAEA Board of Governors, Implementation of the NPT Safeguards Agreement in the Islamic Republic of Iran, Resolution adopted by the Board (GOV/2004/49, 18 June 2004), preambular para (h).

[79] Implementation of the NPT Safeguards Agreement and relevant provisions of Security Council resolutions 1737 (2006), 1747 (2007) and 1803 (2008) in the Islamic Republic of Iran (Report by the Director General) (GOV/2008/15, 26 May 2008), para 16.

[80] IAEA Statute, art VII(F).

relating to the protection of such information, and procedures to deal with breaches of confidentiality.[81]

Similar provisions are included in the Chemical Weapons Convention, drafted in 1993, which has a 'Confidentiality Annex' aimed largely at protection of commercially sensitive information. Among other things, the annex provides that dissemination of confidential information within the Organisation for the Prohibition of Chemical Weapons (OPCW) shall be strictly on a 'need-to-know basis' and that staff shall enter into individual secrecy agreements covering their period of employment and five years afterward. In the case of a serious breach, the Director-General may waive the immunity protecting a staff member from prosecution under national law.[82] These protections exist even though the OPCW has significantly less intrusive inspection powers than available under the IAEA's Model Additional Protocol. The Biological and Toxin Weapons Convention presently lacks any form of inspection regime; the most recent efforts to develop an inspection protocol foundered in mid-2001, in large part due to opposition by the US bio-defence establishment and objections from the US pharmaceutical and biotechnology industries that inspections would be costly and might compromise trade secrets.[83]

One way of avoiding concerns about international organizations handling sensitive information is to bypass them. On 31 May 2003, US President George W Bush announced the creation of the Proliferation Security Initiative (PSI), a partnership of countries drawing upon national capacities to interdict shipments of weapons of mass destruction. As a kind of ongoing coalition of the willing, PSI provides a framework for 'rapid exchange of relevant information' and cooperation in the interception and searching of vessels and aircraft suspected of transporting illicit weapons.[84] It has been effective as a means of enhancing participation in

---

[81] Model Additional Protocol, art 15.

[82] Convention on the Prohibition of the Development, Production, Stockpiling, and Use of Chemical Weapons and on Their Destruction, done at Paris, 13 January 1993, in force 29 April 1997, Annex on the Protection of Confidential Information ('Confidentiality Annex'), paras 2(h), 9.

[83] Convention on the Prohibition of the Development, Production and Stockpiling of Bacteriological (Biological) and Toxin Weapons and on Their Destruction, done at Washington, London, and Moscow, 10 April 1972, in force 26 March 1975; Michael R Gordon, 'Germ Warfare Talks Open in London; US Is the Pariah', *New York Times*, 24 July 2001.

[84] Proliferation Security Initiative: Statement of Interdiction Principles (Washington, DC: The White House, Office of the Press Secretary, 4 September 2003).

this US-led endeavour—primarily intended to deter trade in prohibited weapons with North Korea—but at the cost of criticism for its lack of public accountability and its political divisiveness. PSI is also seen as undermining more traditional (and, it is argued, more legitimate) mechanisms such as the United Nations and the emerging regime of the Law of the Sea.[85]

## 2.4. Targeted Financial Sanctions

Greater energy has been directed towards improving checks on the use of information in the imposition of targeted financial sanctions. This is due to the more diffuse set of interests with a stake in the process of listing and de-listing individuals as opposed to the justification of a given military action. More importantly, however, it is because implementation of sanctions requires the cooperation of many states acting in ways that may be susceptible to judicial review in national courts.

Concerns about the humanitarian consequences of comprehensive economic sanctions, in particular those imposed on Iraq from 1990,[86] led to efforts to make them 'smarter' by targeting sectors of the economy or specific individuals more likely to influence policies—or at least confining sanctions to ensure that those who bore the brunt of their consequences were also those perceived as most responsible for the situation that led to their imposition. This utilitarian approach to minimizing suffering gave rise to different concerns, however, as the identification of individuals (and, in some cases, their immediate families[87]) for the freezing of assets suggested a shift in the way that sanctions were being used.

Though other taxonomies are possible, sanctions tend to be imposed for one of three reasons. First, sanctions may be intended to compel compliance with international law, including acceding to demands by a

---

[85] Mark J Valencia, *The Proliferation Security Initiative: Making Waves in Asia*, Adelphi Paper 376 (Abingdon: Routledge, 2005), 71–3.

[86] See, eg, Roger Normand, 'Human Rights Assessment of Sanctions: The Case of Iraq (1990–1997)', in Willem JM van Genugten and Gerard A de Groot (eds), *United Nations Sanctions— Effectiveness and Effects, Especially in the Field of Human Rights: A Multi-disciplinary Approach* (Antwerp: Intersentia, 1999), 19; Abbas Alnasrawi, *Iraq's Burdens: Oil Sanctions and Underdevelopment* (London: Greenwood Press, 2002), 74–95.

[87] See, eg, SC Res 1173 (1998), para 11.

body such as the UN Security Council. Secondly, sanctions may be designed to contain a conflict, through arms embargoes or efforts to restrict an economic sector that is encouraging conflict. Thirdly, sanctions may be designed primarily to express outrage but without a clear political goal; sanctions are sometimes invoked as a kind of default policy option, where something more than a diplomatic plea is required but a military response is either inappropriate or impossible. Targeted sanctions were initially a subspecies of the first type of regime, employed in an effort to coerce key figures in a regime to comply with some course of action by restricting their ability to travel or access their assets.[88] As the tool came to be applied in the context of counter-terrorism, however, the use of sanctions moved into the second type: individuals were not having their assets frozen in an effort to coerce them to do or refrain from doing anything; instead the assets were frozen as a prophylactic against future support for terrorism.

There is no burden of proof as such for imposing sanctions through a mechanism such as the UN Security Council. The Council, having determined the existence of a threat to the peace, is empowered to decide what measures should be taken 'to maintain or restore international peace and security'.[89] These non-forcible measures are broadly defined:

The Security Council may decide what measures not involving the use of armed force are to be employed to give effect to its decisions, and it may call upon the Members of the United Nations to apply such measures. These may include complete or partial interruption of economic relations and of rail, sea, air, postal, telegraphic, radio, and other means of communication, and the severance of diplomatic relations.[90]

There is a qualitative difference, however, between using economic sanctions as a measure intended to maintain or restore international peace and security in the sense of containing or ending a conflict, and freezing an individual's assets indefinitely on the basis that he or she

---

[88] See generally David Cortright and George A Lopez, *The Sanctions Decade: Assessing UN Strategies in the 1990s*, A Project of the International Peace Academy (Boulder, CO: Lynne Rienner, 2000); David Cortright and George A Lopez, *Sanctions and the Search for Security: Challenges to UN Action*, A Project of the International Peace Academy (Boulder, CO: Lynne Rienner, 2002); Simon Chesterman and Béatrice Pouligny, 'Are Sanctions Meant to Work? The Politics of Creating and Implementing Sanctions Through the United Nations', *Global Governance* 9 (2003) 503.        [89] UN Charter, art 39.        [90] UN Charter, art 41.

might at some unspecified point in the future provide funds to an unidentified terrorist network. The recent practice of freezing individual's assets has also gone well beyond leading members of governments or armed groups (such as the Angolan rebel group UNITA and Afghanistan's Taliban) that are the target of Security Council demands, to embrace a far wider category of 'individuals and entities associated with' al Qaeda as designated by a committee of the Security Council.[91] By the start of 2010, this committee had frozen the assets of over 400 individuals and 100 entities.

Most criticism of the targeted sanctions regimes focuses on alleged violations of the rights of persons whose assets have been frozen, or the inappropriateness of the Security Council 'legislating' by issuing binding orders of general application without adequate checks on its powers.[92] Underlying such human rights and administrative law concerns is the question of how the Council uses information in such circumstances; as that information is frequently sourced from national intelligence services, addressing those concerns must take account of the classified nature of the material. The problem arises at two discrete stages: listing or designation of individuals and entities; and the de-listing process. Discussion here will focus on the most active committee—concerned with al Qaeda—but similar concerns apply to the other Security Council committees managing lists for Sierra Leone, Iraq, Liberia, the Democratic Republic of the Congo, Côte d'Ivoire, Sudan, and Somalia.

The sanctions regime that is now used to freeze al Qaeda-connected assets worldwide was initially established in October 1999 to pressure Afghanistan's Taliban regime to surrender Osama bin Laden for prosecution following his indictment in the United States for the August 1998 bombings of US embassies in Kenya and Tanzania. Resolution 1267 (1999) established a committee (the '1267 Committee') to oversee implementation of the sanctions, including being given the power to 'designate' the relevant funds to be frozen.[93] In December 2000, the regime was expanded to apply to bin Laden himself and 'individuals and entities associated with him as designated by the Committee, including

---

[91] SC Res 1333 (2000), para 8(c).
[92] See, eg, José Alvarez, 'Hegemonic International Law Revisited', *American Journal of International Law* 97 (2003) 873.        [93] SC Res 1267 (1999), para 6(e).

those in the [al Qaeda] organization'.[94] In January 2002, after the
September 11 attacks on the United States and the successful military
operation in Afghanistan, the regime was further expanded with the
removal of a geographic connection to Afghanistan and any time-limit
on its application.[95]

The criteria for inclusion on the list were left intentionally vague. The
threshold established by the Council (being 'associated with' Osama bin
Laden or al Qaeda) was low and ambiguous. Only in January 2004, with
the passage of resolution 1526, were member states proposing individuals
to be listed called upon to provide information demonstrating such an
association. The same resolution 'encouraged' member states to inform
such individuals that their assets were being frozen.[96] In July 2005—
almost six years after the listing regime was first established—resolution
1617 required that when states proposed additional names for the consolidated list they should henceforth provide to the Committee a 'statement
of case describing the basis of the proposal.' This did not affect the more
than 400 individuals and entities that had been listed without such a
formal statement of case. The resolution also requested states to 'inform,
to the extent possible, and in writing where possible, individuals and
entities included in the Consolidated List of the measures imposed on
them, the Committee's guidelines, and, in particular, the listing and
delisting procedures.'[97]

This incremental approach to constraining the discretion of the
Committee is suggestive of the manner in which its activities came to be
seen as more than a simple sanctions regime. When resolution 1267 was
first passed, targeting sanctions specifically at the Taliban regime was
intended to minimize collateral harm to the population of Afghanistan;
in the wake of the September 11 attacks, sanctions became a means of
restricting the flow of terrorist finances. Over time, it became clear that
freezing the assets of an individual or a bank for an indefinite period
raised concerns both in terms of the rights of the affected individuals
and accountability structures for the exercise of this power. By September
2005, a United Nations Summit of world leaders called upon the Security Council to 'ensure that fair and clear procedures exist for placing

---

[94]  SC Res 1333 (2000), para 8(c).       [95]  SC Res 1390 (2002), para 3.
[96]  SC Res 1526 (2004), paras 17–18.       [97]  SC Res 1617 (2005), paras 4–5.

individuals and entities on sanctions lists and for removing them, as well as for granting humanitarian exemptions.'[98]

Such limited protections may be contrasted with the elaborate safe-guards incorporated within the ad hoc tribunals established for the former Yugoslavia and Rwanda, also creatures of the UN Security Council. The resolutions establishing each tribunal contained in their respective stat-utes elaborate protections for the accused, including a presumption of innocence, the right to be informed of the nature and cause of the charge against him or her, and the opportunity of a fair trial including legal assistance and the opportunity to question witnesses; convicted persons also enjoyed a right of appeal over errors of law and fact.[99]

Sanctions are not a form of criminal punishment as such—a point that is frequently emphasized by defenders of the regime and those tasked with implementing it. In a 2005 judgment by the European Court of First Instance, this characterization as preventive rather than punitive was important in determining that the practice, described as 'a temporary precautionary measure restricting the availability of the applicants' prop-erty,' did not violate fundamental rights of the individuals concerned. The Court noted that 'freezing of funds is a precautionary measure which, unlike confiscation, does not affect the very substance of the right of the persons concerned to property in their financial assets but only the use thereof.'[100] Three years later, the European Court of Justice held that the absence of effective judicial protection made the regime inconsistent with European laws, but stayed the implementation of its decision to allow time for new procedures to be worked out.[101]

Nevertheless, once an individual is included on the list it is difficult to be removed. Prior to January 2002, there was no official procedure for managing the sanctions regime. Resolution 1390 (2002) requested the Committee to 'promulgate expeditiously such guidelines and criteria as

[98] 2005 World Summit Outcome Document, UN Doc A/RES/60/1 (2005), para 109.
[99] See section 2.5 in this Chapter.
[100] *Ahmed Ali Yusuf and Al Barakaat International Foundation v Council of the European Union and Commission of the European Communities (Case T-306/01)* (Court of First Instance of the European Communities, 21 September 2005), paras 320, 299.
[101] *Ahmed Ali Yusuf and Al Barakaat International Foundation v Council of the European Union and Commission of the European Communities (Cases C-402/05 P and C-415/05)* (European Court of Justice, 3 September 2008).

may be necessary to facilitate the implementation' of the sanctions regime.[102] In August 2002, a policy for de-listing was announced by the Chairman of the 1267 Committee, requiring a listed person to petition his or her government of residence or citizenship to request review of the case, putting the onus on the petitioner to 'provide justification for the de-listing request, offer relevant information and request support for de-listing.' That government was then expected to review the information and approach the government(s) that first listed the person on a bilateral basis 'to seek additional information and to hold consultations on the de-listing request.'[103] The Committee adopted guidelines implementing this approach in November 2002.[104] In the event that the relevant government of residence or citizenship chose not to request review of the case, there was no provision for an alternative means of petition.

In practice the Committee itself has little direct input into listing or de-listing, instead ratifying decisions made in capitals on the basis of a confidential 'no-objection' procedure. Under this procedure a proposed name is added to the list if no member of the Committee objects within a designated period. Until 2005, this period was 48 hours; it was later extended to five days. In practice, the amount of information provided to identify an individual or entity and justify listing varies. There has been some progress from the days when the Angola Sanctions Committee regarded the *nom de guerre* 'Big Freddy' as sufficient identifying information, but statements of case vary considerably. The average statement of case on the 1267 Committee runs to about a page and a half of information, with some being considerably longer. At the other extreme, one statement of case requesting the listing of 74 individuals included a single paragraph of justification for the entire group.[105] The capacity of members of the Committee to make an informed decision on whether to agree to a listing depends significantly on their access to intelligence information, either through their own services or their relationship with the designating

---

[102]  SC Res 1390 (2002), para 5(d).

[103]  Statement of Chairman of 1267 Committee on De-Listing Procedures (New York: United Nations, UN Press Release SC/7487, 16 August 2002).

[104]  Security Council Committee Established Pursuant to Resolution 1267 (1999) Concerning al-Qaeda and the Taliban and Associated Individuals and Entities, Guidelines of the Committee for the Conduct of Its Work (as amended) (New York: 7 November 2002), para 8.

[105]  Strengthening UN Sanctions, 26, 29 (a hold was placed on this group of 74).

state. In the absence of some national interest in a situation, however, there is little incentive to challenge a specific listing.

Various reform proposals to improve the listing and de-listing process have been developed, including the ongoing work of the 1267 Committee's Monitoring Group, proposals by member states, and policy options being developed by independent bodies.[106] To date no court has held the regime to be invalid in its entirety, though ongoing litigation in European courts may threaten such an outcome. In addition, unlike other sanctions regimes, there is little chance of a political development leading to the al Qaeda/Taliban list itself being wound up—as happened, for example, in 2002 when sanctions against UNITA officials were terminated following the death of Jonas Savimbi and the end of Angola's civil war.[107] As the years pass, the fact that assets may never be unfrozen will lead some to conclude that the regime is, in effect if not in name, a form of confiscation. At present, for example, there is still no agreement on what to do with the frozen assets of an individual who dies.[108]

A basic point of division is whether any improved procedure should incorporate an independent assessment of the evidence used to justify inclusion on the list. Options that have been discussed include an ombudsman-type institution proposed by the Danish government (which held a rotating seat on the Security Council for 2005–06); an administrative review panel comparable to the UN Compensation Commission, Kosovo's Detention Review Commission, or a proposal by the Swiss government for a review panel with representatives of the listing and challenging state; or more formal judicial proceedings comparable to the appeals process in the ad hoc international criminal tribunals.

There has been little progress on such discussions, in part because the human rights and administrative law arguments encouraging independent review are dismissed as essentially irrelevant to the counter-terrorist agenda of the Committee.[109] When the ad hoc tribunals were established,

---

[106] See, eg, Addressing Challenges to Targeted Sanctions (Providence, RI: Watson Institute for International Studies, October 2009).     [107] SC Res 1439 (2002); SC Res 1448 (2002).

[108] Second Report of the Analytical Support and Sanctions Monitoring Team Appointed Pursuant to Resolution 1526 (2004) Concerning al-Qaeda and the Taliban and Associated Individuals and Entities, UN Doc S/2005/83, Annex (2005), 19.

[109] Modest improvements include the creation of a focal point for de-listing petitions and an expansion in the 1267 Committee's review and de-listing procedures: SC Res 1730 (2006); SC Res 1822 (2008).

for example, the UN Office of Legal Affairs was deeply involved. By contrast, the 1267 regime was established without reference to the Legal Counsel at all; when a member state suggested that the office should be consulted, it was told that there were no legal issues involved in listing or de-listing.

The pressure to change is likely to increase, if not through courts striking down asset freezes then through member states refusing to implement them. The main barrier to such reforms, however, is not simply resistance to the human rights arguments or a general reluctance to constrain the discretion of the Security Council by reviewing its decisions. Rather, it is the fact that in many ways the Council and its Committee are not actually making the relevant decisions. As the European Court of First Instance observed in the *Kadi* case, any opportunity for an individual whose assets are frozen to respond to the correctness and relevance of facts used to justify that action is definitively excluded: 'Those facts and that evidence, once classified as confidential or secret by the State which made the Sanctions Committee aware of them, are not, obviously, communicated to him, any more than they are to the Member States of the United Nations to which the Security Council's resolutions are addressed.'[110] Though the obligation to respect procedural constraints is normally clear when a state is seeking to exercise coercive powers over one of its own nationals, it is less clear that such obligations translate to international bodies as a matter of law and certain that there is unwillingness to do so in fact.

This instance of the more general reluctance to share intelligence within an international organization such as the United Nations suggests that a more productive means of challenging specific listings may draw upon the bilateral intelligence relationships described in Chapter one. As the United States proposes the majority of listings, a country's relationship with the United States will therefore be crucial. From the adoption of formal de-listing procedures in November 2002 until December 2005 only two individuals were de-listed. One was a British citizen and the other was a resident of Germany. Both were removed from the list only after intense

---

[110] *Yassin Abdullah Kadi v Council of the European Union and Commission of the European Communities (Case T-315/01)* (Court of First Instance of the European Communities, 21 September 2005), para 273.

lobbying by the respective governments and in one case de-listing was linked to cooperation with the authorities in investigations of terrorist activities.

Such a practice, which favours the citizens and residents of allies of the United States, is unsustainable. Indeed, there are already indications that in countries not in a position like Britain, Germany, Canada, Sweden, or Switzerland to lobby the United States, sanctions are already being implemented selectively. It now seems probable that the greatest problem for the effectiveness of the regime will not be challenges from courts but the reluctance of states to add to the list. This was first identified as a problem in late 2002, with some states citing practical and legal constraints preventing them from submitting the names of individuals and entities under ongoing investigation, or expressing concerns about the legality of listing individuals prior to a judicial finding of culpability.[111]

Advancing this debate would profit from closer examination of the history of intelligence sharing with international organizations, especially in the context of implementing regimes such as weapons inspections in Iraq. Effective use of intelligence by such organizations depends on both a demonstrated ability to receive confidential information appropriately and a capacity to assess its accuracy, relevance, and implications.[112] In the repertoire of the UN Security Council there is, in fact, some experience in drawing upon sensitive information to implement Council decisions: in the practice of the ad hoc international criminal tribunals, which have had to balance the need to protect sources and methods, the rights of an accused, and the integrity of the tribunal itself.

## 2.5. International Criminal Prosecution

International criminal prosecution has seen the most direct discussion of the legal implications of intelligence being used in international forums. Though intelligence provided by member states was extremely useful in

---

[111] UN Doc S/2002/1050/Rev.1, Annex (2002), para 25–27; UN Doc S/2003/1070, Annex (2003), paras 19–20.

[112] See Simon Chesterman, *Shared Secrets: Intelligence and Collective Security* (Sydney: Lowy Institute for International Policy, 2006), 29–38, 60–8.

the investigation of crimes, adducing this evidence in court introduced problems familiar to many jurisdictions in which intelligence and law enforcement bodies operate side by side. The challenges include balancing the need to protect sources and thus ensure an ongoing flow of information to support effectiveness, while at the same time protecting the rights of the accused if the legitimacy of the tribunal is not to be called into question.

The use of intelligence in international criminal prosecution highlights directly the tension between the competing objectives of national security and international legitimacy. The tension is enhanced because the national interest that leads a state to share intelligence concerning war criminals is likely to be less compelling than the other situations discussed in this Chapter; at the same time, the evidentiary threshold for securing a conviction in an international tribunal is considerably more rigorous.

### 2.5.1. Intelligence and Investigation

Access to intelligence, in the sense used here of information obtained covertly, need not be central to the prosecution of an individual before an international tribunal. But it will frequently be very helpful. The nature of situations that fall within the jurisdiction of such tribunals and their limited investigative capacity makes traditional collection of evidence difficult. Intelligence may be a source of leads for interviews with potential witnesses; it may also provide important contextual information that deepens an investigator's understanding of a case. This demand for intelligence may also correspond to a potential supply: if the situation is a conflict zone then there will often be a number of governments collecting intelligence for their own purposes. In some circumstances, these governments may be willing to share at least part of this intelligence with investigators, if not to produce it in open court.[113] At times this discretion may be exercised capriciously. During the Rwandan genocide, for example, the commander of the remaining UN forces in Kigali was informed that the United States had learned of plans for his assassination: 'I guess I should

---

[113] Peter Nicholson, The Function of Analysis and the Role of the Analyst within the Prosecutor's Office of an International Criminal Court (The Hague: International Criminal Court, Office of the Prosecutor, 13 February 2003), 6.

have been grateful for the tip,' Romeo Dallaire later wrote, 'but my larger reaction was that if delicate intelligence like this could be gathered by surveillance, how could the United States not be recording evidence of the genocide occurring in Rwanda?'[114]

The question of whether and how intelligence could and should be used in international criminal prosecution arose shortly after the establishment of the International Criminal Tribunal for the former Yugoslavia (ICTY). The first Chief Prosecutor of the Tribunal, Richard Goldstone, realized the importance of having access to intelligence, especially from the United States. The problem was how to reconcile necessary procedural protection of defendants' rights with the desire of states providing intelligence to avoid compromising their sources and methods.[115] Rule 70 (B) of the ICTY's Rules of Procedure and Evidence was the result. It provides that if the Prosecutor is in possession of information provided on a confidential basis, and which has been used solely to generate new evidence, neither the information nor its origin will be disclosed without the consent of the person or entity that provided it. If such information is to be used in court, it must be shared with the accused first. A further provision was later added to include a national security exemption from the general obligation to produce documents and information.[116]

Louise Arbour, who succeeded Goldstone as Chief Prosecutor, later observed that Rule 70 had been extremely useful: 'It is, frankly, and we have to live in a realistic world, the only mechanism by which we can have access to military intelligence from any source.' That utility had been especially important in the early days of the Tribunal; as its work moved from investigations to trials, the dangers of accepting classified information became apparent as it prevented the Prosecutor from using the information and could curtail the rights of the defence.[117] Such candour about the use of intelligence indicates how much has changed from the days

[114] Roméo Dallaire, *Shake Hands with the Devil: The Failure of Humanity in Rwanda* (Toronto: Random House Canada, 2003), 339.

[115] See Richard J Goldstone, 'Remarks: Intelligence and the Use of Force in the War on Terrorism', *American Society of International Law Proceedings* 98 (2004) 148.

[116] Rules of Procedure and Evidence (The Hague: International Criminal Tribunal for the Former Yugoslavia, IT/32, 14 March 1994), rules 70 (B), 54 *bis*.

[117] Louise Arbour, 'War Crimes Tribunals: The Record and the Prospects: History and Future of the International Criminal Tribunals for the Former Yugoslavia and Rwanda', *American University International Law Review* 13 (1998) 1495 at 1508.

when intelligence itself was a dirty word in the United Nations. Indeed, the International Criminal Court (ICC) now recruits professional staff for the position of 'Criminal Intelligence Analyst'.

In the negotiations leading to the creation of the ICC, a number of delegations also stressed the importance of including provisions for protecting national security information. As in the ICTY, the Rome Statute allows the Prosecutor to conclude agreements not to disclose documents or information obtained 'on the condition of confidentiality and solely for the purpose of generating new evidence.'[118] The openness with which the issue is discussed demonstrates the increasing acceptance of intelligence issues as an important part of the work of the Court, reflected in open briefings on the topic and the creation of posts within the Office of the Prosecutor requiring experience in handling and analysing military intelligence.[119]

The ICC also provides for a national security exception to requests by the Prosecutor or the Court for information or assistance, though it takes the form of a complex mechanism, based in part on an ICTY Appeals Chamber decision in the *Blaškić* case,[120] intended to encourage a state invoking this exception to disclose as much as possible. 'Cooperative means' are first encouraged to reach a resolution through modifying the request or agreeing on conditions to protect the threatened interest. If such means fail and the state refuses to disclose the information or documents, the state must notify the Prosecutor or the Court 'of the specific reasons for its decision, unless a specific description of the reasons would itself necessarily result in such prejudice to the State's national security interests.' If the Court nevertheless determines that the evidence is relevant and necessary for the establishment of the guilt or innocence of an accused, it may refer the matter to the Assembly of States Parties or, if

---

[118] Statute of the International Criminal Court (Rome Statute), UN Doc A/Conf.183/9 (1998), art 54(3)(e). See Michael A Newton, 'The International Criminal Court Preparatory Commission: The Way It Is & the Way Ahead', *Virginia Journal of International Law* 41 (2000) 204 at 212.

[119] See, eg, Peter Nicholson, Testimony at Public Hearing of the Office of the Prosecutor (The Hague: International Criminal Court, Office of the Prosecutor, 17–18 June 2003); Bruno Cathala, Statement of the Registrar: Tenth Diplomatic Briefing of the International Criminal Court (The Hague: International Criminal Court, 26 June 2007).

[120] *Prosecutor v Tihomir Blaškić (Judgement on the Request of the Republic of Croatia for Review of the Decision of Trial Chamber II of 18 July 1997)* (ICTY Appeals Chamber, 29 October 1997) Case No IT-95–14, para 68.

the Security Council referred the matter to the Court, to the Council.[121] An important departure from the *Blaškić* formula is the apparent reversal of the presumption that states are obliged to disclose information; in the ICC Statute the emphasis is on the right of states to deny the Court's request for assistance.[122] In *Blaškić* this obligation was linked to the use of Chapter VII by the Security Council in establishing the Tribunal;[123] as the ICC lacks such coercive powers, specific obligations to disclose information may require action by the Council on a case-by-case basis. The *Blaškić* case also demonstrates the importance of intelligence in providing exculpatory evidence, the release of which led to the defendant on appeal having his sentence drastically reduced and being granted an early release.[124]

## 2.5.2. Maintaining Independence

Though most consideration of intelligence and international criminal prosecution tends to focus on the difficulty of obtaining evidence in a form that may be presented in court, in some circumstances the problem may be too much support. This may call into question the independence of the proceedings, as was alleged in the Special Court for Sierra Leone in 2004. A defence motion argued that the Prosecutor's independence had been compromised by the close relationship between its Chief of Investigations and the FBI. In its response, the Office of the Prosecutor drew a distinction between its dual obligations to investigate and prosecute, emphasizing the important role of external assistance during investigations while distinguishing this from taking instructions from any entity. Rule 39 of the Rules of Procedure and Evidence, for example, provided that in the course of an investigation the Prosecutor could seek 'the assistance of any State authority concerned, as well as of any relevant international body including the International Criminal Police Organization

---

[121] Rome Statute, arts 72, 87(7).

[122] Antonio Cassese, 'The Statute of the International Criminal Court: Some Preliminary Reflections', *European Journal of International Law* 10 (1999) 144 at 166–7.

[123] *Blaškić* (29 October 1997), para 68. See Ruth Wedgwood, 'International Criminal Tribunals and State Sources of Proof: The Case of Tihomir Blaskic', *Leiden Journal of International Law* 11 (1998) 635.

[124] *Prosecutor v Tihomir Blaškić (Judgement)* (ICTY Appeals Chamber, 29 July 2004) Case No IT-95–14.

(INTERPOL).'[125] The Court, setting what appeared to be an unusually high burden of proof, rejected the defence motion on the basis that it had not demonstrated a 'master-servant' relationship between the FBI and the Office of the Prosecutor.[126]

Protecting the integrity of intelligence sources is likely to be important to the medium-term success of international tribunals generally and the International Criminal Court in particular. Soon after the Security Council referred the situation in Darfur to the ICC in March 2005,[127] the Secretary-General transmitted a sealed list of 51 individuals named by the UN International Commission of Inquiry as suspects of grave international crimes;[128] neither the Secretary-General nor the members of the Council knew the contents of this list and transmitted it to the Prosecutor of the ICC unopened. Developing procedures for maintaining confidentiality will help to build trust on the part of those who might provide intelligence to the ICC. At the same time, however, the independence of the ICC and its ad hoc and hybrid cousins depends on more than avoiding a 'master-servant' relationship with the intelligence services of the United States. Avoiding even the impression of inappropriate relationships will depend on diversifying the sources of intelligence and strengthening the capacity to receive and analyse them with a critical and impartial eye.

## 2.5.3. Apprehension

A final area in which intelligence has been both important and troubling is the apprehension of suspects. This had been a particular problem for the ICTY until mid-1997, when the United States and its allies agreed to use intelligence and military capacities to apprehend war criminals. Even then, the failure to locate the two most important suspects from the Bosnian war—Radovan Karadžić and Ratko Mladić—was an embarrassment

---

[125] Rules of Procedure and Evidence (Freetown: Special Court for Sierra Leone, 12 April 2002), Rule 39(iii).

[126] *Prosecutor v Issa Hassan Sesay, Morris Kallon, and Augustine Gbao (Decision on Sesay Motion Seeking Disclosure of the Relationship Between Governmental Agencies of the United States of America and the Office of the Prosecutor)* (Special Court for Sierra Leone, 2 May 2005) Case No SCSL-04-15-T, 14.     [127] SC Res 1593 (2005).

[128] Report of the International Commission of Inquiry on Darfur to the Secretary-General Pursuant to Security Council Resolution 1564 (2004) of 18 September 2004, UN Doc S/2005/60, Annex (2005), 5.

for the ICTY and its supporters. When Karadžić was ultimately arrested in 2008, the ease with which he appeared to have been living in Belgrade was interpreted as an indication that intelligence resources had not been fully devoted to locating him until it suited the purposes of key states to do so.

## 3. THE LIMITS OF COOPERATION

The use of national intelligence in the lead up to the 2003 Iraq war was not limited to spying on Saddam Hussein's regime. As the United States and Britain sought support for a resolution in the Security Council authorizing an invasion, an e-mail was leaked by a translator at the British Government Communications Headquarters (GCHQ) that outlined plans by the US National Security Agency (NSA) to mount a 'surge' against the other 13 members of the Council. This message, sent between the US and British signals intelligence agencies, revealed a concerted effort to tap into the office and home telephone and e-mail communications of delegations on the Council in order to collect information on their positions on the debate over Iraq, including alliances, dependencies, and 'the whole gamut of information that could give US policymakers an edge in obtaining results favorable to US goals or to head off surprises.'[129] Though some feigned shock at the revelation, most diplomats in New York assume that their communications are routinely intercepted by the US and other intelligence services. One Council diplomat, when asked by a reporter in a telephone interview whether he believed his calls were being monitored, replied dryly: 'Let's ask the guy who's listening to us.'[130]

The problematic use of intelligence in international criminal prosecutions points to two larger caveats on increasing access to intelligence, whether in an international tribunal, the Security Council, or any other international body. The first is that intelligence may be overvalued. Officials

---

[129] Martin Bright, Ed Vulliamy, and Peter Beaumont, 'US Dirty Tricks to Win Vote on Iraq War', *Observer* (London), 2 March 2003.
[130] Colum Lynch, 'Spying Report No Shock to UN', *Washington Post*, 4 March 2003.

with limited past access to intelligence sometimes attach disproportionate weight to information bearing the stamp 'secret', or which is
delivered by the intelligence service of a member state. Since any such
material will normally be provided without reference to the sources and
methods that produced it, credulity must be tempered by prudence.
A second caveat is the corresponding danger of undervaluing unclassified or open source material. Intelligence is sometimes likened to quality
journalism; a reasonable corollary is that good journalists frequently
produce material that is comparable to the intelligence product of some
services. The United Nations itself collects large amounts of information
and analysis, though it is not organized systematically. In addition, non-
governmental organizations are increasingly providing better and more
timely policy advice than the United Nations and, on occasion, its
member states.[131]

The use of intelligence, then, creates both opportunities and dangers.
Though it is improbable that states will come to regard it as a kind of
international 'public good' to be provided to international organizations
for collective security purposes,[132] effective peacekeeping and multilateral
responses to the threats of proliferation and terrorism will depend on
intelligence sharing, while international criminal prosecution will
continue to rely on such support at least for the purpose of investigations.
The danger is that passivity on the part of the receiving body will undermine the legitimacy of multilateral institutions and processes by the
reality or the perception of unilateral influence.

Legal standards and accountability for the use of intelligence vary
significantly between the different areas considered here. There has never
been a formal challenge as to whether the United Nations has the power to
undertake intelligence collection activities. It would appear to be included

---

[131] One of the more prominent is Crisis Group: despite its importance to both Australia and
the United States, the best work on the nature and structure of the Southeast Asian terrorist
group Jemaah Islamiyah has been done by Crisis Group's Sidney Jones. See, eg, Crisis Group,
*Indonesia: Jemaah Islamiyah's Publishing Industry* (Jakarta/Brussels: ICG Asia Report No
147, 28 February 2008). Disclosure: the author was seconded to Crisis Group as its Director of
UN Relations in the New York office from late 2003 to early 2004.

[132] Cf Turner, *Secrecy and Democracy*, 280–5; William E Colby, 'Reorganizing Western Intelligence', in Carl Peter Runde and Greg Voss (eds), *Intelligence and the New World Order: Former
Cold War Adversaries Look Toward the 21st Century* (Bustehude: International Freedom Foundation, 1992), 126 at 126–7.

as an implied power necessary to carry out its other responsibilities and apparently accepted by member states—which acknowledged the right of the Organization to use codes in 1946 and have subsequently tolerated its various intelligence-like functions.[133]

Ironically, however, legal controls on the use of intelligence in international forums become stronger as the potential consequences are limited. There is no formal check on the Security Council's authorization to use force against a perceived threat to international peace and security—and ambiguous criteria for evaluating a state's claim to be acting in self-defence. In the case of targeted financial sanctions, stricter limits have been imposed on a regime that freezes the assets of a few hundred people (with elaborate humanitarian exemptions) than applied to the sanctions blamed for killing half a million Iraqis. As for international prosecution, the single alleged war criminal receives by far the greatest protection from dubious recourse to intelligence sources.

This is not to suggest that legal accountability is the only manner in which the exercise of coercive power may be constrained. Other means include negotiation constraints, checks and balances, the threat of unilateral action, and so on, pointing to an important distinction between legal and political accountability discussed in the next Chapter.[134] The UN Security Council was created as an archetypically political body, but as its activities have come to impact on individuals the demands for legal forms of accountability will increase.

Shortly after the Madrid bombings of 11 March 2004, the Council passed a resolution condemning the attacks, which it stated were 'perpetrated by the [Basque] terrorist group ETA'.[135] The resolution was adopted despite German and Russian efforts to include in the text the modifier 'reportedly' to reflect uncertainty about this attribution, which appeared to be intended to bolster the Aznar government's chances in a national election held three days later.[136] It was soon established that the uncertainty was well-founded,

---

[133] *Certain Expenses of the United Nations (Advisory Opinion)* (1962) ICJ Rep 151, 167; Convention on the Privileges and Immunities of the United Nations, 13 February 1946, art III, s 10.

[134] See Chapter seven, section 2.          [135] SC Res 1530 (2004), para 1.

[136] See, eg, Dale Fuchs, 'Investigation of Madrid Bombings Shows No Link to Basque Group, Spanish Minister Says', *New York Times*, 30 March 2004.

though even the subsequent arrest of extremist Islamists did not prompt a correction, an apology, or a statement from the Council.[137]

There are few consequences for the Council itself when it is wrong. Entrusted to deal with 'threats' to international peace and security, it cannot be expected to function as a court of law—though it is no longer tenable to pretend that it does not at least function as a kind of jury. The latter role has been expanded by the Council's move into areas where the determination of a threat to the peace is far more complex than tracking troop movements across international borders. This is only part of a larger transformation in the activities of the Council: instead of merely responding to such threats, it increasingly acts to contain or pre-empt them. Its expanding responsibilities have ranged from the listing of alleged terrorist financiers for the purposes of freezing their assets to administering territories such as Timor-Leste and Kosovo. These activities have prompted calls for greater accountability of the Council, or at least wider participation in its decision-making processes.

As the Council has begun to act in the sphere of counter-terrorism and counter-proliferation, its dependence on intelligence findings has introduced slightly different legitimacy problems. A useful thought experiment is to consider what would have happened if the Council had accepted Colin Powell's February 2003 presentation at face value, voting to authorize a war to rid Iraq of its concealed weapons of mass destruction. For President Bush and Prime Minister Blair, the absence of weapons was a political embarrassment that could be survived. For the Council, it would have undermined the one thing that the United Nations could bring to the issue: some small amount of legitimacy.

With respect to Iraq there appears, with hindsight, to have been little that might have derailed US plans for a military action.[138] The test should not be, however, whether reforms will prevent great powers of the day from pursuing foreign policy objectives decided at the highest levels of government. Rather, more effective use of intelligence would lay a foundation for

---

[137] For a rare mention of the issue, see Letter dated 15 March 2004 from the Permanent Representative of Spain to the United Nations addressed to the President of the Security Council, UN Doc S/2004/204 (2004).

[138] See further Simon Chesterman and Sebastian von Einsiedel, 'Dual Containment: The United States, Iraq, and the UN Security Council', in Paul Eden and Thérèse O'Donnell (eds), *September 11, 2001: A Turning Point in International and Domestic Law?* (New York: Transnational Publishers, 2004), 725.

more effective use of the multilateral forum, making it harder for states participating in that forum to ignore emerging crises or embrace unworkable policies. Over time, it may also encourage greater cooperation between states to address those threats that no one state—even the most powerful—can address alone.

# Part III

# Change

# 7

## Watching the Watchers

> If men were angels, no government would be necessary. If angels
> were to govern men, neither external nor internal controls on govern-
> ment would be necessary. In framing a government which is to be
> administered by men over men, the great difficulty lies in this: you
> must first enable the government to control the governed; and in the
> next place oblige it to control itself. A dependence on the people is,
> no doubt, the primary control on the government; but experience
> has taught mankind the necessity of auxiliary precautions.
>
> James Madison[1]

In late 2003, Khaled el-Masri, a German citizen, was holidaying in
Macedonia. When he attempted to cross the border, he was stopped by
Macedonian officials. Unfamiliar with recent design changes to German
passports, they suspected his was a forgery; his name was also similar to
that of a suspected al Qaeda leader on a list provided by the US government. He was detained on New Year's Eve and many government officials
were on holiday. Even so, there was a division of views about what to do
with him. The head of the CIA's al Qaeda Unit, who had previously been
in the Bin Laden Unit that failed to prevent the September 11 attacks,
argued that the CIA should take him into custody. She overruled doubters
who wanted to wait for German officials to determine whether the passport was indeed a forgery, and by the time the Berlin station became
involved el-Masri had been beaten, sedated, and sent to Afghanistan. The
Kabul station chief later cabled the Counterterrorist Center and accused
them of sending him an innocent person. El-Masri's passport was found
to be genuine but there was continued resistance to his release until CIA

[1] James Madison, Federalist, No 51: 'The Structure of the Government Must Furnish the
Proper Checks and Balances Between the Different Departments', *The Federalist* (New York:
J and A McLean, 1788).

lawyers began lobbying for it. As Jane Mayer recounts, when the matter finally reached CIA Director George Tenet he was stunned: 'Are you telling me we've got an innocent guy stuck in prison in Afghanistan? Oh shit! Just tell me—please—we haven't used "enhanced" interrogation techniques on him, have we?' A dilemma was whether to inform the German government. Condoleezza Rice, then National Security Adviser, insisted that the President could not be put in the position of lying to US allies, a scruple that one of the CIA officers involved thought was somewhat absurd for people essentially running 'Kidnap Inc'. After five months, el-Masri was finally 'reverse rendered' and dumped in Albania, left to make his own way home to a wife and four young sons waiting in Germany.[2]

El-Masri filed lawsuits against Tenet and the owners of the private jets used to transport him, but these were dismissed on the basis of the state secrets privilege. The judge held that, despite wide criticism of the practice of extraordinary rendition, the government could still legitimately refuse to disclose its operational details: any official admission or denial of such claims would reveal the methods employed in the clandestine programme and 'such a revelation would present a grave risk to national security'. If true, the judge noted, el-Masri's allegations showed that he had suffered injuries and deserved a remedy. But that remedy was to be sought from the executive or legislative, rather than the judicial branch.[3] An appeal was dismissed and further recourse to the Supreme Court was denied without comment.[4]

The chapters in Part II addressed some of the basic concerns in the regulation and oversight of intelligence services. Chapter four, looking at the experience of the United States, showed some of the dangers of outsourcing: the extraordinary powers available to intelligence officials can only be justified by the public nature of that power, which should therefore be exercised within a set of political structures accountable to the population. Chapter five considered Britain and the turn to law,

---

[2] Jane Mayer, *The Dark Side: The Inside Story of How the War on Terror Turned Into a War on American Ideals* (New York: Doubleday, 2008), 282–7.

[3] *El-Masri v Tenet*, 437 F Supp 2d 530, 537–8, 541 (ED Va, 2006). See, eg, Report of the Special Rapporteur on the Promotion and Protection of Human Rights and Fundamental Freedoms While Countering Terrorism, UN Doc A/HRC/10/3 (2009), paras 51–3.

[4] *El-Masri v Tenet*, 479 F.3d 296 (4th Cir, 2007); *El-Masri v United States*, 552 US 947 (2007). On the state secrets privilege, see Chapter three, section 1.2.

showing how the uncontroversial point that the mandate and powers of intelligence services must be grounded in law can nevertheless create problems of definition and implementation. Chapter six then examined the unusual situation of the United Nations: lacking an intelligence capacity of its own, it nonetheless demonstrates the accountability questions that flow beyond collection and on to the use of intelligence.

These three basic principles—that intelligence must be publicly-held, legally-grounded, and consequence-sensitive—form the basis for the examination of accountability structures in Part III. Building on the first two principles, this Chapter maps out structural accountability possibilities—mechanisms of control, oversight, and review—applicable to intelligence services. The following Chapter draws upon the third principle to describe how accountability might appropriately move from a focus largely on collection of information to governance of its use.

First it will be necessary to examine the nature and purpose of accountability before turning to structural issues to be resolved in any accountability regime. The intention is not to offer an ideal framework applicable to every society, but rather to set out the structural questions and institutional possibilities that might allow different societies to design a framework appropriate to their needs. Accountability structures must be sensitive to the culture and values of the society in question, its trust in government, its commitment to the rule of law. Ultimately, these latter factors will determine whether a given set of structures can ensure the legitimacy and effectiveness of a country's intelligence services.

## 1. THE NATURE AND PURPOSE OF ACCOUNTABILITY

The term 'accountability' is routinely used in many fields of governance without much concern as to its precise meaning. Though originally denoting a relationship in which an account must be given to a designated authority, it is commonly used in the far wider sense of meaning an unspecified 'responsibility' for a set of actions or decisions. Though of course it is desirable that persons exercising public power behave responsibly, this is an unhelpful blurring of what accountability can and should mean in practice. To clarify the content of the term, it is helpful to examine what relationship of accountability is intended and what that relationship is intended to achieve. Focusing on intelligence services, this may be done by considering *why* there is a need for accountability, *when* it is to be invoked, as well as *to whom* and *for what* a service might be held accountable. The following section then considers how such a regime might be implemented.

## 1.1. Why

There are at least three reasons why one might wish to hold an intelligence service to account. First, and most obviously, to prevent abuse. The twentieth century is replete with stories of unauthorized activities, some of which were catalogued by agencies themselves;[5] following September 11, overzealous efforts to win the twenty-first century 'war on terror' encouraged an environment that appeared to tolerate or encourage mistreatment of detainees and otherwise stretched, bent, or broke the law.[6] This is nothing new, of course: in Hannah Arendt's study of totalitarianism, she noted that the desire of intelligence services to prove their usefulness has always encouraged them to behave badly: 'It appears, for example, that there was not a single anti-government action under the reign of Louis Napoleon which had not been inspired by the police itself.'[7] If one accepts that intelligence services require intrusive powers, it is important that those powers have limits, with consequences for exceeding them.

Limits on such powers are not simply to guard against abuse, however. They may also be needed to justify what would otherwise be a departure from the rule of law. Secondly, then, accountability may legitimize the exercise of intrusive powers within an otherwise open society. This suggests the need to locate intelligence services, in principle, within traditional accountability structures that define the modern state: with political accountability to publicly-appointed representatives, and legal accountability to the institutions of the rule of law.[8]

Accountability is more than a matter of constraining intelligence services. A third reason for holding them to account is that it may lead to

---

[5] See Chapter one, section 1.     [6] See Chapter four, section 1.1.
[7] Hannah Arendt, *The Origins of Totalitarianism*, 2nd edn (New York: Meridian, 1958), 423.
[8] See Chapter two.

better outcomes. One of the key criticisms of the Silberman–Robb Commission that investigated US intelligence failures in Iraq was that the intelligence community is 'not so much poorly managed as unmanaged'.[9] Clearer lines of authority and reporting requirements can ensure that intelligence serves one of its key functions effectively and efficiently: supporting the policy process. As described in Chapter five, a clear mandate may also outline the appropriate functions of a service while providing some measure of protection from political interference.[10]

## 1.2. When

Accountability should not simply be a reaction to scandal. To be effective it should normally exist as of right, which requires the creation of institutions, the elaboration of standards, and the potential for sanctions *before* a scandal takes place. If it is necessary to establish a bipartisan inquiry or Royal Commission to investigate every perceived problem, the threshold for action will be prohibitively high.

In reality, a mix of mechanisms is likely to be required. Focusing on the temporal question, two broad theories of oversight are known as the 'police-patrol' and 'fire-alarm' models. In the former, a sample of activities is investigated with the aim of detecting and remedying problematic behaviour and, through this surveillance, discouraging it. In the latter, a system is put in place where interested groups are empowered to raise an alarm and thus set in motion a response. The authors who developed these models were focused on congressional oversight and sought to challenge conventional wisdom in the United States that denounced the legislature's neglect of its oversight responsibilities. They argued, instead, that Congress had implicitly chosen the more efficient fire-alarm model of reactive rather than centralized and continuous intervention.[11]

---

[9] The Commission on the Intelligence Capabilities of the United States Regarding Weapons of Mass Destruction (Silberman–Robb Commission Report) (Washington, DC: Laurence H Silberman and Charles S Robb, co-chairs, 31 March 2005), 18.

[10] See Chapter five, section 2.2.

[11] Mathew D McCubbins and Thomas Schwartz, 'Congressional Oversight Overlooked: Police Patrols versus Fire Alarms', *American Journal of Political Science* 28 (1984) 165 at 166–76.

Given the barriers to discovering wrongdoing by an intelligence service, complete reliance on reactive investigations is undesirable. Some measure of ongoing oversight will therefore be required, supplemented by mechanisms put in place to respond to issues that arise, with the further possibility of inquiries or commissions to consider structural or high political problems not able to be handled through regular procedures. The appropriate mechanism may also depend on the precise subject matter in question, with the obvious need for caution when considering specific operations as opposed to more general policies and practices.

### 1.3. To Whom

As indicated earlier, one reason for accountability is to locate intelligence services within the institutions of the state. The most influential relationship will be control through a service's internal structures. For this reason, some of the more effective institutions may be internal, such as an inspector general who is part of a service and understands its culture. Purely internal checks, however, place too high a burden on—or too much trust in—the agency, with the additional risk of regulatory capture.[12] Other relationships should therefore be invoked.

Central will be the role of the executive, with elected officials bearing political responsibility for the acts of agencies under their control. In the Westminster tradition, ministerial responsibility embraces the notion that a cabinet minister is politically accountable for any action taken within his or her department, even if he or she had no direct knowledge of it. The US style of executive government places more responsibility in the hands of the President, at whose pleasure the various secretaries and heads of agencies serve. One consequence of this distinction is that there is less of a tradition of resignation in the United States; in some circumstances it may in fact suit a sitting president to keep an appointee in place in order to insulate him- or herself from culpability.[13]

---

[12] See Chapter three, section 2.3.

[13] Matthew SR Palmer, 'Toward an Economics of Comparative Political Organization: Examining Ministerial Responsibility', *Journal of Law, Economics, and Organization* 11(1) (1995) 164.

The legislature offers various forms of possible oversight. The mandate and powers of intelligence services are now generally found in statutes, which may also provide the remedies available to wronged individuals. Congress or Parliament may also have some form of budgetary control. Individual members may serve on committees established as a further form of oversight, such as the US Senate and House Select Committees on Intelligence, and the British Intelligence and Security Committee.

The judiciary naturally plays an important role in interpreting and applying the law, typically in the course of resolving disputes that are brought before it.[14] Procedural variations may be adopted when dealing with intelligence matters. These include the use of *in camera* and *ex parte* proceedings, meaning that hearings may be conducted in closed session or with only one party—normally representatives of the government—present.[15] Specially constituted courts may be formed with judges who develop an expertise in intelligence matters, such as the US Foreign Intelligence Surveillance Court, which consists of 11 federal district court judges appointed by the Chief Justice, each serving a seven year term. Judges may also be called upon to serve in their individual capacity to investigate specific matters, such as the Canadian Commission of Inquiry into the Maher Arar case, led by the Associate Chief Justice of Ontario.[16]

Other arrangements are possible. Tribunals, such as Britain's Investigatory Powers Tribunal, may have a partial relationship to the judiciary: its members are appointed by the Queen but must be senior members of the legal profession; the President and Vice President of the Tribunal must hold or have held high judicial office.[17] Commissioners and ombudspersons may be appointed by government to oversee specific agencies or government functions, as in the case of Britain's various commissioners.[18]

---

[14] An important case in Britain concerned administrative law, arising when the government tried to prohibit employees of the signals intelligence agency GCHQ from belonging to trade unions. See *Council of Civil Service Unions v Minister for the Civil Service (GCHQ case)* [1985] AC 374.

[15] For a discussion in the Canadian context, see *Ruby v Canada (Solicitor General)* (1996) 136 DLR (4th) 74. In the United States, the Classified Information Procedures Act 1980 governs the use of intelligence in criminal trials. See generally Daphne Barak-Erez and Matthew C Waxman, 'Secret Evidence and the Due Process of Terrorist Detentions', *Columbia Journal of Transnational Law* 48 (2009) 3.   [16] See Chapter eight.

[17] Regulation of Investigatory Powers Act (RIPA) 2000 (UK), Schedule 3.

[18] See section 2.2 in this Chapter and Chapter five, section 2.4.

There is, in addition, an important if informal role for those outside the government. As shown in Chapter three, civil society organizations—and, especially, the media—in practice serve as an extremely important check on the activities of intelligence services.[19] This relationship may be cultivated through appropriate levels of transparency, freedom of information laws, and outreach activities. Ultimately, the relationship of accountability must flow to the public itself, though it would be naïve to expect this relationship to be a direct and candid one, unmediated by other institutions of the state.[20]

## 1.4. For What

Accountability may be targeted in a variety of ways. It may focus narrowly on ensuring compliance with the law or internal protocols, similar to the responsibilities of judges issuing warrants for wiretaps or searches. It may also consider the broader policy questions driving the intelligence community, such as the annual threat assessment presented by the US intelligence community to Congress, which includes an unclassified version that is then released to the public. This reflects a distinction between accountability for the *means* used by intelligence services and an examination of the proper *ends* of the powers they exercise.

Particularly in the United States, the many actors in the intelligence community—16 agencies with over 200,000 employees—may pose accountability difficulties through sheer complexity. The fragmentation of authority can pose practical problems in ensuring appropriate oversight for the various agencies; it may also be used precisely to avoid oversight through delegation to the least accountable agency, or through the creation of a new entity. For this reason, some countries have sought to provide for functional as opposed to institutional accountability, with the emphasis on the activity being regulated, regardless of the identity of the actor.[21]

---

[19] See Chapter three, section 3.

[20] Cf the discussion of Oren Gross's extra-legal measures in Chapter two, section 1.2.3.

[21] Commission of Inquiry into the Actions of Canadian Officials in Relation to Maher Arar, A New Review Mechanism for the RCMP's National Security Activities (Arar Commission Policy Review) (Ottawa: Government of Canada, 2006), 313; Loch K Johnson, 'Governing in the Absence of Angels: On the Practice of Intelligence Accountability in the United States', in

Given the separation of powers and the secrecy of many activities, a key point of leverage for legislatures may be the appropriation of funding. Budgetary controls may therefore be an important form of accountability— though even these tend to be considered at a high degree of abstraction.[22] In practice, the most high profile focus of accountability tends to be after the fact accounting for a scandal that generates significant political interest.

## 2. STRUCTURAL QUESTIONS

How, then, might accountability be implemented? The barriers to effective accountability for intelligence activities are considerable. The necessary secrecy of the enterprise may encourage abuse, facilitate cover-ups, make it hard to ask the right questions, or allow regulatory capture. Agencies have little incentive to share more than they must and it may in fact be convenient for politicians to know as little as they can.[23] The Maxwell-Fyfe Directive, discussed in Chapter five, was an internal document and therefore unusually candid in its injunction that the head of MI5 should 'maintain the well-established convention whereby Ministers do not concern themselves with the detailed information' concerning operations under their authority.[24]

It is also important to note that intelligence services have legitimate and important functions to serve that may be rendered impossible if they are subject to excessive transparency or burdensome legal and bureaucratic requirements. To be effective, it is necessary to encourage flexibility and adaptability; in some circumstances it will be appropriate to allow greater discretion or to restrict individual rights in the name of preserving national security. Striking the right balance requires a realistic assessment of the appropriate functions of intelligence services, the proper purpose of an accountability mechanism, and an understanding of the

Hans Born, Loch K Johnson, and Ian Leigh (eds), *Who's Watching the Spies: Establishing Intelligence Service Accountability* (Washington, DC: Potomac Books, 2005), 57.

[22] See Chapter three, section 1.2.    [23] See Chapter three, section 2.
[24] See Chapter five, section 1.

probable impact on the behaviour of the agencies to be regulated. Such a regime should thereby provide the context within which discretion will be exercised.

Discussion of accountability often focuses on convictions, resignations, and compensation, but there are many ways of holding power to account in the broader sense understood here. *Legal* accountability requires that a decision-maker has a convincing reason for a decision or act, in the absence of which that decision or act is outside the law. *Political* accountability, by contrast, can be entirely arbitrary. In an election, for example, voters are not required to have reasons for their decision—indeed, the secrecy of the ballot implies the exact opposite: it is generally unlawful even to ask a voter why he or she voted one way or another.[25] These forms of accountability may be seen as lying on a spectrum, with other variations possible.[26] Four broad structural categories will be adopted here, reflecting different relationships between those who delegate power, those who make decisions, and those who bear the consequences: control, oversight, review, and culture.

## 2.1. Control

Control denotes a hierarchical relationship within a bureaucracy or supervisory powers that may be exercised in a direct manner and on a daily basis. The former would include the senior management of an intelligence agency; the latter points to the political responsibility of the relevant secretary or minister, and ultimately the President or Prime Minister.

Administrative controls should ensure that the agency operates within the law and require sufficient information and offer adequate penalties to deter violations. This includes ensuring proportional use of any special powers that an agency might have: investigative techniques should be proportionate to the threat and weighed against the potential damage to civil liberties and democratic structures; where there is a choice, the least

[25] John Ferejohn, 'Accountability and Authority: Toward a Theory of Political Accountability', in Adam Przeworski, SC Stokes, and B Manin (eds), *Democracy, Accountability, and Representation* (Cambridge: Cambridge University Press, 1999), 131.

[26] See also Simon Chesterman, 'Globalization Rules: Accountability, Power, and the Prospects for Global Administrative Law', *Global Governance* 14 (2008) 39 at 44 and sources there cited.

intrusive alternative should be chosen. Such powers may also require variable authorization, with a higher level of approval required for more intrusive methods. Where such matters are too sensitive to regulate by law, clear internal procedures should be developed with additional oversight. There should be no incentive for staff to pursue less-regulated means, and protections should be offered to whistleblowers who bring possible wrongdoing to light. A code of conduct should ensure that staff are aware of relevant rules and procedures, while also addressing the ethical boundaries of their work.[27]

Political control should provide governance of an agency while protecting it from political abuse. To be effective, this requires the ability to direct the broad policy for an agency as well as to demand information; it does not mean direct managerial responsibility, which should vest with the head of the agency. How this line will be drawn will vary by country and by agency; its precise route is less important than its clarity and effectiveness in avoiding both 'off-the-book' actions by a rogue agency and abuse of 'plausible deniability' by a political principal. Such control should be non-delegable, but should also provide for a right of access from the agency head to the relevant secretary or minister.[28]

## 2.2. Oversight

Oversight also points to an ongoing relationship of accountability, but without the level of direction implied by 'control'. It is typically used to refer to the role of legislative bodies that receive regular briefings on intelligence activities, but may also include the 'police-patrol' responsibilities of inspectors general and commissioners tasked with examining and reporting on intelligence services or their functions on a regular basis.

The appropriateness of a role for the legislature is obvious, but it nonetheless presents operational and prudential difficulties. Operational concerns relate to the necessary secrecy of many activities; related prudential concerns are the possibility that national security questions may be

---

[27] See Hans Born and Ian Leigh, *Making Intelligence Accountable: Legal Standards and Best Practice for Oversight of Intelligence Agencies* (Oslo: Parliament of Norway, 2005), 29–51, 68–71.  [28] Ibid, 55–9.

politicized. For these reasons, many countries carry out this function through committees that meet, at least partly, in closed session. Their responsibilities may include scrutiny of the budget, in some cases linked to confirmation of the appointment of senior personnel and general approval of policies. In some cases, notably the United States, the relevant committees enjoy subpoena powers to compel testimony. Such committees may also be empowered to conduct investigations or audits of problematic programmes.[29]

Oversight may also be exercised by other bodies. In the United States, inspectors general exist within various departments and agencies and are tasked with preventing and detecting fraud and abuse, as well as promoting economy, efficiency, and effectiveness in the various programmes they oversee.[30] For the most part appointed by the President, the inspectors general file semi-annual reports to their respective congressional committees. They also conduct audits and process complaints, as well as carrying out investigations if requested by the head of the agency or Congress, or at their own initiative. Though they are under the general supervision of the agency head, they enjoy a dual and independent reporting relationship to Congress. The head of an agency has the power to stop an investigation or prevent its publication, but this must be reported to Congress with the reasons for the decision. The power appears to be rarely used.[31]

In Britain, the various intelligence agencies are overseen by commissioners. The Intelligence Services Commissioner, the Interception of Communications Commissioner, and the Chief Surveillance Commissioner issue annual reports to the Prime Minister that are later published, though these have tended to be formulaic recitations of the legal framework with a limited amount of statistical data on warrants issued and

---

[29] See generally Frank Smist, *Congress Oversees the United States Intelligence Community*, 2nd edn (Knoxville: University of Tennessee Press, 1994); Loch K Johnson, 'Congressional Supervision of America's Secret Agencies: The Experience and Legacy of the Church Committee', *Public Administration Review* 64 (2004) 3; Serge Grossman and Michael Simon, 'And Congress Shall Know the Truth: The Pressing Need for Restructuring Congressional Oversight of Intelligence', *Harvard Law & Policy Review* 2 (2008) 435.

[30] 5 App USC § 2.

[31] 5 App USC § 8ff; Born and Leigh, *Making Intelligence Accountable*, 110; Arar Commission Policy Review, 391.

complaints lodged. The Intelligence Services Commissioner's reports for 2007 and 2008 were nine and ten pages long respectively, with the first seven essentially identical.[32]

One advantage of the British system is the functional nature of their mandates. The Interception of Communications Commissioner, for example, exercises modest powers of review over hundreds of agencies authorized to intercept communications. Though this points to the troublingly wide range of actors enjoying such powers, there is some merit to having a centralized entity to oversee their use.[33] Nevertheless, with a staff consisting of one chief inspector and five inspectors, the capacity for meaningful oversight is limited. The annual reports helpfully provide a survey of breaches in interception protocols, though the vast majority are reported by agencies themselves, attributed to human or technical error, and said to have been without injury. The reports are generally enthusiastic about the benefits of interceptions in law enforcement and national security. Indeed, it is striking that the strongest policy argument proposed to date is an *expansion* of interception powers. Specifically, the Commissioner has repeatedly argued that the 'Wilson Doctrine'—a ban on tapping the telephones of British Members of Parliament named after the famously paranoid British Prime Minister who established it in 1966—be overturned. A recent report concluded with a telling observation: 'Why should Members of Parliament not be in the same position as everyone else?'[34]

## 2.3. Review

Review processes scrutinize activities as to their lawfulness or propriety, normally conducted by a separate entity at arm's length and after the fact. The paradigm of such a review process is a lawsuit that is commenced after alleged wrongdoing. To be sure, these categories are not exact: judges may also play a role in more of an oversight capacity when issuing warrants

---

[32] Report of the Intelligence Services Commissioner for 2007 (London: House of Commons, HC 948, 2008); Report of the Intelligence Services Commissioner for 2008 (London: House of Commons, HC 902, 2009).     [33] See also Chapter five, section 2.4.

[34] Report of the Interception of Communications Commissioner for 2008 (London: House of Commons, HC 901, 2009), para 7.3.

in advance of a wiretap, and legislative and other oversight bodies may conduct after the fact investigations. It is the institutional relationship that is of particular interest here, however.[35]

The advantages of review are that it is normally conducted by an independent body, can be tailored to respond to the needs of a victim of injustice, and typically results in a public finding. These are also the disadvantages. Independence can mean unfamiliarity with the agency being examined, leading to practical and political problems such as access to information or sensitivity to context. The responsive nature of review makes it necessarily ad hoc and thus inadequate to respond to systemic problems, though the demonstration effect of punishing bad behaviour may have a wider impact than resolving any given case. The extent to which the external review will lead to public disclosure may also impose limitations on the cases that can be brought and the dissemination of their resolution.

Specialized tribunals are therefore a common variation on judicial review, as seen in the US Foreign Intelligence Surveillance Court and Britain's Investigatory Powers Tribunal.[36] Such an arrangement allows the development of expertise in adjudicating intelligence matters and procedures for handling sensitive information. It may also allow for judges and lawyers to be vetted in order to have access to classified information, though this is of little assistance to a victim of misconduct unless his or her counsel is similarly privy to the information.

A mechanism used in many jurisdictions—though not in the US or British intelligence services—is an ombudsperson, an individual appointed to receive and investigate complaints against one or more agencies. The powers of such individuals are often limited, and the primary output is a report and recommendations. Ombudspersons may therefore seem inferior to a judicial process, but the relative informality may facilitate the resolution of individual grievances, and the reporting process may be more amenable to addressing problems of policy than a judicial determination.[37]

---

[35] See also Frederic F Manget, 'Another System of Oversight: Intelligence and the Rise of Judicial Intervention', *Studies in Intelligence* 39(5) (1996) 43.

[36] See section 1.3 in this Chapter.

[37] The CIA does have internal ombudsperson institutions that have been cited in unclassified documents. An Ombudsman for Politicization was created in 1992 to serve as an

## 2.4. Culture

Though control, oversight, and review are important means of encouraging good behaviour and discouraging bad, a final influence shaping the behaviour of an intelligence agency is the culture within which it operates. This is particularly true of potentially abusive behaviour, where the first and most important check is self-restraint.

Culture operates at the level of the agency and the society it exists to serve. Within an agency, culture reflects the values and customs that it develops over time. This can and should be codified through codes of practice with clear guidelines on both the purpose the agency serves and the limits on its powers: the ends and the means. Such codes should be enforced, but even without enforcement the presence of clear guidelines can encourage the peer accountability that shapes individual behaviour in any organization. Intelligence officials are bureaucrats, but they are also people, aspiring to maintain credibility and influence among their colleagues. This will be further shaped by the extent to which an agency internalizes broader political values such as democracy and the rule of law—manifesting in a respect for dissenting ideas and acceptance of the agency's accountability to the public that it serves.[38]

At a wider level, the expectations of society—often mediated through the political process or the media—will also play a role in determining the possibility of holding intelligence services to account. After examining the British system of oversight, for example, Ian Leigh concludes that on paper the British scheme appears to be weak, due to the influence of the executive over all aspects of oversight. One would hardly recommend these arrangements as a model to other countries, yet in a stable democratic

independent, informal, and confidential counsellor for analysts concerned about politicization. Silberman–Robb Commission Report, 188. A second ombudsman appears to have been created in 2008 to receive complaints from employees about the work of the CIA Inspector General. Joby Warrick, 'CIA Sets Changes To IG's Oversight, Adds Ombudsman', *Washington Post*, 2 February 2008. The latter appeared intended to reduce the authority and significance of the Inspector General. Neither is included in the government's Coalition of Federal Ombudsmen.

[38] See Ruth W Grant and Robert O Keohane, 'Accountability and Abuses of Power in World Politics', *American Political Science Review* 99(1) (2005) 1; Marina Caparini, 'Controlling and Overseeing Intelligence Services in Democratic States', in Hans Born and Marina Caparini (eds), *Democratic Control of Intelligence Services: Containing Rogue Elephants* (Aldershot: Ashgate, 2007), 3 at 17.

system they work 'tolerably well'.[39] A key determinant will be the trust of the public in the institutions of the state, though this is in turn shaped by the larger political environment. The United States before Vietnam and Watergate reflected a high level of trust in government institutions; the erosion of that trust saw greatly increased scrutiny of intelligence services prior to September 11.[40] After the attacks on New York and Washington, DC, faith in the agencies and support for President Bush increased dramatically, eroding only gradually as abuses of power came to light.[41] In Britain, by contrast, tolerance for the government's surveillance powers appears to remain relatively high, with resistance to specific measures, such as the national identity card, based more on concerns about cost and the government's competence than on abuse.[42]

## 3. INSTITUTIONAL POSSIBILITIES

These questions are rarely considered in the abstract. Major transformations tend to happen in response to scandal, most prominently the excesses revealed in the Watergate saga in the United States, but also the failure to prevent the September 11 attacks. Britain is an unusual case of a country that went through significant change due to legal challenges and the threat of further suits. A third driver of change is constitutional upheaval such as the transition from military to civilian rule, seen in Eastern Europe after the end of the Cold War, or South Africa's transition after apartheid.[43]

Reforms will generally be responsive to the pressures that justify them— leading in different directions, for example, if the scandal is abuse of powers or failure to prevent an attack. If the motivating factor is the perceived weakness of intelligence, or of an increase in the threats requiring greater surveillance powers or coordination of agencies, changes to the legal framework—particularly if being made in haste after some kind of attack— should normally be of limited duration, enabling a more sober reflection

---

[39] Ian Leigh, 'Accountability of Security and Intelligence in the United Kingdom', in Born, Johnson, and Leigh (eds), *Who's Watching the Spies*, 79 at 95.

[40] See Chapter one, section 1.　　[41] See Chapter four, section 4.

[42] See Chapter five, section 3.

[43] See generally Born and Caparini (eds), *Democratic Control of Intelligence Services*.

on the balancing of security and liberty at a later date.[44] In the same vein, scandal in the form of abuse of powers might lead to an overreaction, making the legitimate work of intelligence services unnecessarily difficult.

It is possible, however, to distil some general principles concerning accountability. First, all four structures of accountability discussed in the previous section—control, oversight, review, culture—are important. The precise arrangements may vary significantly, but some aspect of each is a necessary component if accountability is to be effective. There must be some scope for wide-ranging examination of intelligence activities as well as responding to specific complaints of wrongdoing. Whatever structures are established must be able to deal with the increasing integration of intelligence, either through a body with jurisdiction over multiple agencies, or establishing ways of ensuring information exchange and cooperation between different accountability bodies.

Secondly, although it is true that the most important check on abuse is self-restraint, an agency cannot be given the lead role in policing itself. Access to information relevant to accountability must be available to external bodies, whether an ombudsperson reporting to the executive, a legislative committee with oversight responsibility, periodic judicial investigations, and so on. An agency should not be put in the position of determining what information is and is not relevant to those who are scrutinizing its activities.

Thirdly, people matter. Individuals put in the most prominent positions for ensuring accountability must be credible and well-resourced. They should be knowledgeable about the craft of intelligence without being beholden to it; they should have access to political principals without themselves being driven by political fortune.[45]

These principles—that accountability must be multifaceted, independent, and credible—are necessarily general. Nevertheless, their importance is easily illustrated drawing on examples from Part II. In the United States, reliance on narrow constraints on executive power enabled their circumvention prior to Watergate and after September 11. The use of contractors in particular was seen as a means of avoiding scrutiny of questionable conduct, pointing to gaps in the accountability mechanisms

---

[44] See Chapter two, section 1.2.2.
[45] Cf Born and Leigh, *Making Intelligence Accountable*; Arar Commission Policy Review, 316.

available.[46] Britain's faith in the integrity of its intelligence services was long premised on a larger trust in government. Yet this arrangement was also consistent with the desire of politicians to maintain a level of deniability as to the actions taken in their name. Such accountability mechanisms as exist today continue to rely too heavily on information provided by agencies themselves.[47] As for the United Nations, the absence of any credible capacity to evaluate intelligence renders the organization entirely dependent on the states that supply it. That reliance poses obvious political problems, but also jeopardizes the legitimate exercise of powers to maintain international peace and security, most obviously the use of targeted financial sanctions and international criminal prosecution.[48]

## 4. AUXILIARY PRECAUTIONS

Ambrose Bierce, in his *Devil's Dictionary* first published a century ago, defined accountability as 'the mother of caution'.[49] Structures of accountability should certainly inspire hesitation when an intelligence official contemplates wrongdoing, but they should also serve to legitimize the special powers enjoyed by such actors even when operating within their mandate. In addition, they may help to ensure that such actors carry out their functions effectively, as well as legitimately.

The necessary secrecy involved reduces the value of traditional structures such as political accountability through democratic institutions and legal accountability through the courts. Yet there are many more ways in which accountability can be sought. As James Madison noted, these questions were not new even in the late eighteenth century.[50] In the early twenty-first century, the case of Khaled el-Masri suggests the ongoing deficiencies when a court observes apparent—and widely reported—wrongdoing, but is constrained from offering a remedy. The subsequent repudiation of abusive interrogation practices points to the ability of the government to 'control itself', even as it shows the ongoing need for 'auxiliary precautions' against those who would protect us from harm.

---

[46] See Chapter four.    [47] See Chapter five.    [48] See Chapter six.
[49] Ambrose Bierce, *The Devil's Dictionary* (New York: Neale, 1911).
[50] Madison, Federalist, No 51.

# 8

## The Transparent Community

Interested policy-makers quickly learn that intelligence can be used the way a drunk uses a lamp post—for support rather than illumination.

Thomas Hughes, *The Fate of Facts in a World of Men*[1]

You have zero privacy. Get over it.

Scott McNealy, CEO of Sun Microsystems[2]

In September 2002, a Canadian citizen named Maher Arar was detained by US officials while transiting through New York's John F Kennedy International Airport. He was held for 12 days before being flown to Jordan and then Syria, the country of his birth, where he was interrogated and tortured. After being imprisoned for nearly a year in a grave-sized underground cell, he was released and returned to Canada. Arar was never charged with an offence in any of these countries. Although Canadian officials had wanted to interview him as part of a terrorism-related investigation, they did not consider him a suspect or target of that investigation. A public inquiry cleared him of any suspicion, sharply criticized the actions of the Royal Canadian Mounted Police (RCMP) and other Canadian government departments, and led to a formal protest to the United States over his treatment. The Canadian Prime Minister gave Arar an apology and ten million dollars in an out-of-court settlement for the ordeal. A lawsuit against various senior officials in the Bush administration was dismissed at first instance and on appeal. A further appeal was dismissed without comment by the US Supreme

---

[1] Thomas L Hughes, *The Fate of Facts in a World of Men: Foreign Policy and Intelligence-Making* (New York: Foreign Policy Association, 1976), 24.

[2] Deborah Radcliff, 'A Cry for Privacy', *Computer World*, 17 May 1999.

Court in June 2010. Arar remains on a terrorist watch-list used by US authorities.[3]

The reasons for Arar's detention by US authorities can be traced to the mishandling of intelligence by Canadian officials. In the wake of the September 11 attacks, the Canadian Security Intelligence Service (CSIS) transferred responsibility for certain investigations of alleged terrorists to the RCMP, Canada's national police force. One consequence of this blurring of the line between policing and intelligence was that individuals with limited national security experience were put in charge of highly sensitive matters in a tense atmosphere with little guidance. Arar became a person of interest because he met with one of the targets of an investigation and listed that person as the emergency contact on a rental agreement. On the basis of this fairly thin evidence, border lookouts were placed on him and his wife, designating them 'terrorism' suspects. The lookout requests were shared with the United States, in a manner that suggested that Arar and his wife were part of a 'group of Islamic Extremist individuals suspected of being linked to the al Qaeda terrorist movement'— baseless and potentially inflammatory language to use in the United States in the fall of 2001.[4]

Canadian privacy protections exceed those in either the United States or Britain; the powers given to its relatively small intelligence services are more limited than their Anglo-American counterparts. Yet the Arar case demonstrates a problem that is certain to grow in coming years: though no serious challenge has been made against the collection activities of the Canadian agencies, their *use* of intelligence had devastating effects for Arar and his family. This Chapter considers the rise of collection activities that, as a legal or practical matter, are unlikely to be restrained by the type of accountability mechanisms discussed in Chapter seven. It then examines the most important effort to check the use of intelligence information in the late twentieth century—by constructing a 'wall' between intelligence and law enforcement—and why it failed. The last two sections then outline the contours of a more promising

---

[3] Commission of Inquiry into the Actions of Canadian Officials in Relation to Maher Arar, Report of the Events Relating to Maher Arar: Analysis and Recommendations (Arar Commission Factual Inquiry) (Ottawa: Government of Canada, 2006); *Arar v Ashcroft*, 532 F.3d 157 (2nd Cir, 2008); *Arar v Ashcroft*, 585 F.3d 559 (2nd Cir (en banc), 2009).

[4] Arar Commission Factual Inquiry, 16–30.

approach to regulating the use of intelligence and what this means for our understanding of privacy.

## 1. FROM COLLECTION TO USE

The literature on intelligence and privacy tends to approach the expansion of collection activities in one of two ways. Privacy advocates urge restraint, suggesting absolute limits on the powers available to government and tight regulation of those powers that are granted, such as through a system of warrants where cause must precede surveillance.[5] These battles will continue and may slow the expansion of surveillance powers. But they will not stop it. The combination of threats, technology, and culture has ensured the inexorable expansion of government surveillance powers.

In response, some have argued for *greater* surveillance—in particular, greater transparency of the agencies themselves so that government and the public can scrutinize the scrutinizers. The notion that greater exposure can itself serve as a form of accountability is not new. Louis Brandeis famously extolled the virtues of sunlight as a disinfectant, seeing it as a useful remedy for social as well as industrial diseases.[6] Edward Shils argued that liberal democracy required defending the privacy of individuals and denying it to the government.[7] David Brin applied such insights to the Internet age, embracing the idea of a 'transparent society' in which neither government nor citizens enjoy much privacy.[8]

These are useful thought experiments. Such debates are marginal to the larger discourse of national security, however. This is partly because of the

---

[5] See, eg, A Michael Froomkin, 'The Death of Privacy?', *Stanford Law Review* 52 (2000) 1461; Christopher Slobogin, *Privacy at Risk: The New Government Surveillance and the Fourth Amendment* (Chicago: University of Chicago Press, 2007); Jon L Mills, *Privacy: The Lost Right* (Oxford: Oxford University Press, 2008).

[6] Louis D Brandeis, *Other People's Money and How the Bankers Use It* (New York: Stokes, 1914), 92.

[7] Edward A Shils, *The Torment of Secrecy: The Background and Consequences of American Security Policies* (London: Heinemann, 1956), 21–5.

[8] David Brin, *The Transparent Society: Will Technology Force Us to Choose Between Privacy and Freedom?* (Reading, MA: Addison-Wesley, 1998).

transformed threat environment, with the traditional division between domestic and foreign threats being eroded by the possibility of mass-casualty terrorist attacks. The discourse is also shaped by the greater technical capacities of governments today, as well as the apparent toleration of surveillance by a culture that implicitly trades privacy for the conveniences of modern life and protection from modern threats. The debates are also marginal because traditional collection activities that raise privacy concerns constitute a diminishing proportion of 'intelligence'. Returning to a distinction highlighted earlier, intelligence in the sense of acquiring secrets is becoming less important than piecing together information to solve mysteries.[9]

Much information that one might consider private—aspects of one's family life, finances, medical records, for example—was traditionally protected through the 'practical obscurity' of paper records.[10] Court proceedings, for example, might technically be public documents, but if stored in a single hard copy in a government office they were unlikely to be accessed by social and professional acquaintances. When the same records are computerized and stored in a form accessible through the Internet, this practical obscurity disappears.

## 1.1. Connecting the Dots

The importance of computerization was recognized as early as the 1960s, with prescient warnings that the retrieval of 'documentary fingerprints and footprints' would give governments power that could not be achieved with armies of investigators.[11] For the most part, however, government was slow to move on these possibilities even when motivated to do so. During the mole-hunt that revealed CIA spy Aldrich Ames in 1994, for example, a

---

[9] See the Introduction to this volume, section 1. Cf Philip HJ Davies, 'Ideas of Intelligence: Divergent National Concepts and Institutions', *Harvard International Review* 24(3) (2002) 62 at 64.

[10] *United States Department of Justice v Reporters Committee for Freedom of the Press*, 489 US 749, 762 (1989). Specific types of information have also received protection through legislation. See Chapter four, section 1. See generally Arminda Bradford Bepko, 'Public Availability or Practical Obscurity: The Debate over Public Access to Court Records on the Internet', *New York Law School Law Review* 49 (2005) 968.

[11] Alan F Westin, *Privacy and Freedom* (New York: Atheneum, 1967), 158.

senior official has noted how striking it was that his creditors knew much more about his finances than the CIA did.[12]

In the aftermath of the September 11 attacks, it became clear that the US government had been in possession of much information that might have linked those responsible and, perhaps, warned of their intentions. What was required was not greater collection, but more creativity in piecing together the information already available. Two men, Nawaf al-Hazmi and Khalid al-Midhar, were on lists of suspected terrorists and purchased tickets using their real names, addresses, telephone numbers, and frequent flyer cards. Publicly available address information would have revealed that Salem al-Hazmi and Mohamed Atta shared the same address as al-Hazmi; Marwan al-Shehhi had the same address as al-Midhar. Five other men, Fayez Ahmed, Mohand al-Shehri, Wail al-Shehri, Waleed al-Shehri, and Abdulaziz al-Omari used the same Florida phone number as Atta; all were booked on flights on September 11. Public records show that Satam al-Suqami shared a post office box with al-Shehri; Hani Hanjour was a former roommate of the first two men, al-Hazmi and al-Midhar. The INS watch-list for expired visas had flagged Ahmed al-Ghamdi, who was booked together with al-Shehhi, Ahmed, and al-Shehri. And so on.[13]

Such accounts must, of course, be treated cautiously. Quite apart from the danger of hindsight bias—with the benefit of which all these connections now seem obvious—it is far from clear how the information could have been used prior to the attacks. Nevertheless, the larger lesson that intelligence services have taken from this is that a key priority is more effective aggregation and analysis of the data that are available to them.[14]

Problems remain. In August 2009, the National Security Agency (NSA) intercepted communications in Yemen concerning a planned attack by a Nigerian citizen. Three months later, a former Nigerian government official and prominent banker expressed alarm at his son's turn to radical Islam and asked Nigerian and US authorities to intervene before his son did harm. CIA officials began compiling biographical information on

[12] Gregory F Treverton, 'President Obscured the Case for Spying', *San Francisco Chronicle*, 5 February 2006 (Treverton was Vice Chair of the National Intelligence Council from 1993–95).

[13] See, eg, Newton N Minow, 'Seven Clicks Away', *Wall Street Journal*, 3 June 2004.

[14] See, eg, 9/11 Commission Report: Final Report of the National Commission on Terrorist Attacks upon the United States (Washington, DC: US Government Printing Office, 2004), 269–72, 423–8.

Umar Farouk Abdulmutallab, but did not share it with any other agencies. The US embassy sent a 'visas viper'—jargon for a terrorist warning—but he was merely added to the largest of four government intelligence databases, a list of more than half a million names of possible terrorist suspects. Though Abdulmutallab purchased his ticket with cash and checked no luggage, he was not prevented from boarding a flight from Amsterdam to Detroit on Christmas Day 2009, in the course of which he attempted to detonate an explosive device before being subdued by passengers and flight attendants.[15]

One aspect of the trend towards closer examination of available data has been the move to embrace anthropological models in intelligence assessments. The aim is to develop a 'thick description' of an environment, based explicitly on the work of anthropologists such as Clifford Geertz.[16] The intelligence to be gained might include an understanding, for example, of the make-up and dynamics of a given community with a view to identifying individuals of influence and the potential for radicalization. In Britain this approach came to be known as 'Rich Picture', referring to an MI5 project of the same name. The FBI's comparable initiative was called 'Domain Management', intended to mark a move away from case-based investigations to a more forward-looking approach to the threat posed by terrorism. Both efforts led to concerns about the civil liberties implications of profiling—selecting individuals for additional scrutiny based on ethnicity or religion—though such concerns do not appear to have significantly impeded the programmes.[17] The most extensive application of anthropological models in intelligence has been focused not on communities in Britain or the United States, but on insurgent groups in Iraq and Afghanistan. From 2007, the US military's 'Human Terrain System' embedded anthropologists and social scientists in military units with a view to providing 'socio-cultural knowledge' in support

---

[15] Mark Mazzetti and Eric Lipton, 'Spy Agencies Failed to Collate Clues on Terror', *New York Times*, 30 December 2009.

[16] See, eg, Clifford Geertz, *The Interpretation of Cultures* (New York: Basic Books, 1973), 3–30.

[17] Jason Bennetto, 'MI5 Conducts Secret Inquiry into 8,000 al-Qa'eda "Sympathisers"', *Independent*, 3 July 2006; Scott Shane and Lowell Bergman, 'FBI Struggling to Reinvent Itself to Fight Terror', *New York Times*, 10 October 2006; Samuel Rascoff, 'Domesticating Intelligence', *Southern California Law Review* 83 (2010) 575. See Chapter nine, section 2.

of the commander's objectives. Though credited with some successes in the US counterinsurgency campaign in Iraq in particular, the American Anthropological Association criticized the enterprise as dangerous, unethical, and unscholarly.[18]

## 1.2. Aggregating the Dots

In addition to these more fine-grained analyses, the most important transformation has been the routine aggregation of vastly more data using telecommunication, financial, and other records. In 2006, for example, it was revealed that the NSA had obtained extensive telephone records from major US phone companies, described in some reports as the 'largest database ever assembled in the world'.[19] A month later the *New York Times* reported that the US government had accessed bank records from the Society for Worldwide Interbank Financial Transactions (SWIFT), the organization that manages global financial transactions for thousands of banks.[20]

Privacy theorists have struggled to respond to the shift from protection of sensitive personal information to the consequences of aggregation of data about an individual.[21] The difficulties can be illustrated in a 1989 US Supreme Court case concerning publication of an FBI 'rap sheet', which compiles basic descriptive information as well as a history of arrests, indictments, convictions, and sentences. A Freedom of Information Act request for a rap sheet had initially been rejected due to privacy concerns, but was then modified to limit the request to matters of public record. The Court accepted that the information on the sheet had already been disclosed to the

---

[18] AAA Commission on the Engagement of Anthropology with the US Security and Intelligence Communities (CEAUSSIC), Final Report on the Army's Human Terrain System Proof of Concept Program (Arlington, VA: American Anthropological Association, 14 October 2009).

[19] Leslie Cauley, 'NSA Has Massive Database of Americans' Phone Calls', *USA Today*, 11 May 2006.

[20] Eric Lichtblau and James Risen, 'Bank Data Sifted in Secret by US to Block Terror', *New York Times*, 23 June 2006.

[21] See, eg, Helen Nissenbaum, 'Protecting Privacy in an Information Age: The Problem of Privacy in Public', *Law and Philosophy* 17 (1998) 559; Lisa M Austin, 'Privacy and the Question of Technology', *Law and Philosophy* 22 (2003) 119; Daniel J Solove, *Understanding Privacy* (Cambridge, MA: Harvard University Press, 2008), 70.

public, but still held that the rap sheet attracted a privacy interest sufficient to prevent disclosure: 'Plainly there is a vast difference between the public records that might be found after a diligent search of courthouse files, county archives, and local police stations throughout the country and a computerized summary located in a single clearinghouse of information.'[22]

How that difference is conceived is the central problem. Many of the publicly articulated concerns about data mining tend to focus either on misrepresentation in the collection of data, such as 'warranty cards' that are in fact used to gather information for targeted advertising, or on incompetence in the handling of records, which might lead to unauthorized release of data or the facilitation of identity theft.[23] These are legitimate concerns, but do not address the larger problem of whether there is a meaningful privacy interest in the mere aggregation of data.

The better view of the privacy concern would seem to be that it relates to the changed context, where information collected for one purpose may assume a larger significance when combined with other data. Much as the mosaic theory has been used by governments to resist the release of apparently innocuous data, the compilation of diverse data points from an individual's life might reveal information they would be unwilling to share with others.[24] Richard Posner, who adopts a notoriously narrow conception of privacy as being an individual's right 'to conceal discreditable facts about himself',[25] has argued that the automated collection and analysis of vast amounts of data cannot as such invade privacy as a 'computer is not a sentient being'.[26] This slightly miscasts the privacy question—individual officials do set the parameters for the analysis and examine the results—but rightly points to the need to balance possible privacy implications against the potential national security gains.[27]

[22] *Reporters*, 489 US 749, 764 (1989).

[23] Daniel J Solove, *The Digital Person: Privacy and Technology in the Information Age* (New York: New York University Press, 2004), 53–5.

[24] See, eg, Alessandro Acquisti and Ralph Gross, 'Predicting Social Security Numbers from Public Data', *Proceedings of the National Academy of Sciences* 106(27) (2009) 10975. On the mosaic theory, see Chapter three, section 1.1.

[25] Richard A Posner, *The Economic Analysis of the Law*, 5th edn (New York: Aspen, 1998), 46.

[26] Richard A Posner, 'Our Domestic Intelligence Crisis', *Washington Post*, 21 December 2005.

[27] Daniel J Solove, '"I've Got Nothing to Hide" and Other Misunderstandings of Privacy', *San Diego Law Review* 44 (2007) 745 at 753.

The definitional question of privacy will be revisited below, but for present purposes it is sufficient to note that the various concerns raised have been unsuccessful in stemming the expansion of data mining. Although attempts to establish massive new capacities have provoked public outrage and government retreat, the trend towards greater and more effective use of data mining has continued unabated. In the United States, for example, attempts by the Johnson and Ford administrations in the 1960s and 1970s to consolidate or link government databases were abandoned after public protests.[28] The Total Information Awareness project proposed after September 11 would have brought together data concerning finance, education, health, travel, and other matters with a view to identifying potential terrorists. In response to the public outcry, it was renamed 'Terrorist Information Awareness' and privacy protections were introduced, but it was eventually abandoned as a policy.[29] Despite such symbolic victories, however, government capacity to aggregate and analyse data has continued to increase—in each case soon exceeding the capacities proposed in the various cancelled programmes.[30]

## 2. INTELLIGENCE VERSUS LAW ENFORCEMENT

The most sustained effort to draw a line as to the manner in which intelligence may be used has been at the door of the courtroom. The distinctions between intelligence and law enforcement are, on their face, obvious. Intelligence is intended to aid policy; it is generally forward-looking and based on an assessment of available data. Law enforcement upholds the criminal law, tends to be backward-looking, and is held to the courtroom standards of beyond reasonable doubt. Because of their different functions and powers, a conscious effort has been made in some jurisdictions to separate intelligence from law enforcement agencies completely. Britain's

---

[28] Charles J Sykes, *The End of Privacy: Personal Rights in the Surveillance Society* (New York: St Martin's Griffin, 1999), 44.    [29] See the Introduction to this volume.

[30] Solove, *Digital Person*, 169–75. See also Technology and Privacy Advisory Committee, Safeguarding Privacy in the Fight Against Terrorism (Washington, DC: Department of Defense, March 2004).

MI5 and MI6, for example, have no executive policing powers. In the United States, the National Security Act that established the CIA prohibited it having domestic law enforcement powers.

The FBI, by contrast, has long occupied a more conflicted position, serving as both a federal criminal investigative body and a domestic intelligence agency. This has led to periodic shifts in its self-understanding. In 1924, following alleged abuses during the 'Red Scare', Attorney General Harlan Fiske Stone ordered that what was then the Bureau of Investigations should not concern itself with the opinions of individuals but 'only with their conduct and then only with such conduct as is forbidden by the laws of the United States.'[31] The idea that the FBI should not gather intelligence without an allegation of criminal activity did not last long. J Edgar Hoover quickly pushed back against these limits, later supported by President Franklin Delano Roosevelt's desire to understand the threat posed by communists and fascists.

Hoover notoriously expanded the powers of the FBI, harassing civil rights activists, compiling vast files on politicians, and engaging in patently illegal activities. By the late 1960s, however, the FBI began reining in its activities, among other things requiring that wiretap requests from other agencies such as the CIA and NSA (previously issued routinely and in secret) be referred to the Attorney General for approval. The change had less to do with legal scruples than with political prudence, as the altered political climate heralded more aggressive efforts to contain the intelligence services—something seen by Hoover before most.[32] A decade later, in the wake of the Church and Pike hearings, new guidelines were announced by Attorney General Edward Levi concerning the FBI's domestic intelligence activities that shifted its activities away from strategic intelligence and towards case-specific investigations.[33] The 9/11 Commission memorably described this in basketball terms as the difference between the FBI's 'man-to-man' approach and the CIA's 'zone defence'.[34]

---

[31] Regin Schmidt, *Red Scare: FBI and the Origins of Anticommunism in the United States, 1919–1943* (Copenhagen: Museum Tusculanum Press, 2000), 325.

[32] Athan Theoharis, *The Quest for Absolute Security: The Failed Relations Among US Intelligence Agencies* (Chicago: Ivan R Dee, 2007), 170–208.

[33] John T Elliff, 'The Attorney General's Guidelines for FBI Investigations', *Cornell Law Review* 69 (1984) 785. See Chapter one, section 1.     [34] 9/11 Commission Report, 268.

The law enforcement culture of the 'Feds' became well entrenched, shaping careers and policy, but arguably failing to prepare the Bureau to address the threats posed by terrorism.[35] After the September 11 attacks, various attempts to reorganize the FBI's intelligence capacities were undertaken, with a Directorate of Intelligence being added in 2004, incorporated the following year within a larger National Security Branch. The law enforcement culture remains, however. In many respects this is appropriate and even admirable, as seen in the rift between the FBI and the CIA over interrogation practices: FBI officials objected to methods such as waterboarding and were supported by their superiors who made it clear that 'we don't do that'. The current challenge for the FBI is to balance these positive aspects of its concern for rule of law in its policing capacity with the need to function as a proactive intelligence service in addressing the very real threat of terrorism.[36]

## 2.2. The Rise and Fall of the 'Wall'

The other major change that followed the Church and Pike hearings was a warrant-based system to authorize wiretaps. The Foreign Intelligence Surveillance Act (FISA) sought to regularize electronic surveillance for foreign intelligence purposes. Whereas the standard for placing a wiretap in a criminal context requires a judge to find probable cause that an individual is committing, has committed, or is about to commit a particular offence,[37] FISA allows a warrant to be issued if there is probable cause to believe that the target is a foreign power or an agent of a foreign power.[38] Put simply, the criminal law required evidence as to a person's *behaviour*, while FISA allowed a wiretap based on a person's *status*. The latter is clearly a lower threshold and from the outset there were concerns that FISA would be used as a simpler way of obtaining wiretaps that might not pass muster in a normal court of law.

---

[35] See Chapter four, section 2.2.

[36] Ali Soufan, 'My Tortured Decision', *New York Times*, 22 April 2009; A Review of the FBI's Involvement in and Observations of Detainee Interrogations in Guantanamo Bay, Afghanistan, and Iraq (Washington, DC: US Department of Justice, Office of the Inspector General, October 2009). See generally Amy B Zegart, *Spying Blind: The CIA, the FBI, and the Origins of 9/11* (Princeton: Princeton University Press, 2007); Rascoff, 'Domesticating Intelligence'.

[37] 18 USC § 2518(3).     [38] 50 USC § 1805(a)(3). See also Chapter three.

The manner in which FISA came to be interpreted demonstrates the complexity of distinguishing intelligence from law enforcement, as well as confusion about how the law should be applied. From the early 1980s, based on a case concerning surveillance before FISA was enacted, courts interpreted FISA as requiring that the 'primary purpose' of surveillance be the collection of foreign intelligence information and not law enforcement.[39] Though there was some support for this interpretation in the history of FISA, such as a House of Representatives report stating that FISA surveillance should not be 'primarily for the purpose of gathering evidence of a crime', the requirement was not based on explicit language in the statute.[40] The law did require that a FISA request certify that 'the purpose' of surveillance was obtaining foreign intelligence information, but that was defined in the statute as including evidence of crimes such as espionage, sabotage, and terrorism.[41] Nonetheless, the view that intelligence had to be separated from law enforcement completely came to be reinforced in bureaucracy and policy. The division was known as the 'wall' between those elements within the Department of Justice, leading in some cases to parallel investigations by discrete squads of FBI agents who were prevented from consulting freely with one another.[42]

The 'wall' later came to be blamed as one of the barriers to the United States being able to fight terrorism effectively. The 9/11 Commission Report cited examples of FBI agents being hampered in their investigations, including an extraordinary scene in which one of the investigators from the October 2000 terrorist attack on the *USS Cole* was told to destroy his copy of information concerning efforts to locate one of the men ultimately responsible for the September 11 attacks. The agent, who was designated 'criminal' for internal FBI purposes—as opposed to intelligence— angrily fired off an e-mail less than two weeks before the hijackings:

Whatever has happened to this—someday someone will die—and wall or not—the public will not understand why we were not more effective and throwing

---

[39]  *United States v Truong Dinh Hung*, 629 F.2d 908 (4th Cir, 1980).

[40]  House of Representatives Report on Foreign Intelligence Surveillance Act of 1978 (Washington, DC: Permanent Select Committee on Intelligence, Report 95–1283, 8 June 1978), 36.          [41]  50 USC §§ 1801(e), 1804(a)(7)(B).

[42]  David S Kris, 'The Rise and Fall of the FISA Wall', *Stanford Law & Policy Review* 17 (2006) 487 at 488.

every resource we had at certain 'problems'. Let's hope the National Security Law Unit will stand behind their decisions then, especially since the biggest threat to us now, [Osama bin Laden], is getting the most 'protection'.[43]

Following the attacks, two moves were made to try to reduce the constraints imposed by the wall. First, the Patriot Act replaced the requirement that 'the purpose' of surveillance be foreign intelligence with a requirement that it be 'a significant purpose'.[44] The clear intention was to increase coordination between intelligence and law enforcement officials. Secondly, the Attorney General issued new intelligence-sharing procedures that would have largely removed prior barriers to how the FBI could direct surveillance and use the information thus acquired.

The matter came before the Foreign Intelligence Surveillance Court, the body established to consider FISA warrants, which issued its first ever published opinion. The Court essentially defended the wall, holding in particular that law enforcement officials were still prohibited from directing or controlling the use of FISA procedures.[45] The Department of Justice appealed to the Foreign Intelligence Surveillance Court of Review, the first time that body had ever convened to hear a case. The Court of Review examined the history of FISA and concluded that the law had been misinterpreted almost from its enactment. Since the definition of foreign intelligence included evidence of crimes, the judges found it 'quite puzzling' that FISA had come to be seen as unable to assist in the prosecution of, for example, foreign intelligence crimes.[46]

The 'wall', therefore, never existed. In an unusual twist, however, the Court of Review concluded that in trying to dismantle the wall, the Patriot Act had actually given it a legal foundation. Legislation that had been intended to enhance the government's authority under FISA had in fact *reduced* it. Where FISA under this new interpretation could originally have been used exclusively to prosecute a person for international terrorism prior to the Patriot Act, the amended law required that the government have a measurable foreign intelligence purpose other than prosecution. This would be satisfied, the Court of Review concluded, provided that the

[43] 9/11 Commission Report, 271.      [44] Patriot Act 2001 (US) § 218.
[45] *In re All Matters Submitted to the Foreign Intelligence Surveillance Court*, 218 F Supp 2d 611, 625 (FISC, 2002).      [46] *In re Sealed Case*, 310 F.3d 717, 723 (FISA Ct Rev, 2002).

government entertains a 'realistic option' of dealing with the person other than through criminal prosecution.[47] That would be true of virtually any case. The consequences, therefore, were negligible.

## 2.2. Spies Versus Cops

As with Britain's move to put its intelligence services on a legislative footing, this short history of FISA is interesting as an example of the need for careful drafting of the mandate and powers of intelligence services.[48] It is also a useful illustration of the difficulties of drafting and implementing a clear division between intelligence and law enforcement.

There are various arguments in favour of maintaining a division, beginning with the view that the Court of Review was simply wrong in its interpretation of the law. The judges expressed puzzlement that other courts had assumed that the government might seek foreign intelligence information 'for its own sake—to expand its pool of knowledge—because there is no discussion of how the government would use that information outside criminal prosecution.'[49] This is an exceptionally narrow understanding of intelligence, however: intelligence is often used precisely to inform government policy more generally. The fact that prosecution of a foreign intelligence crime might be a *consequence* of surveillance does not mean that a distinction cannot be made between the purposes of gathering information and prosecuting crimes.[50]

On the broader policy question, the history of FISA also suggests the potential for abuse if the line is not drawn carefully. This was evident in the decision of the Foreign Intelligence Surveillance Court. Unlike the Court of Review, the judges on this court deal with FISA requests on a regular basis and they appear to have been frustrated at the 'alarming number of incidences' when information sharing guidelines had been violated; in one case this reached the point that an FBI agent had been banned from requesting further FISA warrants.[51] The potential for abuse is clear in individual cases where it may be easier to get a FISA warrant based on a person's status rather than their behaviour, but a larger concern

---

[47] Ibid, 735.    [48] See Chapter five, section 2.4.    [49] *In re Sealed Case*, 727.
[50] *In re All Matters Submitted to the FISC*, 625.    [51] Ibid, 620–1.

is the use of FISA for sweeping surveys of groups based, for example, on their attendance at a certain religious institution.[52]

Another reason to be wary of blurring the line between intelligence and law enforcement is the impact it may have on prosecutions. Much as international criminal investigators confronted problems when they switched from investigations to indictments, information gathered through surveillance might be inadmissible in court due to rules of evidence or out of concerns that sources and methods might be revealed.[53] Together with the case-based approach typical of the FBI criminal division, this was one of the factors that strengthened the wall as agents had a clear incentive to proceed on the assumption that every piece of information they gathered would ultimately have to be produced in court.[54] The risks are far from theoretical: when the Bush administration belatedly attempted to prosecute detainees held in Guantánamo Bay under the criminal law it was necessary to establish 'clean teams' isolated from interrogations that had used methods unlikely to be acceptable to US courts.[55] (It appears that Khalid Sheikh Mohammed, who had been water-boarded 183 times, was later enticed to provide comparable information with Starbucks coffee.[56])

Yet in practice, a clear distinction between intelligence and law enforcement will be difficult to maintain. Though governments remain conflicted as to the appropriate manner of dealing with alleged terrorists, the imperative to detect and prevent terrorism will lead to ever greater cooperation between different parts of government, including the sharing of information. Some optimistic accounts suggest that this could actually be good for civil liberties. David Kris, later appointed head of the US Department of Justice's National Security Division, has argued that lawyers will now play an increased role in intelligence investigations. Maintaining the wall, he intimated, might have discouraged the government from using civilian courts in favour of 'alternative remedies':

[52] Cf John Yoo, 'The Terrorist Surveillance Program and the Constitution', *George Mason Law Review* 14 (2007) 565 at 590.      [53] See Chapter six, section 2.5.

[54] See Stewart A Baker, 'Should Spies be Cops?', *Foreign Policy* 97 (1994–95) 36.

[55] Morris D Davis, 'Historical Perspective on Guantánamo Bay: The Arrival of the High Value Detainees', *Case Western Reserve Journal of International Law* 42 (2009) 115.

[56] Josh White, Dan Eggen, and Joby Warrick, 'US to Try 6 on Capital Charges over 9/11 Attacks', *Washington Post*, 12 February 2008.

A civilian prosecution—with counsel provided by the government, an Article III judge and a jury of twelve peers, the benefits of the Federal Rules of Evidence, conducted in full view of the press and public—is a far better prospect to most civil libertarians than military detention, a military tribunal, or a Hellfire missile.[57]

Such apocalyptic warnings aside, it does seem accurate that many of the debates over intelligence are likely to move from whether a wiretap should be authorized to how information so gathered might be used.

## 3. SAFEGUARDS

As the Arar case demonstrated, incautious use of intelligence can have serious consequences. That incident pointed to two types of problems, however. The first was the failure to attach a caveat, such as a requirement that neither the content nor the source of the information shared could be disseminated further without the consent of the originator, in this case Canada. This is the principle of 'originator control', also known as the 'third party rule', frequently applied in intelligence-sharing relationships. The second problem was the sloppy manner in which information was recorded at the outset. Arar had become a person of interest when he met with the target of an investigation in a café; another person interviewed was not sure if Arar had a business relationship with the man. When approached for an interview Arar agreed, provided that his lawyer could be present; five months later he travelled to Tunisia. This information was recorded erroneously as being that Arar had travelled from Quebec to attend a meeting, the two men had a business relationship, Arar had refused to be interviewed, and then 'suddenly' left for Tunisia. As the Arar Commission warned, written labels tend to stick to an individual, spreading to others and becoming accepted fact or wisdom.[58]

The most common approach to addressing the danger of misuse of data has been the adoption of protocols such as the European Data Protection Directive, discussed in Chapter five. In the United States, a Code of Fair Information Practices was proposed in 1973 by an advisory committee to

---

[57] Kris, 'Rise and Fall', 529.        [58] Arar Commission Factual Inquiry, 24–8.

the Department of Health, Education, and Welfare. The basic provisions continue to be cited and would require that there can be no record-keeping systems whose very existence is secret, a person must be able to find out what information is in a record and how it is used, information gathered for one purpose cannot be used for another without consent, there must be a way to correct or amend information, and the organization controlling the data must ensure its reliability and take reasonable precautions to prevent misuse.[59]

Such approaches are of limited relevance to intelligence services, of course. In Britain, legislation implementing the European directive gives the Minister broad discretion to certify that data should be exempted from the requirements for national security reasons with a right of review that—since one would never know that the information has been exempted—is largely theoretical.[60] In the United States, the Privacy Act 1974 allows the Director of the CIA to exempt entire recording systems from its provisions without any meaningful possibility of review;[61] other legislation concerning financial and electronic privacy also has broad carve-outs for the intelligence services.[62]

More importance is therefore attached to internal processes intended to guard against misuse of data. Such 'minimization' practices tend to fall into three categories. The first is *acquisition*, meaning that if, in the course of collecting intelligence on one person information is mistakenly acquired on another, then the activity would be discontinued. If a wiretap is authorized on a shared phone, for example, conversations by a person not connected with the target should not be recorded. The second is *retention*, requiring that information be destroyed when it is no longer necessary. This has certain obvious attractions in that it limits the amount of information held on individuals, though in some situations the destruction of information may limit legal accountability for the manner in which it was collected or used. The third form of minimization concerns *dissemination*, limiting the sharing of information to officials with a need for such information.[63]

---

[59] Records, Computers and the Rights of Citizens, Report of the Secretary's Advisory Committee on Automated Personal Data Systems (HEW Report) (Washington, DC: Department of Health, Education, and Welfare, July 1973), viii.

[60] See Chapter five, section 3.1.       [61] Privacy Act 1974 (US); 5 USC § 552a(j)(1).

[62] See Chapter four, section 1.       [63] See, eg, 50 USC § 1801(h).

In light of the discussion of accountability in Chapter seven, however, it is striking that these efforts focus almost exclusively on only one of the reasons for seeking accountability: the prospect of abuse. The special status accorded to intelligence services would also seem to support the need for an accountability regime justifying that status. As the Arar case implies, greater accountability may improve not just the legitimacy but also the quality of intelligence. A broader approach is therefore required.

### 3.1. Public

A starting point would be to affirm the essentially public nature of the power in question. Exemptions from civil liberties protections may be justifiable in the interests of national security, but only when those exemptions apply to entities that are directly accountable in other ways to a given population—typically through democratic accountability to an electorate. Any such regime should establish clear and transparent lines of responsibility that lead to an individual official who is in turn accountable to the citizenry.

Though the details of specific programmes can and should remain secret, this principle would require at least internal clarity about responsibility for all such programmes. In this way, even if absolute transparency to the public is impossible, incentives can be put in place to avoid deniability. That may sound like a weak constraint—and it is—but examples of it working are not hard to find. Consider Hoover's efforts to avoid exposing the FBI (and himself) to legal and political jeopardy in the years before the Watergate scandal broke.[64] Whistleblowers and the media will continue to play an important role in exposing wrongdoing, as can be seen in the more recent examples of torture, extraordinary rendition, and warrantless electronic surveillance in the United States.[65]

Importantly, the principle would also limit the activities of private entities. Unless fully incorporated into government accountability structures, such bodies should be denied the protections offered to government actors. The retrospective immunity granted to telecommunications companies that violated the law in cooperating with US surveillance after September 11

---

[64] See section 2 in this Chapter.    [65] See Chapter three, section 3.

sends precisely the wrong message to both government agencies and corporations.[66]

## 3.2. Legal

A second requirement is that the intelligence services should be grounded in the rule of law. The notion that government activity should be legal sounds obvious. Yet, as the case of Britain showed, it is a notion of fairly recent vintage. Israel's Mossad, for example, continues to operate on the basis of a six-sentence letter written by Prime Minister David Ben-Gurion in 1949.[67]

Even if operational details must be left classified, the entities carrying out intelligence functions of the government must themselves be established by laws that are publicly available. Among other things, such laws must outline the mandate for an agency in clear terms that allow for a discussion of the purposes for which it may exercise its powers. The contours of those powers should also be spelled out, along with the remedies available when powers are exceeded or when innocent persons are harmed. Perhaps most importantly, building on the requirement of publicness, the law must establish the governance structure applicable to these entities: who exercises day-to-day control, what measures of oversight are in place, and in what circumstances decisions may be reviewed externally and by whom.

These provisions are general and they are intended to be. One lesson of the past decades of intelligence activities is that the precise details of an accountability regime are less important than clarity as to its existence and scope. Rather than putting faith in perfect structures, the intent is to ensure that there is sufficient information for meaningful debate.

## 3.3. Consequence-sensitive

A third general prescription is that the activities of intelligence services and the accountability regime should focus on the consequences of their activities.

---

[66] See Chapter four, section 3.1.1.
[67] Ronald Payne, *Mossad: Israel's Most Secret Service* (London: Bantam, 1990), 22–31; Ian Black and Benny Morris, *Israel's Secret Wars: A History of Israel's Intelligence Services* (Grove Press: New York, 1992), 83.

Most of the structures set up to limit the powers of intelligence agencies tend to assume a model of individualized searches. Such a regime can be regulated through individual warrants, but it does not reflect the reality of how many agencies operate today. The move to more systematic surveillance of the entire population—through widespread CCTV, the linking of government databases, and sweeping data searches of telecommunications and financial records—requires a different regime. Warrants will still be important for narrowly targeted surveillance or to authorize searches of property, but accountability for systematic surveillance will necessarily be more general.

As with the requirements of publicness and legality, a key aspect is transparency. This might include regular reports as to the nature and purpose of surveillance, why and how it is analysed, and for what purposes it is used. Technology itself could assist in this process, by recording precisely who accesses data and what is done with it. Clear lines of internal authority and oversight by the legislature would provide a measure of accountability, with appropriately sanitized reports released to the public on a regular basis. It is certain that there would be misuse or abuse of the vastly increasing amount of data in government hands. For such situations a compensation regime could be developed, offering financial or other assistance to those whose identity is stolen, personal details revealed, or whose life is disrupted by inclusion on a list to be screened specially before boarding a flight or entering a building.

## 4. AFTER PRIVACY

What, then, of privacy?

As discussed in the Introduction, the desire to prevent the disclosure of certain information about oneself is both ancient and widespread. Yet most legal protections of a right to privacy date only to the late nineteenth century, as a reaction to changes in threats, technology, and culture. These two aspects of privacy—the ostensibly self-evident basis for the concept but the reactive nature of efforts to protect it—have led to incoherence in both the theory and the doctrine of privacy.

Theories of privacy typically seek to identify a foundation for the various intuitions commonly shared concerning privacy. One approach focuses on the information in question. Some scholars emphasize the element of *intimacy*, with privacy embracing intimate information, access, and decisions. Such an approach is extremely narrow, however, as much information one might wish to keep private—one's financial records, political affiliations—could not accurately be described as 'intimate' unless the word is defined so broadly as to become, in essence, a synonym for 'private'.[68]

A second approach therefore emphasizes the relations between individuals and the right to be 'let alone'. Privacy is compromised when others obtain information about an individual, pay attention to him or her, or gain physical access. Privacy should therefore protect secrecy, anonymity, and solitude. This definition may be too broad, however, as it would appear to include rights—not to be pushed, for example—that go well beyond a meaningful definition of privacy.[69]

These first two conceptions of privacy are often associated with the approach adopted in the United States that sees privacy primarily as protecting a liberty interest, a freedom from external interference. This may be distinguished from what is sometimes termed a 'European' understanding that focuses more on protection of the personal honour or dignity of individuals.[70] A third approach focuses on this notion of dignity, which is said to be stripped away if a person is denied a meaningful private life.[71] The need for a 'private place' finds support in among psychologists, yet as a theory it is imprecise, as a life with dignity requires more than merely the possibility of seclusion from society.[72]

An alternative conception is therefore to focus not on the benefits to the individual of preventing inconvenient or embarrassing disclosures, but on

[68] See, eg, Julie C Inness, *Privacy, Intimacy, and Isolation* (Oxford: Oxford University Press, 1992); Solove, 'Nothing to Hide', 755.

[69] See, eg, Ruth Gavison, 'Privacy and the Limits of Law', *Yale Law Journal* 89 (1980) 421; Solove, 'Nothing to Hide', 755.

[70] James Q Whitman, 'The Two Western Cultures of Privacy: Dignity Versus Liberty', *Yale Law Journal* 113 (2004) 1153.

[71] See, eg, EJ Bloustein, 'Privacy as an Aspect of Human Dignity: An Answer to Dean Prosser', *New York University Law Review* 39 (1964) 962.

[72] SM Jourard, 'Some Psychological Aspects of Privacy', *Law and Contemporary Problems* 31 (1966) 307; Tim Frazer, 'Appropriation of Personality—A New Tort?', *Law Quarterly Review* 99 (1983) 281 at 296.

the benefits to society of maintaining a sphere of life that is insulated from the public gaze.[73] This is a promising line of inquiry, but if privacy is considered to be an individual right in tension with societal interests (such as security), the individual right will generally lose.[74] In any case, the sphere that can be insulated in this way has now diminished to the point where its physical borders are probably the confines of one's home, with temporal limits determined by the moments when one's telecommunications devices are switched off or out of range.

Despairing of conceptual clarity, some scholars resort to argument by intuition alone: the 'twinges of indignation' that are said to be suggestive of the breaching of social norms.[75] That may well be how most people think of privacy, but intuitionism is a highly dubious basis for law. Taken seriously, it requires a pluralism that would make a choice between the different conceptions of privacy outlined above impossible; accepting that such pluralism derives from different social conditioning undermines the claim that the relevant intuitions are self-evident.[76] Others have gamely attempted to develop taxonomies based not on doctrinal coherence but 'family resemblances'.[77] None of these approaches is satisfactory, supporting Jonathan Franzen's pithy account of privacy as 'the Cheshire cat of values: not much substance, but a very winning smile.'[78]

Not surprisingly, the legal protection of privacy—in the United States in particular—is confusing and confused. Courts loosely embraced the idea of a right to be 'let alone' articulated in the late nineteenth century, but a proliferation of cases ended up coalescing around four distinct kinds of interference with different interests of the plaintiff. These were linked by the name privacy but otherwise had little in common. Writing in 1960, William Prosser grouped them into an analytical framework that continues to be recognized today: (1) intrusion upon seclusion; (2) public disclosure of private facts; (3) publicity that places a person in a false light in

---

[73] Robert C Post, 'The Social Foundations of Privacy: Community and Self in the Common Law Tort', *California Law Review* 77 (1989) 957; Austin, 'Privacy and the Question of Technology', 164–5.

[74] Cf Amitai Etzioni, *The Limits of Privacy* (New York: Basic Books, 1999).

[75] Nissenbaum, 'Protecting Privacy', 583.

[76] Cf John Rawls, *A Theory of Justice* (Oxford: Clarendon Press, 1972), 34–40.

[77] Solove, 'Nothing to Hide', 756.

[78] Jonathan Franzen, *How to Be Alone* (London: Harper Collins, 2002), 42.

the public eye; and (4) appropriation of a person's name or likeness for another's advantage.[79]

The European Convention on Human Rights establishes a quasi-constitutional basis for privacy protection, unlike the common law approach developed in the United States. As described in Chapter five, this requires any interference with the right to 'respect for private and family life' to be in accordance with the law, and necessary in a democratic society in the interests of 'national security, public safety or the economic well-being of the country, for the prevention of disorder or crime, for the protection of health or morals, or for the protection of the rights and freedoms of others.'[80] Privacy protections in Europe are significantly stronger than the United States, with the result that European standards often become global in areas such as Internet policy.[81] Nevertheless, the European Court of Human Rights has concluded that it would not be possible or desirable to attempt an exhaustive definition of 'private life' for the purposes of its convention, instead developing specific protections that can be tied to that vague term incrementally.[82]

In this way, the protection of privacy has been conceived in terms of functional restrictions: an activity is identified—the collection, storage, or use of information characterized as private—and a legal regime is developed in the hope of restricting that activity to legitimate purposes.[83] Conceptual clarity is not helped by the routine inclusion of matters not properly tied to privacy. The ability to correct information about oneself, for example, may be an important aspect of living in a world of computer databases and central to notions of data protection, but it is not helpful to link this to a core understanding of privacy.[84]

It is not the intent here to add yet another definition of privacy to the literature. Rather, it is to suggest that the incoherence of privacy as a concept in theory and the reactive approach to its protection by law in

---

[79] William Prosser, 'Privacy', *California Law Review* 484 (1960) 383. See *Restatement of the Law, Second, Torts* (Philadelphia: American Law Institute, 1977), § 652A.

[80] [European] Convention for the Protection of Human Rights and Fundamental Freedoms, done at Rome, 4 November 1950, in force 3 September 1953, art 8. See Chapter five.

[81] Jack Goldsmith and Timothy Wu, *Who Controls the Internet? Illusions of a Borderless World* (Oxford: Oxford University Press, 2006), 174.

[82] See, eg, *Niemietz v Germany* (1992) 16 EHRR 97, para 29.

[83] Jonathan Zittrain, *The Future of the Internet—and How to Stop It* (New Haven, CT: Yale University Press, 2008), 202.          [84] Austin, 'Privacy and the Question of Technology', 165.

practice help explain why privacy activists have been so unsuccessful in drawing lines in the sand to stop the encroachment of the surveillance state. Many writers have tried and failed to reconcile the apparent sincerity of individuals claiming to be concerned about their privacy with the nonchalant behaviour of those same individuals in revealing personal information voluntarily or engaging in activities where there is manifestly no reasonable expectation to privacy. Paraphrasing Jane Austen, one concludes that 'privacy is a value that everyone speaks well of, but no-one remembers to do anything about. No-one disparages privacy to its face. They simply choose to emphasize the public's right to know, national security, personal safety, conveniences, economic opportunity, politics, ideology, or the pursuit of virtue.'[85]

There is also a generational element to the transformation underway. Whereas in the 1960s activists opposed even the creation of files, today's fears tend to stress the potential for abuse by private actors—identity theft, stalking—rather than nefarious activity by governments. This may change: high profile scandals might lead to a reining in of intelligence services comparable to the aftermath of Watergate. But it seems unlikely. The scandals that have emerged in places like the United States and Britain have largely been confined in their impact to visible minorities, such as the Syrian-Canadian Maher Arar, allowing a certain complacency on the part of the majority. A more probable scenario is that the activists, like the generation that used to write, sign, and seal envelopes, or confide in diaries locked with a key, will be succeeded by the generation that sends e-mails with all the privacy of a postcard and blogs about the most intimate details of their lives.[86]

Are we, then, 'sleepwalking into a surveillance society' as Britain's Information Commissioner Richard Thomas warned in 2004?[87] The answer would seem to be: no, we are walking in that direction with our eyes wide open.

---

[85] Sykes, *End of Privacy*, 8.

[86] Cf Thomas S Kuhn, *The Structure of Scientific Revolutions*, 3rd edn (Chicago: University Of Chicago Press, 1996), 151–2.

[87] Quoted in Richard Ford, 'Beware Rise of Big Brother State, Warns Data Watchdog', *The Times* (London), 16 August 2004.

# 9

# A New Social Contract

Hitherto I have set forth the nature of Man, (whose Pride and other Passions have compelled him to submit himselfe to Government;) together with the great power of his Governour, whom I compared to *Leviathan*, taking that comparison out of the two last verses of the one and fortieth of *Job*; where God having set forth the great power of *Leviathan*, calleth him King of the Proud. *There is nothing*, saith he, *on earth, to be compared with him. He is made so as not to be afraid. Hee seeth every high thing below him; and is King of all the children of pride.* But because he is mortall, and subject to decay, as all other Earthly creatures are; and because there is that in heaven, (though not on earth) that he should stand in fear of, and whose Lawes he ought to obey; I shall in the next following Chapters speak of his Diseases, and the causes of his Mortality; and of what Lawes of Nature he is bound to obey

Thomas Hobbes, *Leviathan*[1]

At his inauguration in 2009, US President Barack Obama sought to draw a line between his administration and a White House that had unlawfully spied on its citizens, established secret prisons, and embraced torture. 'We reject as false,' he declared, 'the choice between our safety and our ideals.'[2] Presenting the security dilemmas of a modern state as a choice between its safety or its ideals is indeed false, but the 'enduring convictions' of which President Obama later spoke do evolve over time. As this book has shown, the new threats posed by terrorism, the opportunities offered by technological innovation, and the acceptance of a public willing to compromise its privacy have changed the context within which such decisions on national security matters are made.

[1] Thomas Hobbes, *Leviathan* [1651] (Cambridge: Cambridge University Press, 1991), ch xxviii.     [2] 'Barack Obama's Inaugural Address', *New York Times*, 20 January 2009.

For although it is not *either* safety *or* ideals, decisions must still be made. Writing in 1971, Alan Westin argued that a 'free society should not have to choose between more rational use of authority and personal privacy'. Westin remains one of the most important writers on privacy of his era, but this line of argument is deeply flawed.[3] Societies do choose how to manage the relationship between rational authority and privacy, and they must choose carefully.

This final Chapter examines the choices that must be made—and the false dilemmas that frequently confuse debates over intelligence. It does so using the device of a social contract. This has been selected in part because the concept is sometimes invoked, albeit in imprecise terms, by the intelligence community itself. Michael Hayden, Director of the CIA from 2006 to 2009, used the language of social contract in his confirmation hearing and in a number of speeches during his tenure, but confined its meaning to requiring that the CIA obey the law and maintain the trust of the American people.[4] Trust is important, but suggests a fiduciary rather than a contractual relationship. In law, a fiduciary relationship exists when one party, typically in a position of vulnerability, puts its faith in another to act on its behalf. The person that agrees to act in this way is subject to high standards of loyalty, but is also given a significant measure of discretion in determining what is in the best interests of the other party.[5]

A contract, by contrast, implies an agreement negotiated between two parties. Here the social contract is used in a somewhat broader sense to frame the relevant choices: not as a choice between safety or ideals, between security or liberty, but as a dynamic relationship negotiated between governor and governed that, to remain legitimate, must be premised on some measure of consent.

---

[3] Alan F Westin, 'Civil Liberties Issues in Public Databanks', in Alan F Westin (ed), *Information Technology in a Democracy* (Cambridge, MA: Harvard University Press, 1971), 301 at 310. Cf James B Rule, *Privacy in Peril* (Oxford: Oxford University Press, 2007), 149–50.

[4] Michael V Hayden, Testimony to the Judiciary Committee of the US Senate (Washington, DC: Judiciary Committee, 26 July 2006). Cf The National Intelligence Strategy (Washington, DC: Office of the Director of National Intelligence (ODNI), 2009), 2.

[5] Matthew Conaglen, *Fiduciary Loyalty: Protecting the Due Performance of Non-Fiduciary Duties* (Oxford: Hart Publishing, 2010); James Edelman, 'When Do Fiduciary Duties Arise?', *Law Quarterly Review* 126 (2010) 302.

## 1. LEVIATHAN

The term 'social contract' has come to be embraced by a range of traditions in political philosophy. The central idea is that coercive political authority can be legitimized through the notion—either historical or hypothetical—of some kind of pact.[6]

In its original formulation, Thomas Hobbes grounded this pact in a fairly base self-interest. Life in what he termed the state of nature was 'solitary, poore, nasty, brutish, and short'; to escape this existence—'that miserable condition of Warre'—individuals ceded their natural right to govern themselves to establish a commonwealth, creating centralized political authority in exchange for order. Hobbes named this commonwealth, a multitude united in one person, 'Leviathan', after the sea monster described in the Bible. The frontispiece to the first edition depicted a giant figure towering over the landscape, crowned and bearing a sword; viewed closely the arms and body are revealed to be composed of hundreds of smaller figures, all looking up towards the majestic head.[7]

Critics such as David Hume have long pointed to the absurdity of grounding the origins of government upon any actual agreement, and the dubiousness of asserting that citizens continue tacitly to agree to government today. In any case, Hume argued, such a promise could not provide the basis for ongoing political obligations, as promises themselves are part of those political obligations rather than the foundation for them.[8] More nuanced contractarian theorists, such as John Rawls, follow Immanuel Kant in rejecting the literal contractual basis for political authority, but still use the idea of a social contract to describe a form of political association based on some measure of reasoned consent.[9] Such an approach finds support in the constitutional structures of liberal democracies.

---

[6] See generally David Boucher and Paul Kelly, 'The Social Contract and Its Critics', in David Boucher and Paul Kelly (eds), *The Social Contract from Hobbes to Rawls* (New York: Routledge, 1994), 1. Moral contractarianism, by contrast, grounds moral principles in the enlightened self-interest of individuals who adopt constraints on their behaviour in order to maximize benefits. David Gauthier, *Morals by Agreement* (Oxford: Oxford University Press, 1986).

[7] Hobbes, *Leviathan*, chs xiii, xvii.

[8] David Hume, 'Of the Original Contract [1748]', in Ernest Barker (ed), *Social Contract: Essays by Locke, Hume, and Rousseau* (Oxford: Oxford University Press, 1962), 147.

[9] John Rawls, *A Theory of Justice* (Oxford: Clarendon Press, 1972).

In the case of the United States it was implicit in the Declaration of Independence, which provided that 'to secure these rights, Governments are instituted among Men, deriving their just powers from the consent of the governed'.[10]

What we are witnessing today is the formulation of a new social contract that goes beyond the centralization of political authority to make organized society possible. Instead of ceding powers of coercion—a monopoly over the legitimate use of force, the ability to levy taxes, and so on—this new social contract is premised on granting access to information. In return, the benefit is not political order as such, but a measure of increased security and the convenience of living in the modern world. The diminishing sphere of life that may truly be regarded as 'private' is not being taken, but given in exchange for these benefits. There is some truth to the claim that this happens without much reflection, but leaving aside abstract privacy concerns in theory, the vast majority of the population appears to accept the transfer in practice.[11]

One reason for that acceptance is the understanding that there are legitimate security threats that require a governmental response. We tolerate billions of dollars being spent on intelligence, we submit to video surveillance in public buildings and spaces, and we allow ourselves to be fingerprinted before entering countries like the United States.[12] Extreme cases aside, much of modern intelligence is not legally problematic: the primary constraint is therefore political. A key problem here is that the history of intelligence shows that public debate on the subject is reactive and highly dependent on the manner in which a question is posed. A large new government initiative that aspires to 'Total Information Awareness' is opposed, but incremental growth of data mining or detention of non-citizens is not.[13]

The second reason for accepting the loss of privacy is the extent to which it is connected to the practicalities of modern life. Some of these benefits are mere convenience, such as the ability to use a mobile phone, send and receive e-mails, pay with a credit card, earn points through a loyalty scheme, and so on. Many involve private actors entrusted with information on the basis of an explicit contract, though the terms of these

---

[10] US Declaration of Independence (4 July 1776).     [11] See Chapter eight, section 4.
[12] See Chapter two, section 2.     [13] See Chapter eight, section 1.2.

agreements are routinely approved or signed unread. Other benefits more explicitly link convenience and security, such as trusted traveller programmes that allow approved individuals expedited clearance through border procedures. 'Approval' involves an interview and background check, as well as the storing of biometric identification data.

The result is governments with vastly more information about their citizens than at any point in human history. Though difficult to measure, much of this information does enhance security and simplify daily communications and transactions. It also increases the possibility of abuse: the loss or misuse of data, especially the discriminatory treatment of particular groups. More generally, however, the very fact of knowledge, or indeed the *possibility* of such knowledge, may impact on individuals and society in deleterious ways. The manner in which governments use information to produce self-policing subjects has long been a subject of postmodern social theorists. Michel Foucault used Jeremy Bentham's ideal of a Panopticon—a prison in which all inmates could be watched at all times but would never know when they were being observed—to illustrate a new power dynamic through which a society could produce individuals who would discipline themselves.[14] There is, clearly, some truth to this: one reason why notices advise that closed-circuit television (CCTV) cameras are in operation is to avoid privacy challenges, but they are also regarded as most effective when people know that they are being watched.[15]

Yet there are important ways in which this new pact differs from the traditional conception of the social contract. Unlike the traditional social contract, it is theoretically possible to opt out of this new set of arrangements—at least in part. Though one cannot legally avoid a modern government having any record concerning one's birth, taxable income, and death, it is possible to minimize one's digital footprint. One can abstain from having a mobile phone, an e-mail address, or a credit card; refrain from travelling or obtaining a driving licence. Few choose this path. Alternatively, encryption software can be used for telecommunications and anonymizing services when accessing the Internet. The market for such products is steadily increasing, with governments also turning to the private

[14] Michel Foucault, *Discipline and Punish: The Birth of the Prison* [1975] (London: Penguin, 1979).     [15] See Chapter five, section 3.1.

sector for assistance.[16] Europe's response to the revelation that the United States routinely intercepted its telecommunications was to invest in stronger quantum cryptography that was launched in 2008.[17]

Such responses point to another difference in the new social contract, which is that the transfer of information is not merely to a central political authority but to a far broader array of actors. That breadth is attributable to choice by government, but also to the nature of a globalized economy. As Chapter four showed, governments—especially, but not only, in the United States—have turned to the private sector for an extraordinary range of intelligence assistance. It may be that technologically sophisticated surveillance is only possible with the cooperation of telecommunications and other companies. Nevertheless, the turn to outsourcing went far beyond that practical requirement to include the use of private aircraft in extraordinary rendition and contractors in interrogation, suggesting a desire to hide or deny legally questionable conduct.

Privacy theorists and lawyers have struggled to respond to these moves, in part because of the diminishing sphere of truly private activity and the growing coercive powers of the state. A more fundamental problem may be conceiving the question as how to maintain the distinction between what is public and what is private. Here, again, it is helpful to draw upon a contractarian analysis that is premised not on a dichotomy between public and private but on a dynamic relationship between government and governed. Existing rules have been inadequate to the task. New rules are required.

## 2. NEW RULES

The content of those rules—how the precise terms of this new bargain is struck—will depend on the politics and culture of the society in question. Canada and the United States, for example, have much in common but have adopted strikingly different postures with regard to privacy, with Canada far closer to a European model of data protection than the United States. The reasons for the divergence are complex, including the

---

[16] See Chapter four, section 3.1.          [17] See Chapter one, section 1.2.

different political and legal systems, as well as the distinct threat percep-tions of the two countries. At the same time, Americans generally regard their government with far more suspicion than Canadians and yet entrust it with more intrusive powers. Popular culture reflects these inconsisten-cies: the CIA and FBI are the subject of extensive and largely positive representation in films and television. There is nothing comparable with respect to the far weaker Canadian Security Intelligence Service (CSIS), which tends to be the part of the Canadian government that is eyed most suspiciously.

Some of the explanation lies in the scandals that drive change. Chapter one described the manner in which the powers of US intelligence agencies expanded during the Cold War before being reined in after Watergate. Following September 11 there was a concerted push to expand them once more.[18] Canada is unusual in that the scandals that have precipitated reform were disproportionally scandals of abuse rather than omission—indeed, CSIS itself was created not because of a threat but following revela-tions of misconduct by the Royal Canadian Mounted Police, which had its national security powers stripped away in 1984.[19] Concerns about abuse were reinforced by the Maher Arar scandal, which from an early stage alerted Canadians to the danger of aggressive new powers in a 'war on terror'.[20]

Britain, by contrast, has seen relatively few scandals of abuse to check the growth of surveillance technologies. Though nominally European in its human rights obligations, Chapter five showed how the roll-out of CCTV and the development of a DNA database in advance of legal constraints makes it highly unlikely that the law will prove a meaningful check on such collection activities. That said, Britain is also a rare example of a country that developed a comprehensive identity card regime during the Second World War and then dismantled it after the conclusion of hostilities, apparently to the dismay of many in law enforcement circles. In 2010, another identity card regime was the subject of bitter attacks, though this had less to do with privacy concerns than the expense involved,

---

[18] See Chapter one, section 3.
[19] See Commission of Inquiry Concerning Certain Activities of the Royal Canadian Mounted Police by Justice DC McDonald (Ottawa: Government of Canada, 1979–1981); Canadian Security Intelligence Service (CSIS) Act 1984 (Canada).
[20] See Chapter eight.

concerns about government incompetence in managing the data, and a general wariness that the whole enterprise looked a little too 'European'.[21]

National variations aside, global economic forces will require some measure of harmonization. Many European standards, for example, have been adopted as de facto global standards for Internet policy.[22] On security matters, however, the United States will essentially impose many of its requirements on the rest of the world. This is already happening with biometric passports, which are required to enter the United States under the Visa Waiver Program, and the mandatory electronic transfer by airlines of passenger data prior to arrival, which has pressed ahead despite European privacy concerns. Databases are now routinely used to check passports, making them harder to fake.[23] These standards will eventually apply to all international travel. Maintaining dominance in telecommunications has been more problematic: US officials have stressed the security interest it has in keeping a majority of Internet traffic flowing through the switching equipment of companies based in the United States, but the fragmented nature of the Web makes this difficult.[24]

It does seem possible and necessary, then, to distil some common principles for this new social contract that should apply across jurisdictions. Building on the safeguards articulated in Chapter eight, these can be reduced to three basic ideas.

First, and fundamental to the consensual premise of a contract, the intelligence powers exercised must be *public*. Claims of national security are most credibly made by entities accountable to the nation; outsourcing such responsibilities to private actors both undermines the legitimacy of the actions taken and perverts the incentives that are intended to deter abuse.[25] The requirement of publicness also acknowledges that the limits on these powers will be those fought over in the political process. There will be different answers to where the line should be drawn, based in part

---

[21] See Chapter five, section 3 and Chapter seven, section 2.4.

[22] See Chapter eight, section 4.

[23] When a Hamas leader was assassinated in Dubai in January 2010, the two dozen agents—widely suspected as working for the Israeli intelligence agency Mossad—appear to have used the identities of real nationals of five countries, most of them holding dual citizenship with Israel.

[24] See, eg, Hayden, Testimony; John Markoff, 'Internet Traffic Begins to Bypass the US', *New York Times*, 30 August 2008.     [25] See Chapter eight, section 3.1.

on competing visions of a good life. Some will prefer a more secure, more efficient, less dangerous world at the expense of significant limits on privacy; others would choose privacy even if the cost is living a little less comfortably or more dangerously.[26] It has been the argument of this book that privacy will generally lose in these battles, but each political community should make that determination on its own.

Secondly, and implied by the notion of a formalized agreement, the entities carrying out these functions must be *legal*: each agency itself, its mandate, and its powers must be established by law.[27] This requirement of legality recognizes the need for clear limits for officers working in an intelligence agency, as well as to guide the politicians to whom they report. The history of efforts to govern intelligence is, in many ways, a series of haphazard efforts by the legislature and judiciary to restrain or direct intelligence-gathering powers, followed by determined efforts by the executive to continue on its path.[28] Enforcement of these laws may take a variety of forms, as seen in the range of accountability mechanisms described in Chapter seven. There will be some restrictions on collection, particularly when it involves intrusive interference with person or property, but a general conception of privacy seems unlikely to pose much of a barrier. Despite the erosion of the distinction between foreign and domestic threats, there will continue to be a need for separate rules concerning what can be done domestically and abroad. Most countries will therefore maintain different agencies for these purposes, but with far greater collaboration than is currently exhibited between the FBI and the CIA. For the United States, a logical consequence would be the formal division of the FBI into a federal policing agency and a domestic intelligence service along the lines of Britain's MI5.[29]

The requirement of legality also makes clear that there are limits to what the government can do and what the public will accept. As Chapter two argued, it is inevitable that threats will drive the executive to push at

---

[26] Cf Rule, *Privacy in Peril*, xvii.     [27] See Chapter eight, section 3.2.

[28] Cf Laura K Donohue, 'Anglo-American Privacy and Surveillance', *Journal of Criminal Law & Criminology* 96 (2006) 1059 at 1073.

[29] See, eg, Charles Cogan, 'Hunters not Gatherers: Intelligence in the Twenty-First Century', *Intelligence and National Security* 19(2) (2004) 304; Philip Bobbitt, *Terror and Consent: The Wars for the Twenty-First Century* (New York: Allen Lane, 2008), 301–2. See also Chapter four, section 2.2.

the boundaries of law in its efforts to safeguard the nation; in some cases, the law may even be broken. The rule of law can survive a breach—the fact that many murders are left unsolved does not mean that the crime of homicide ceases to be meaningful. It may not survive subjugation to a ruler that sets him- or herself above the law completely.[30]

Thirdly, going to the purpose of the contract, accountability for the activities of intelligence services must be *consequence-sensitive*. Accountability through a warrant-based system of individualized searches is largely irrelevant in an era of systematic surveillance of entire populations; the focus instead needs to be on what is done with the information gathered.[31] Historically, minimization protocols sought to reduce acquisition, limit retention, and constrain dissemination of data. Systematic surveillance and expanding storage capacities have reduced the significance of the first two elements; all three narrowly assume that the purpose of accountability is simply to deter or respond to abuse. There will be abuse, of course: identities will be stolen, CCTV footage will be uploaded to YouTube, personal information will be lost. There will also be discrimination. The most prominent example of this—implicit in the very notion of systematic surveillance—is profiling.

Profiling raises legitimate concerns about explicit or implicit racism and other forms of bigotry. Yet it is also clearly a part of the investigative method currently used by police and intelligence officers. The debate as it is often presented sets the civil liberties of the profiled group against the security interests of the population as a whole. It is misleading, however, to say that the choice is between profiling and lost lives. A better analysis might be that the use of ethnicity as a basis for profiling imposes a cost on innocent members of the targeted group—for example, younger Muslim men of Middle Eastern backgrounds. It might be preferable to distribute that cost more equitably, perhaps by excluding the factor perceived as relevant but offensive, and increasing the scrutiny of the population as a whole. One scholar concludes that profiling does not pose the question of whether ethnic sensitivity must be bought at the price of thousands of lives, but whether such sensitivity should be bought at the price of arriving half an hour earlier at the airport.[32]

---

[30] See Chapter two, section 1.2.4.    [31] See Chapter eight, section 3.3.
[32] Frederick Schauer, *Profiles, Probabilities, and Stereotypes* (Cambridge, MA: Harvard University Press, 2003), 174.

Such an analysis is misleading in a different way, however, as it still implicitly accepts the 'trade-off thesis' that gains for liberty necessarily entail a loss of security. The metaphor of a balance is compelling and routinely used by both civil libertarians and security hawks. Yet it is distorting in that it fails to consider that liberty may in fact *contribute* to security.[33] In the case of profiling, for example, pre-selecting all young Muslim men might well offend public 'sensitivities', but it may also contribute to the problem that it is intended to solve. Much as the invocation of a 'global war on terror'—a term now rightly abandoned by the US government—falsely implied that groups with diverse aims and widely varied capacities were in fact part of a worldwide conspiracy pitted against the United States, putting all individuals of one ethnicity or religion in a category labelled 'dangerous' may in fact undermine identification with the larger community and encourage radicalization.[34]

As systematic surveillance and the capacity for data retention and analysis expand, an alternative to profiling may emerge. Rather than targeting a specific group for closer examination, it may be possible to gather information on the entire population in such depth that human intervention—with the subjectivity and potential for bias that this brings—is significantly reduced. Bias may still affect the manner in which data are organized and analysis prioritized, but it should at least be more evident than the personal choices of individual analysts. It will leave a trail.

An area in which this is already happening is the expansion of DNA databases. Many countries collect DNA samples from convicted felons; an increasing number collect samples from individuals arrested but never charged or subsequently acquitted. Britain today holds samples of the DNA of around a tenth of the population.[35] The FBI's Combined DNA Index System (CODIS) has recently overtaken it in absolute size: as of January 2010 CODIS had nearly 8 million 'offender profiles'. The growth of such databases follows the conviction and arrest patterns of the different countries, with critics arguing—correctly—that certain minorities are overrepresented in the database. One way of dealing with this concern

---

[33] Stephen Holmes, 'In Case of Emergency: Misunderstanding Tradeoffs in the War on Terror', *California Law Review* 97 (2009) 301 at 313.

[34] Bernard E Harcourt, 'Muslim Profiles Post-9/11: Is Racial Profiling an Effective Counterterrorist Measure and Does It Violate the Right to be Free from Discrimination?', in Benjamin J Goold and Liora Lazarus (eds), *Security and Human Rights* (Oxford: Hart Publishing, 2007), 73. See also Chapter four, section 1.2.      [35] See Chapter five, section 4.

and the larger privacy implications of storing individuals' DNA is to limit collection, confining the collection of samples to those convicted of serious crimes, or limiting the length of time that a sample may be retained before destruction. Such approaches have had little success, with the trend going very much in the opposite direction. Another approach to the discrimination question would be far simpler in theory, if difficult in practice: collect and store DNA samples from the entire population. Even if not adopted as a policy, serious debate on the topic would refocus attention of a sometimes apathetic public on the questions of who is controlling the information collected, with what powers and safeguards, and to what purposes and with what consequences.

These three principles—that intelligence should be public, legal, and consequence-sensitive—may sound obvious, if not trite. Nevertheless, as this book has shown, established democracies founded on the rule of law and the most important international organization on the planet have not lived up to them. The United States only terminated a contract outsourcing assassinations to a private company in June 2009.[36] Britain has the most extensive CCTV regime in the world and it is, for the most part, unregulated. And, as described in Chapter six, the United Nations continues to maintain lists of hundreds of individuals whose assets are frozen worldwide without requiring any evidence of wrongdoing.

The principles may also sound weak, or pessimistic. The argument is not that this represents the best framework for intelligence, however—simply that it is the most likely one to have traction. Returning to the idea of a contract, embracing these principles should help to ensure that its terms are, at least, clear. That element of clarity—as to the framework within which intelligence services operate, if not the precise details of their operations—is relatively new to intelligence. But it must be encouraged. Transparency can also help educate the public so that better choices are made concerning the diminishing sphere of privacy. Education is essential if the consent of the population is to be informed.

This marks an important distinction from the manner in which intelligence services have previously justified their special powers, based on

---

[36] See Chapter four. Revelations of similar arrangements in Afghanistan and Pakistan under the auspices of the Department of Defense emerged in March 2010. Dexter Filkins and Mark Mazzetti, 'Contractors Tied to Effort to Track and Kill Militants', *New York Times*, 14 March 2010.

trust. The Cold War era motto of the US Air Force's 9th Reconnaissance Wing was 'In God we trust, all others we monitor.' That dictum might now be applied to the agencies themselves. There are now a range of best practices that can be drawn upon to ensure that their work is both legitimate and effective, ranging from executive control and legislative oversight to judicial review.[37] In addition, however, culture can and should play a role within the agency and in its relationship with the public at large. As Chapter three showed, one of the most important aspects of this has been the media, which historically played a vital role in checking the excesses of intelligence services; the decline of many quality newspapers leaves it uncertain as to what might take their place.[38]

One possibility is new media. A distinctive feature of the move to systematic surveillance is that it has coincided with the emergence of technology that cannot be confined, at least in its entirety, to government hands. During the controversy over Total Information Awareness, for example, Web sites quickly appeared with extensive information about its head, John Poindexter: his telephone number and address, where he shopped, what he bought, and where he had last been seen. More recently, a law professor teaching privacy at Fordham Law School set an assignment for his students of building a dossier on Supreme Court Justice Antonin Scalia, based on what could be found on the Internet. The selection of Justice Scalia was linked to his statement at a conference that it is 'silly' to assert that every datum about one's life deserves privacy protection. The students subsequently compiled a 15-page dossier that included the judge's home address and telephone number, his wife's personal e-mail address, and the television shows and food he prefers. When the project became public, Scalia reaffirmed his position that not every datum about his life should be protected by law. He continued:

It is not a rare phenomenon that what is legal may also be quite irresponsible. That appears in the First Amendment context all the time. What can be said often should not be said. Professor Reidenberg's exercise is an example of perfectly legal, abominably poor judgment. Since he was not teaching a course in judgment, I presume he felt no responsibility to display any.[39]

---

[37] See Chapter seven, section 2.  [38] See Chapter three, sections 3 and 4.
[39] Noam Cohen, 'Law Students Teach Scalia About Privacy and the Web', *New York Times*, 17 May 2009.

These examples show that it is possible for citizens to use the technology that enables much of modern surveillance against their own governments. In developed democracies this may mitigate the decline of investigative journalism. In others—Iran and China are the most prominent recent examples—technology has become one of the primary battlegrounds on which the openness of their societies will be determined.

## 3. FALSE CHOICES

In the opening scene of *The History Boys*, Alan Bennett's play about education and childhood, a schoolteacher who has become a celebrity through populist iconoclasm advises a group of elected officials on the best way to sell a distasteful piece of legislation curtailing civil liberties to a sceptical electorate. 'I would try not to be shrill or earnest,' he suggests. 'An amused tolerance always comes over best, particularly on television. Paradox works well and mists up the windows, which is handy. "The loss of liberty is the price we pay for freedom" type thing.'[40] Debates over the appropriate response to threats to the nation often invoke paradox, with an assumed conflict between liberty and security leading to impassioned and often irreconcilable debate. The assumption of a zero-sum relationship reduces many of these debates to political theatre.

Framing the problem as a tension between liberty and security is also a category error, as it adopts an emergency paradigm as the lens through which to view the threat. Terrorism may well present the most significant threat of violence to the countries discussed in this book, but it is unlikely to constitute an existential threat to organized political life as such. In the event that a dirty bomb is detonated in Manhattan, civil liberties will certainly be curtailed. That is not an argument for abandoning those liberties today. Instead, what is needed now is a reasoned examination of the framework within which the growing surveillance powers of the state should be exercised. Three key elements of that framework are agreement that special powers can only be granted to actors accountable directly to the public, that the extent and the purpose of those powers must be provided

---

[40] Alan Bennett, *The History Boys* (London: Faber and Faber, 2004).

for in law, and that a regime is set up to ameliorate and compensate the intended and unintended consequences of the use of those powers.

The US Pledge of Allegiance was first published in an 1892 issue of a Boston magazine called *The Youth's Companion*. In the following decades it was widely distributed to schools, with millions of children pledging their allegiance to the US flag and the republic for which it stands, 'one Nation indivisible, with liberty and justice for all.' In 1954, the US Congress added the words 'under God', resulting in the current text of 'one Nation under God'.[41] The addition was partly an evangelical project of the Knights of Columbus, a lay Catholic organization. Even in the dying days of the McCarthy period, it struck a chord as a means of distinguishing a God-fearing United States from the atheistic Soviet Union. On the day in which he signed it into law, President Dwight Eisenhower declared that the revised pledge reaffirmed 'the transcendence of religious faith in America's heritage and future; in this way we shall constantly strengthen those spiritual weapons which forever will be our country's most powerful resource in peace and war.'[42]

Two generations later, the United States and Britain no longer confront a global threat on the scale of communism, but are part of a globalized world in which a far wider range of threats capitalize on the very openness that defines that globalization. The United Nations, originally paralysed by the Cold War, is now part of a network of institutions that offer varying degrees of global governance. The threats are also global—terrorist networks, weapons proliferation—as is the technology that enables governments to disrupt at least some of those threats through the interception of telecommunications, the tracking of financial transactions, or the use of video surveillance. The rise of these forms of surveillance has been greeted with extraordinary equanimity, perhaps characterized by an equal mix of acceptance and apathy. The hope of this book is that it offers some modest tools to assert more agency in the negotiation of these arrangements, a new social contract between government and governed, even as we find ourselves living in one nation under surveillance.

---

[41] 4 USC § 4.

[42] 'President Hails Revised Pledge—He Endorses Congress' Action in Inserting "Under God" in Allegiance Vow', *New York Times*, 15 June 1954; Dianne Kirby, 'Harry Truman's Religious Legacy: The Holy Alliance, Containment, and the Cold War', in Dianne Kirby (ed), *Religion and the Cold War* (New York: Palgrave Macmillan, 2003), 77 at 96–7; John W Baer, *The Pledge of Allegiance: A Revised History and Analysis* (Annapolis, MD: Free State Press, 2007).

# Select Bibliography

Ackerman, Bruce, *Before the Next Attack: Preserving Civil Liberties in an Age of Terrorism* (New Haven, CT: Yale University Press, 2006).

Acquisti, Alessandro and Ralph Gross, 'Predicting Social Security Numbers from Public Data', *Proceedings of the National Academy of Sciences* 106(27) (2009) 10975.

Agamben, Giorgio, *State of Exception* [2003], translated by Kevin Attell (Chicago: University of Chicago Press, 2005).

——'Bodies Without Words: Against the Biopolitical Tatoo', *German Law Journal* 5 (2004) 168.

Alexander, Larry and Frederick Schauer, 'On Extrajudicial Constitutional Interpretation', *Harvard Law Review* 110 (1997) 1359.

Alexander, Matthew, *How to Break a Terrorist: The US Interrogators Who Used Brains, Not Brutality, to Take Down the Deadliest Man in Iraq* (New York: Free Press, 2008).

Alnasrawi, Abbas, *Iraq's Burdens: Oil Sanctions and Underdevelopment* (London: Greenwood Press, 2002).

Alpern, David M, 'America's Secret Warriors', *Newsweek*, 10 October 1983, 38.

Alvarez, José, 'Hegemonic International Law Revisited', *American Journal of International Law* 97 (2003) 873.

Andrew, Christopher M, *The Defence of the Realm: The Authorised History of MI5* (London: Allen Lane, 2009).

Annan, Kofi A, *The Question of Intervention: Statements by the Secretary-General* (New York: UN Department of Public Information, 1999).

Arbour, Louise, 'War Crimes Tribunals: The Record and the Prospects: History and Future of the International Criminal Tribunals for the Former Yugoslavia and Rwanda', *American University International Law Review* 13 (1998) 1495.

Arendt, Hannah, *The Origins of Totalitarianism*, 2nd edn (New York: Meridian, 1958).

Ashcroft, John, 'Memorandum for Heads of all Federal Departments and Agencies', *FOIA Post* 19 (2001).

Auden, WH, 'The Unknown Citizen', *New Yorker*, 6 January 1940, 19.

Austin, Lisa M, 'Privacy and the Question of Technology', *Law and Philosophy* 22 (2003) 119.

Baer, John W, *The Pledge of Allegiance: A Revised History and Analysis* (Annapolis, MD: Free State Press, 2007).

Baer, Robert, *See No Evil: The True Story of a Ground Soldier in the CIA's War on Terrorism* (New York: Three Rivers, 2002).

Baker, Christopher, 'Tolerance of International Espionage: A Functional Approach', *American University International Law Review* 19 (2004) 1091.

Baker, Stewart A, 'Should Spies be Cops?', *Foreign Policy* 97 (1994–95) 36.

Balkin, Jack M, 'The Constitution in the National Surveillance State', *Minnesota Law Review* 93 (2008) 1.

Bamford, James, *The Puzzle Palace: A Report on America's Most Secret Agency* (Boston: Houghton Mifflin, 1982).

—— *Body of Secrets: Anatomy of the Ultra-Secret National Security Agency from the Cold War Through the Dawn of a New Century* (New York: Doubleday, 2001).

—— *The Shadow Factory: The Ultra-Secret NSA from 9/11 to the Eavesdropping on America* (New York: Doubleday, 2008).

Barak-Erez, Daphne and Matthew C Waxman, 'Secret Evidence and the Due Process of Terrorist Detentions', *Columbia Journal of Transnational Law* 48 (2009) 3.

Barnett, Hilaire, *Constitutional & Administrative Law*, 6th edn (Oxford: Routledge-Cavendish, 2006).

Baxter, Richard R, 'So-called "Unprivileged Belligerency": Spies, Guerrillas, and Saboteurs', *British Yearbook of International Law* 28 (1951) 323.

Belair, Robert R and Charles D Bock, 'Police Use of Remote Camera Systems for Surveillance of Public Streets', *Columbia Human Rights Law Review* 4 (1972) 143.

Benjamin, Daniel and Steven Simon, *The Age of Sacred Terror* (New York: Random House, 2002).

Bennett, Alan, *The History Boys* (London: Faber and Faber, 2004).

Bennett, Colin J and Rebecca Grant (eds), *Visions of Privacy: Policy Choices for the Digital Age* (Toronto: University of Toronto Press, 1999).

Bepko, Arminda Bradford, 'Public Availability or Practical Obscurity: The Debate over Public Access to Court Records on the Internet', *New York Law School Law Review* 49 (2005) 968.

Berdal, Mats R, 'Fateful Encounter: The United States and UN Peacekeeping', *Survival* 36(1) (1994) 34.

Berkowitz, Bruce D and Allan E Goodman, *Best Truth: Intelligence in the Information Age* (New Haven, CT: Yale University Press, 2000).

Bernstein, Barton J, 'The Road to Watergate and Beyond: The Growth and Abuse of Executive Authority Since 1940', *Law and Contemporary Problems* 40(2) (1976) 58.

Best, Geoffrey, *War and Law Since 1945* (Oxford: Oxford University Press, 1994).

Betts, Richard K, 'Analysis, War, and Decision: Why Intelligence Failures Are Inevitable', *World Politics* 31(1) (1978) 61.

—— *Enemies of Intelligence: Knowledge and Power in American National Security* (New York: Columbia University Press, 2007).

Bickel, Robert D, Susan Brinkley, and Wendy White, 'Seeing Past Privacy: Will the Development and Application of CCTV and Other Video Security Technology Compromise an Essential Constitutional Right in a Democracy, or Will the Courts Strike a Proper Balance?', *Stetson Law Review* 33 (2003) 299.

Biddle, Francis, *In Brief Authority* (Garden City, NY: Doubleday, 1962).

Bidwell, Bruce W, *History of the Military Intelligence Division, Department of the Army General Staff: 1775–1941* (Frederick, MD: University Publications of America, 1986).

Bierce, Ambrose, *The Devil's Dictionary* (New York: Neale, 1911).

Bignami, Francesca, 'Transgovernmental Networks vs Democracy: The Case of the European Information Privacy Network', *Michigan Journal of International Law* 26 (2005) 807.

—— 'European Versus American Liberty: A Comparative Privacy Analysis of Antiterrorism Data Mining', *Boston College Law Review* 48 (2007) 609.

Bignell, Jonathan, *Big Brother: Reality TV in the Twenty-First Century* (New York: Palgrave Macmillan, 2005).

Black, Ian and Benny Morris, *Israel's Secret Wars: A History of Israel's Intelligence Services* (Grove Press: New York, 1992).

Blackstone, William, *Commentaries on the Laws of England* (Oxford: Clarendon Press, 1769) vol 4.

Blix, Hans, *Disarming Iraq* (New York: Pantheon, 2004).

Bloustein, EJ, 'Privacy as an Aspect of Human Dignity: An Answer to Dean Prosser', *New York University Law Review* 39 (1964) 962.

Bobbitt, Philip, *Terror and Consent: The Wars for the Twenty-First Century* (New York: Allen Lane, 2008).

Born, Hans and Marina Caparini (eds), *Democratic Control of Intelligence Services: Containing Rogue Elephants* (Aldershot: Ashgate, 2007).

Born, Hans, Loch K Johnson, and Ian Leigh (eds), *Who's Watching the Spies: Establishing Intelligence Service Accountability* (Washington, DC: Potomac Books, 2005).

Born, Hans and Ian Leigh, *Making Intelligence Accountable: Legal Standards and Best Practice for Oversight of Intelligence Agencies* (Oslo: Parliament of Norway, 2005).

Boucher, David and Paul Kelly (eds), *The Social Contract from Hobbes to Rawls* (New York: Routledge, 1994).

Bowman, ME, 'Intelligence and International Law', *International Journal of Intelligence and Counterintelligence* 8(3) (1995) 321.

Braddon, Derek, *Exploding the Myth? The Peace Dividend, Regions and Market Adjustment* (New York: Routledge, 2000).

Brandeis, Louis D, *Other People's Money and How the Bankers Use It* (New York: Stokes, 1914).

Brin, David, *The Transparent Society: Will Technology Force Us to Choose Between Privacy and Freedom?* (Reading, MA: Addison-Wesley, 1998).

Brown, Jeremy, 'Pan, Tilt, Zoom: Regulating the Use of Video Surveillance of Public Places', *Berkeley Technology Law Journal* 23 (2008) 755.

Burgess, John W, *Political Science and Comparative Constitutional Law* (Boston: Ginn, 1891) vol 1.

Burke, Susan, 'Accountability for Corporate Complicity in Torture', *Gonzaga Journal of International Law* 10 (2006) 81.

Burrows, Quentin, 'Scowl Because You're on Candid Camera: Privacy and Video Surveillance', *Valparaiso University Law Review* 31 (1997) 1079.

Campbell, Lisa Madelon, 'Rising Governmental Use of Biometric Technology: An Analysis of the United States Visitor and Immigrant Status Indicator Technology Program', *Canadian Journal of Law and Technology* 4 (2005) 99.

Carey, Peter, *Data Protection*, 2nd edn (Oxford: Oxford University Press, 2004).

Carlisle, Rodney P (ed), *Encyclopedia of Intelligence and Counter-Intelligence* (Armonk, NY: Sharpe Reference, 2005).

Carne, Greg, 'Thawing the Big Chill: Reform, Rhetoric, and Regression in the Security Intelligence Mandate', *Monash University Law Review* 22 (1996) 379.

Casey, Timothy, 'Electronic Surveillance and the Right to Be Secure', *UC Davis Law Review* 41 (2008) 977.

—— *The USA PATRIOT Act: The Decline of Legitimacy in the Age of Terrorism* (Oxford: Oxford University Press, 2009).

Cassese, Antonio, 'The Statute of the International Criminal Court: Some Preliminary Reflections', *European Journal of International Law* 10 (1999) 144.

Cate, Fred H, 'Government Data Mining: The Need for a Legal Framework', *Harvard Civil Rights-Civil Liberties Law Review* 43 (2008) 435.

Chayes, Abraham, *The Cuban Missile Crisis* (Oxford: Oxford University Press, 1974).

Chesney, Robert M, 'Leaving Guantánamo: The Law of International Detainee Transfers', *University of Richmond Law Review* 40 (2006) 657.

—— 'State Secrets and the Limits of National Security Litigation', *George Washington Law Review* 75 (2007) 1249.

Chesterman, Simon, 'Last Rights: Euthanasia, the Sanctity of Life and the Law in the Netherlands and the Northern Territory of Australia', *International and Comparative Law Quarterly* 47 (1998) 362.

——*Just War or Just Peace? Humanitarian Intervention and International Law*, Oxford Monographs in International Law (Oxford: Oxford University Press, 2001).

——*Shared Secrets: Intelligence and Collective Security* (Sydney: Lowy Institute for International Policy, 2006).

——(ed), *Secretary or General? The UN Secretary-General in World Politics* (Cambridge: Cambridge University Press, 2007).

——'An International Rule of Law?', *American Journal of Comparative Law* 56 (2008) 331.

——'Globalization Rules: Accountability, Power, and the Prospects for Global Administrative Law', *Global Governance* 14 (2008) 39.

Chesterman, Simon and Sebastian von Einsiedel, 'Dual Containment: The United States, Iraq, and the UN Security Council', in Paul Eden and Thérèse O'Donnell (eds), *September 11, 2001: A Turning Point in International and Domestic Law?* (New York: Transnational Publishers, 2004).

Chesterman, Simon and Angelina Fisher (eds), *Private Security, Public Order: The Outsourcing of Public Services and Its Limits* (Oxford: Oxford University Press, 2009).

Chesterman, Simon and Chia Lehnardt (eds), *From Mercenaries to Market: The Rise and Regulation of Private Military Companies* (Oxford: Oxford University Press, 2007).

Chesterman, Simon and Béatrice Pouligny, 'Are Sanctions Meant to Work? The Politics of Creating and Implementing Sanctions Through the United Nations', *Global Governance* 9 (2003) 503.

Chowdhury, Subrata Roy, *Rule of Law in a State of Emergency: The Paris Minimum Standards of Human Rights Norms in a State of Emergency* (London: Palgrave Macmillan, 1989).

Clark, Kathleen, '"A New Era of Openness?" Disclosing Intelligence to Congress Under Obama', *Constitutional Commentary* 26 (2010) forthcoming.

Clark, Robert M, *Intelligence Analysis: A Target-Centric Approach*, 2nd edn (Washington, DC: CQ Press, 2007).

Clarke, Richard A, *Against All Enemies: Inside America's War on Terror* (New York: Free Press, 2004).

Cogan, Charles, 'Hunters not Gatherers: Intelligence in the Twenty-First Century', *Intelligence and National Security* 19(2) (2004) 304.

Colby, William E, 'Reorganizing Western Intelligence', in Carl Peter Runde and Greg Voss (eds), *Intelligence and the New World Order: Former Cold War*

*Adversaries Look Toward the 21st Century* (Bustehude: International Freedom Foundation, 1992) 126.

Conaglen, Matthew, *Fiduciary Loyalty: Protecting the Due Performance of Non-Fiduciary Duties* (Oxford: Hart Publishing, 2010).

Conan Doyle, Arthur, 'Silver Blaze', *Strand Magazine* 4 (1892) 645.

Cooley, Thomas M, *A Treatise on the Law of Torts, or the Wrongs Which Arise Independent of Contract*, 2nd edn (Chicago: Callaghan & Co, 1888).

Copeland, Thomas E, *Fool Me Twice: Intelligence Failure and Mass Casualty Terrorism* (Leiden: Koninklijke Brill NV, 2007).

Cortright, David and George A Lopez, *The Sanctions Decade: Assessing UN Strategies in the 1990s*, A Project of the International Peace Academy (Boulder, CO: Lynne Rienner, 2000).

——*Sanctions and the Search for Security: Challenges to UN Action*, A Project of the International Peace Academy (Boulder, CO: Lynne Rienner, 2002).

Corwin, Edward S, *The President: Office and Powers* (New York: New York University Press, 1940).

Couillard, David A, 'Defogging the Cloud: Applying Fourth Amendment Principles to Evolving Privacy Expectations in Cloud Computing', *Minnesota Law Review* 93 (2009) 2205.

Curtis, Mark, *The Great Deception: Anglo-American Power and World Order* (London: Pluto Press, 1998).

Dallaire, Roméo, *Shake Hands with the Devil: The Failure of Humanity in Rwanda* (Toronto: Random House Canada, 2003).

Davies, Philip HJ, 'Ideas of Intelligence: Divergent National Concepts and Institutions', *Harvard International Review* 24(3) (2002) 62.

Davies, Simon, *Big Brother: Britain's Web of Surveillance and the New Technological Order* (London: Pan Books, 1996).

Davis, Morris D, 'Historical Perspective on Guantánamo Bay: The Arrival of the High Value Detainees', *Case Western Reserve Journal of International Law* 42 (2009) 115.

Delupis, Ingrid, 'Foreign Warships and Immunity for Espionage', *American Journal of International Law* 78 (1984) 53.

Demarest, Lt Col Geoffrey B, 'Espionage in International Law', *Denver Journal of International Law and Policy* 24 (1996) 321.

Denza, Eileen, *Diplomatic Law: A Commentary on the Vienna Convention on Diplomatic Relations* [1976], 2nd edn (Oxford: Clarendon Press, 1998).

Der Derian, James, The Rise and Fall of the Office of Strategic Influence, (Info Tech War Peace, posted 5 December 2005), available at <http://www.watson-institute.org/infopeace/911/index.cfm?id=9>.

Dershowitz, Alan M, *Why Terrorism Works: Understanding the Threat, Responding to the Challenge* (New Haven, CT: Yale University Press, 2002).

Dicey, AV, *Introduction to the Study of the Law of the Constitution* [1885], 8th edn (London: Macmillan, 1915).

Divine, Robert A (ed), *The Cuban Missile Crisis* (Chicago: Quadrangle Books, 1971).

Donnelly, Eric, 'The United States-China EP-3 Incident: Legality and Realpolitik', *Journal of Conflict and Security Law* 9 (2004) 25.

Donohue, Laura K, 'Anglo-American Privacy and Surveillance', *Journal of Criminal Law & Criminology* 96 (2006) 1059.

Dorn, A Walter, 'The Cloak and the Blue Beret: Limitations on Intelligence in UN Peacekeeping', *International Journal of Intelligence and Counterintelligence* 12(4) (1999) 414.

Dorril, Stephen, *MI6: Inside the Covert World of Her Majesty's Secret Intelligence Service* (New York: Free Press, 2000).

Dosman, E Alexandra, 'For the Record: Designating "Listed Entities" for the Purposes of Terrorist Financing Offences at Canadian Law', *University of Toronto Faculty Law Review* 62 (2004) 1.

Dyzenhaus, David, 'The Rule of (Administrative) Law in International Law', *Law and Contemporary Problems* 68 (2005) 127.

Edelman, James, 'When Do Fiduciary Duties Arise?', *Law Quarterly Review* 126 (2010) 302.

Eickelman, Dale F, 'Intelligence in an Arab Gulf State', in Roy Godson (ed), *Comparing Foreign Intelligence: The US, the USSR, the UK, and the Third World* (Washington, DC: Pergamon-Brassey's, 1988) 89.

Elliff, John T, 'The Attorney General's Guidelines for FBI Investigations', *Cornell Law Review* 69 (1984) 785.

Etzioni, Amitai, *The Limits of Privacy* (New York: Basic Books, 1999).

Falk, Richard A, 'Foreword', in Roland J Stanger (ed), *Essays on Espionage and International Law* (Columbus, OH: Ohio State University Press, 1962) v.

Feldman, Noah, 'Ugly Americans', in Karen J Greenberg (ed), *The Torture Debate in America* (Cambridge: Cambridge University Press, 2006) 267.

Ferejohn, John, 'Accountability and Authority: Toward a Theory of Political Accountability', in Adam Przeworski, SC Stokes, and B Manin (eds), *Democracy, Accountability, and Representation* (Cambridge: Cambridge University Press, 1999) 131.

Ferejohn, John and Pasquale Pasquino, 'The Law of the Exception: A Typology of Emergency Powers', *International Journal of Constitutional Law* 2 (2004) 210.

Findlay, Trevor, *The Use of Force in UN Peace Operations* (Oxford: SIPRI & Oxford University Press, 2002).

Foucault, Michel, *Discipline and Punish: The Birth of the Prison* [1975] (London: Penguin, 1979).

Franck, Thomas M, *Recourse to Force: State Action Against Threats and Armed Attacks*, Hersch Lauterpacht Memorial Lectures (Cambridge: Cambridge University Press, 2002).

Frankel, Joseph, *Contemporary International Theory and the Behavior of States* (Oxford: Oxford University Press, 1973).

Franklin, Benjamin, 'Pennsylvania Assembly: Reply to the Governor, November 11, 1755', in Leonard W Labaree (ed), *The Papers of Benjamin Franklin* (New Haven, CT: Yale University Press, 1963) vol 6, 242.

Franzen, Jonathan, *How to Be Alone* (London: Harper Collins, 2002).

Frazer, Tim, 'Appropriation of Personality—A New Tort?', *Law Quarterly Review* 99 (1983) 281.

Friedman, William F, 'From the Archives: A Brief History of the Signal Intelligence Service (June 1942; declassified 1979)', *Cryptologia* 15(3) (1991) 263.

Froomkin, A Michael, 'The Death of Privacy?', *Stanford Law Review* 52 (2000) 1461.

Gallagher, Caoilfhionn, 'CCTV and Human Rights: The Fish and the Bicycle? An Examination of *Peck v United Kingdom* (2003) 36 EHRR 41', *Surveillance & Society* 2 (2004) 270.

García-Mora, Manuel R, 'Treason, Sedition, and Espionage as Political Offenses Under the Law of Extradition', *University of Pittsburgh Law Review* 26 (1964–65) 65.

Gaston, EL, 'Mercenarism 2.0? The Rise of the Modern Private Security Industry and Its Implications for International Humanitarian Law Enforcement', *Harvard International Law Journal* 49 (2008) 221.

Gauthier, David, *Morals by Agreement* (Oxford: Oxford University Press, 1986).

Gavison, Ruth, 'Privacy and the Limits of Law', *Yale Law Journal* 89 (1980) 421.

Geertz, Clifford, *The Interpretation of Cultures* (New York: Basic Books, 1973).

Goedhuis, D, 'The Changing Legal Regime of Air and Outer Space', *International and Comparative Law Quarterly* 27 (1978) 576.

Goldsmith, Jack, *The Terror Presidency* (New York: Norton, 2007).

Goldsmith, Jack and Timothy Wu, *Who Controls the Internet? Illusions of a Borderless World* (Oxford: Oxford University Press, 2006).

Goldstone, Richard J, 'Remarks: Intelligence and the Use of Force in the War on Terrorism', *American Society of International Law Proceedings* 98 (2004) 148.

Gollin, James, 'Stirring Up the Past: KAL Flight 007', *International Journal of Intelligence and Counterintelligence* 7(4) (1994) 445.

Gomersall, Chris, 'A Closer Look at Video Analytics', *GIT Security + Management*, November–December 2007, 36.

Goold, Benjamin J, *CCTV and Policing: Public Area Surveillance and Police Practices in Britain* (Oxford: Oxford University Press, 2004).

——and Liora Lazarus (eds), *Security and Human Rights* (Oxford: Hart Publishing, 2007).

Gourevitch, Philip and Errol Morris, 'Exposure: Behind the Camera at Abu Ghraib', *New Yorker*, 24 March 2008.

Granholm, Jennifer Mulhern, 'Video Surveillance on Public Streets: The Constitutionality of Invisible Citizen Searches', *University of Detroit Law Review* 64 (1987) 687.

Grant, Ruth W and Robert O Keohane, 'Accountability and Abuses of Power in World Politics', *American Political Science Review* 99(1) (2005) 1.

Gras, Marianne L, 'The Legal Regulation of CCTV in Europe', *Surveillance & Society* 2 (2004) 216.

Greenberg, Karen J and Joshua L Dratel (eds), *The Torture Papers: The Road to Abu Ghraib* (Cambridge: Cambridge University Press, 2005).

Greenberg, Murice R and Richard Haass (eds), *Making Intelligence Smarter: The Future of US Intelligence* (New York: Council on Foreign Relations, 1996).

Grey, Stephen, *Ghost Plane: The True Story of the CIA Torture Program* (New York: St Martin's Press, 2006).

Gross, Emanuel, 'The Struggle of a Democracy Against Terrorism: Protection of Human Rights', *Cornell International Law Journal* 37 (2004) 27.

Gross, Oren, 'Chaos and Rules: Should Responses to Violent Crises Always be Constitutional?', *Yale Law Journal* 112 (2003) 1011.

Gross, Oren and Fionnuala Ní Aoláin, *Law in Times of Crisis: Emergency Powers in Theory and Practice* (Cambridge: Cambridge University Press, 2006).

Grossman, Serge and Michael Simon, 'And Congress Shall Know the Truth: The Pressing Need for Restructuring Congressional Oversight of Intelligence', *Harvard Law & Policy Review* 2 (2008) 435.

Grotius, Hugo, *De iure belli ac pacis libri tres* [1646], translated by Francis W Kelsey, Classics of International Law (Oxford: Clarendon Press, 1925).

Hager, Nicky, *Secret Power: New Zealand's Role in the International Spy Network* (Nelson, NZ: Craig Potton, 1996).

Hakimi, Monica, 'The Council of Europe Addresses CIA Rendition and Detention Program', *American Journal of International Law* 101 (2007) 442.

Halleck, HW, *International Law; or, Rules Regulating the Intercourse of States in Peace and War*, 1st edn (San Francisco: H Bancroft, 1861).

Hamilton, Keith and Richard Langhorne, *The Practice of Diplomacy: Its Evolution and Administration* (New York: Routledge, 1995).

Harding, AJ, 'Singapore', in AJ Harding and J Hatchard (eds), *Preventive Detention and Security Law: A Comparative Survey* (Dordrecht: Martinus Nijhoff, 1993) 193.

Hardy, Michael, *Modern Diplomatic Law* (Manchester: Manchester University Press, 1968).

Harris, Candida, Peter Jones, David Hillier, and David Turner, 'CCTV Surveillance Systems in Town and City Centre Management', *Property Management* 16(3) (1998) 160.

Harris, John, 'Euthanasia and the Value of Life', in John Keown (ed), *Euthanasia Examined: Ethical, Clinical and Legal Perspectives* (Cambridge: Cambridge University Press, 1995) 6.

Hart, Gary, *The Shield and the Cloak: The Security of the Commons* (Oxford: Oxford University Press, 2007).

Herman, Michael, *Intelligence Power in Peace and War* (Cambridge: Cambridge University Press, 1996).

——*Intelligence Services in the Information Age: Theory and Practice* (London: Frank Cass, 2001).

Hersh, Seymour M, 'Saddam's Best Friend', *New Yorker*, 5 April 1999.

Heymann, Philip B and Juliette N Kayyem, *Protecting Liberty in an Age of Terror* (Cambridge, MA: MIT Press, 2005).

Higgins, Rosalyn, 'UK Foreign Affairs Committee Report on the Abuse of Diplomatic Immunities and Privileges: Government Response and Report', *American Journal of International Law* 80 (1986) 135.

Hinsley, FH and Alan Stripp (eds), *Codebreakers: The Inside Story of Bletchley Park* (Oxford: Oxford University Press, 2001).

Hitchens, Christopher, 'Weapons of Mass Distraction', *Vanity Fair*, March 1999, 92.

Hitz, Frederick P, *The Great Game: The Myth and Reality of Espionage* (New York: Alfred A Knopf, 2004).

——*Why Spy? Espionage in an Age of Uncertainty* (New York: Thomas Dunne, 2008).

Hixson, Richard F, *Privacy in a Public Society* (Oxford: Oxford University Press, 1987).

Ho, Soyoung, 'EU's Quantum Leap', *Foreign Policy* 144, September 2004, 92.

Hobbes, Thomas, *Leviathan* [1651] (Cambridge: Cambridge University Press, 1991).

Hocking, Jenny, 'Charting Political Space: Surveillance and the Rule of Law', *Social Justice* 21(4) (1994) 66.

——*Terror Laws: ASIO, Counter-Terrorism, and the Threat to Democracy* (Sydney: UNSW Press, 2004).

Hogan, Jenny, 'Your Every Move Will Be Analysed', *New Scientist*, 12 July 2003, 4.

Hohfeld, Wesley Newcomb, *Fundamental Legal Conceptions as Applied in Judicial Reasoning and Other Legal Essays* (New Haven, CT: Yale University Press, 1923).

Holmes, Stephen, 'In Case of Emergency: Misunderstanding Tradeoffs in the War on Terror', *California Law Review* 97 (2009) 301.

Hor, Michael, 'Terrorism and the Criminal Law: Singapore's Solution', *Singapore Journal of Legal Studies* [2002] 30.

Horn, Carl von, *Soldiering for Peace*, 1st American edn (New York: David McKay, 1967).

Hoversten, Michael R, 'US National Security and Government Regulation of Commercial Remote Sensing from Outer Space', *Air Force Law Review* 50 (2001) 25.

Hughes, Thomas L, *The Fate of Facts in a World of Men: Foreign Policy and Intelligence-Making* (New York: Foreign Policy Association, 1976).

Hulnick, Arthur S, *Keeping Us Safe: Secret Intelligence and Homeland Security* (Westport, CT: Praeger, 2004).

Hume, David, 'Of the Original Contract [1748]', in Ernest Barker (ed), *Social Contract: Essays by Locke, Hume, and Rousseau* (Oxford: Oxford University Press, 1962) 147.

Humphreys, Stephen, 'Legalizing Lawlessness: On Giorgio Agamben's *State of Exception*', *European Journal of International Law* 17 (2006) 677.

Hyde, Charles Cheney, 'Aspects of the Saboteur Cases', *American Journal of International Law* 37 (1943) 88.

Ignatieff, Michael, *The Lesser Evil: Political Ethics in an Age of Terror* (Princeton: Princeton University Press, 2004).

Ignatius, David, *Agents of Innocence* (New York: Norton, 1987).

Inderfurth, Karl F and Loch K Johnson (eds), *Fateful Decisions: Inside the National Security Council* (Oxford: Oxford University Press, 2004).

Inness, Julie C, *Privacy, Intimacy, and Isolation* (Oxford: Oxford University Press, 1992).

International Peace Academy, *Peacekeeper's Handbook* (New York: Pergamon Press, 1984).

Issacharoff, Samuel and Richard H Pildes, 'Emergency Contexts Without Emergency Powers: The United States' Constitutional Approach to Rights During Wartime', *International Journal of Constitutional Law* 2 (2004) 296.

James, Alan, *Peacekeeping in International Politics* (New York: St Martin's Press, 1990).

Jay, Rosemary, *Data Protection: Law and Practice*, 3rd edn (London: Sweet & Maxwell, 2007).

Jefferson, Thomas, 'Letter from Thomas Jefferson to John B Colvin, 20 September 1810', in Paul Leicester Ford (ed), *The Works of Thomas Jefferson* (New York: GP Putnam's Sons, 1905) vol 11, 146.

Jervis, Robert, *Why Intelligence Fails: Lessons from the Iranian Revolution and the Iraq War* (Ithaca, NY: Cornell University Press, 2010).

Johnson-Woods, Toni, *Big Bother: Why Did That Reality TV Show Become Such a Phenomenon?* (Brisbane: University of Queensland Press, 2002).

Johnson, Loch K, *A Season of Inquiry: The Senate Intelligence Investigation* (Lexington, KY: University Press of Kentucky, 1985).

—— 'Congressional Supervision of America's Secret Agencies: The Experience and Legacy of the Church Committee', *Public Administration Review* 64 (2004) 3.

Johnson, Loch K and James J Wirtz (eds), *Intelligence and National Security: The Secret World of Spies*, 2nd edn (Oxford: Oxford University Press, 2007).

Jones, Alex S, *Losing the News: The Future of the News That Feeds Democracy* (Oxford: Oxford University Press, 2009).

Jourard, SM, 'Some Psychological Aspects of Privacy', *Law and Contemporary Problems* 31 (1966) 307.

Kanwar, Vik, 'Review Essay: Giorgio Agamben, *State of Exception*', *International Journal of Constitutional Law* 4 (2006) 567.

Kaplan, Arthur, *Dictatorships and 'Ultimate' Decrees in the Early Roman Republic, 501–202 BC* (New York: Revisionist Press, 1977).

Keefe, Patrick Radden, 'Cat-and-Mouse Games', *New York Review* LII(9), 26 May 2005, 41.

—— *Chatter: Inside the Secret World of Global Eavesdropping* (New York: Random House, 2005).

Keith, Linda Camp and Steven C Poe, 'Are Constitutional State of Emergency Clauses Effective? An Empirical Exploration', *Human Rights Quarterly* 26 (2004) 1071.

Kennedy, Robert F, *Thirteen Days: A Memoir of the Cuban Missile Crisis* (New York: WW Norton, 1969).

Kenyon, Andrew T and Megan Richardson (eds), *New Dimensions in Privacy Law: International and Comparative Perspectives* (Cambridge: Cambridge University Press, 2006).

Keown, John (ed), *Euthanasia Examined: Ethical, Clinical, and Legal Perspectives* (Cambridge: Cambridge University Press, 1995).

Kessler, Ronald, *The CIA at War: Inside the Secret Campaign Against Terror* (New York: St Martin's Press, 2003).

Khattab, Mohab Tarek, 'Revised Circular A-76: Embracing Flawed Methodologies', *Public Contract Law Journal* 34 (2005) 469.

Kingsbury, Benedict, Nico Krisch, and Richard B Stewart, 'The Emergence of Global Administrative Law', *Law and Contemporary Problems* 68 (2005) 15.

Kirby, Dianne, 'Harry Truman's Religious Legacy: The Holy Alliance, Containment, and the Cold War', in Dianne Kirby (ed), *Religion and the Cold War* (New York: Palgrave Macmillan, 2003) 77.

Kissinger, Henry, *Years of Upheaval* (Boston: Little, Brown, 1982).

Koh, Harold Hongju, *The National Security Constitution: Sharing Power after the Iran–Contra Affair* (New Haven, CT: Yale University Press, 1990).

Krepon, Michael and Amy E Smithson (eds), *Open Skies, Arms Control, and Cooperative Security* (New York: St Martin's Press, 1992).

Kris, David S, 'The Rise and Fall of the FISA Wall', *Stanford Law & Policy Review* 17 (2006) 487.

Kruegle, Herman, *CCTV Surveillance* (Amsterdam: Elsevier Butterworth Heinemann, 2007).

Kruh, Louis, 'Stimson, the Black Chamber, and the "Gentlemen's Mail" Quote', *Cryptologia* 12(2) (1988) 65.

Kuhn, Thomas S, *The Structure of Scientific Revolutions*, 3rd edn (Chicago: University Of Chicago Press, 1996).

Kunzendorf, Volker, *Verification in Conventional Arms Control*, Adelphi Paper 245 (London: IISS/Brassey's, 1989).

Laffont, Jean-Jacques and Jean Tirole, 'The Politics of Government Decision-Making: A Theory of Regulatory Capture', *Quarterly Journal of Economics* 106 (1991) 1089.

Lazar, Nomi Claire, *States of Emergency in Liberal Democracies* (Cambridge: Cambridge University Press, 2009).

le Carré, John, *The Spy Who Came In from the Cold* (London: Gollancz, 1963).

—— *The Russia House* (New York: Knopf, 1989).

—— *The Constant Gardener* (London: Hodder & Stoughton, 2001).

Leahy, Patrick, 'The Uniting and Strengthening America Act of 2001', *Congressional Record (Senate)* 147(134) (2001) S10365.

Lefkon, Owen Philip, 'Culture Shock: Obstacles to Bringing Conflict Prevention Under the Wing of UN Development…and Vice Versa', *New York University Journal of International Law and Politics* 35 (2003) 671.

Levine, Michael E and Jennifer L Forrence, 'Regulatory Capture, Public Interest, and the Public Agenda: Toward a Synthesis', *Journal of Law, Economics, and Organization* 6 (1990) 167.

Lewis, Margaret K, 'Note: An Analysis of State Responsibility for the Chinese-American Airplane Collision Incident', *New York University Law Review* 77 (2002) 1404.

Lim Yee Fen, *Cyberspace Law: Commentary and Materials*, 2nd edn (Oxford: Oxford University Press, 2007).

Locke, John, *Two Treatises of Government* [1690] (Cambridge: Cambridge University Press, 1988).

Lorber, Steven, 'Data Protection and Subject Access Requests', *Industrial Law Journal* 33(2) (2004) 179.

Lowenthal, Mark M, *Intelligence: From Secrets to Policy*, 3rd edn (Washington, DC: CQ Press, 2006).

Luneburg, William V, 'Contracting by the Federal Government for Legal Services: A Legal and Empirical Analysis', *Notre Dame Law Review* 63 (1988) 399.

Lustgarten, Laurence and Ian Leigh, 'The Security Service Act 1989', *Modern Law Review* 52 (1989) 801.

——*In from the Cold: National Security and Parliamentary Democracy* (Oxford: Clarendon Press, 1994).

Lynn, Jonathan and Antony Jay, *The Complete Yes Minister* (London: British Broadcasting Corporation, 1984).

Machiavelli, Niccolò, *The Discourses* [1531], translated by Leslie J Walker (London: Penguin, 1970).

Maddrell, Paul, *Spying on Science: Western Intelligence in Divided Germany 1945–1961* (Oxford: Oxford University Press, 2006).

Malone, David M and Ramesh Thakur, 'UN Peacekeeping: Lessons Learned?', *Global Governance* 7(1) (2001) 11.

Manget, Frederic F, 'Another System of Oversight: Intelligence and the Rise of Judicial Intervention', *Studies in Intelligence* 39(5) (1996) 43.

Mann, James, *Rise of the Vulcans: The History of Bush's War Cabinet* (New York: Viking, 2004).

Markesinis, BS, 'The Royal Prerogative Revisited', *Cambridge Law Journal* 32 (1973) 287.

Markesinis, Basil, Colm O'Cinneide, Jorg Fedtke, and Myriam Hunter-Henin, 'Concerns and Ideas About the Developing English Law of Privacy (and How Knowledge of Foreign Law Might Be of Help)', *American Journal of Comparative Law* 52 (2004) 133.

Martin, Kathryn, 'The USA PATRIOT Act's Application to Library Patron Records', *Journal of Legislation* 29 (2003) 283.

Martin, P, 'Destruction of Korean Air Lines Boeing 747 over Sea of Japan, 31 August 1983', *Air Law* 9(3) (1984) 138.

Martin, Samantha L, 'Interpreting the Wiretap Act: Applying Ordinary Rules of "Transit" to the Internet Context', *Cardozo Law Review* 28 (2006) 441.

Martin, Shannon E, *Bits, Bytes, and Big Brother: Federal Information Control in the Technological Age* (Westport, CT: Praeger, 1995).

Mattingly, Garrett, *Renaissance Diplomacy* (London: Jonathan Cape, 1962).

Maugham, W Somerset, *Ashenden; or: The British Agent* [1928] (New York: Doubleday, 1941).

Mayer, Jane, 'Outsourcing: The CIA's Travel Agent', *New Yorker*, 30 October 2006.

—— 'Whatever It Takes: The Politics of the Man Behind "24"', *New Yorker*, 19 February 2007, 66.

—— *The Dark Side: The Inside Story of How the War on Terror Turned Into a War on American Ideals* (New York: Doubleday, 2008).

McClanahan, Grant V, *Diplomatic Immunity: Principles, Practices, Problems* (New York: St Martin's Press, 1989).

McCubbins, Mathew D and Thomas Schwartz, 'Congressional Oversight Overlooked: Police Patrols versus Fire Alarms', *American Journal of Political Science* 28 (1984) 165.

McDougal, Myres S, Harold D Lasswell, and W Michael Reisman, 'The Intelligence Function and World Public Order', *Temple Law Quarterly* 46 (1973) 365.

Mead, Margaret, 'Margaret Mead Re-Examines Our Right to Privacy', *Redbook*, April 1965, 15.

Mills, Jon L, *Privacy: The Lost Right* (Oxford: Oxford University Press, 2008).

Minow, Martha, 'Outsourcing Power: How Privatizing Military Efforts Challenges Accountability, Professionalism, and Democracy', *Boston College Law Review* 46 (2005) 989.

Moynihan, Daniel Patrick, *Secrecy: The American Experience* (New Haven, CT: Yale University Press, 1998).

Nagel, Thomas, 'Concealment and Exposure', *Philosophy & Public Affairs* 27 (1998) 3.

Newton Lyons, Carrie, 'The State Secrets Privilege: Expanding Its Scope Through Government Misuse', *Lewis & Clark Law Review* 11 (2007) 99.

Newton, Michael A, 'The International Criminal Court Preparatory Commission: The Way It Is & the Way Ahead', *Virginia Journal of International Law* 41 (2000) 204.

Nissenbaum, Helen, 'Protecting Privacy in an Information Age: The Problem of Privacy in Public', *Law and Philosophy* 17 (1998) 559.

Normand, Roger, 'Human Rights Assessment of Sanctions: The Case of Iraq (1990–1997)', in Willem JM van Genugten and Gerard A de Groot (eds), *United Nations Sanctions—Effectiveness and Effects, Especially in the Field of Human Rights: A Multi-disciplinary Approach* (Intersentia, Antwerp: 1999) 19.

Norris, Clive and Gary Armstrong, *The Maximum Surveillance Society: The Rise of CCTV* (Oxford: Berg, 1999).

Norris, Clive, Mike McCahill, and David Wood, 'The Growth of CCTV: A Global Perspective on the International Diffusion of Video Surveillance in Publicly Accessible Space', *Surveillance & Society* 2 (2004) 110.

Norris, Clive and Dean Wilson (eds), *Surveillance, Crime and Social Control* (Aldershot: Ashgate, 2006).

Nye, Joseph S, 'Peering into the Future', *Foreign Affairs* 73(4) (1994) 82.

O'Brien, Connor Cruise, *To Katanga and Back* (New York: Simon & Schuster, 1962).

O'Neill, Brendan, 'Watching You Watching Me', *New Statesman*, 2 October 2006.

Orwell, George, *Nineteen Eighty-Four* (London: Secker and Warburg, 1949).

Oudraat, Chantal de Jonge, 'UNSCOM: Between Iraq and a Hard Place', *European Journal of International Law* 13 (2002) 139.

Packer, George, 'Knowing the Enemy: Can Social Scientists Redefine the "War on Terror"?', *New Yorker*, 18 December 2006, 60.

Palmer, Matthew SR, 'Toward an Economics of Comparative Political Organization: Examining Ministerial Responsibility', *Journal of Law, Economics, and Organization* 11(1) (1995) 164.

Parker, John, *Total Surveillance: Investigating the Big Brother World of E-Spies, Eavesdroppers and CCTV* (London: Piatkus, 2000).

Payne, Ronald, *Mossad: Israel's Most Secret Service* (London: Bantam, 1990).

Phelps, Major John T, 'Aerial Intrusions by Civil and Military Aircraft in Time of Peace', *Military Law Review* 107 (1985) 255.

Philby, Kim, *My Silent War* (New York: Grove Press, 1968).

Philips, Edward, 'Drastic Solutions: A Comparative Study of Emergency Powers in the Commonwealth', *Denning Law Journal* 5 (1990) 57.

Pillar, Paul R, 'Intelligence, Policy, and the War in Iraq', *Foreign Affairs* 85(2) (2006) 15.

Pither, Kerry, *Dark Days: The Story of Four Canadians Tortured in the Name of Fighting Terror* (Toronto: Viking Canada, 2008).

Plame Wilson, Valerie, *Fair Game: My Life as a Spy, My Betrayal by the White House* (New York: Simon & Schuster, 2007).

Posner, Richard A, *The Economic Analysis of the Law*, 5th edn (New York: Aspen, 1998).

—— 'The Best Offense', *New Republic*, 2 September 2002, 28.

—— *Preventing Surprise Attacks: Intelligence Reform in the Wake of 9/11* (Stanford, CA: Hoover, 2005).

—— 'Wire Trap: What If Wire-Tapping Works?', *New Republic*, 6 February 2006.

Post, Robert C, 'The Social Foundations of Privacy: Community and Self in the Common Law Tort', *California Law Review* 77 (1989) 957.

Pozen, David E, 'The Mosaic Theory, National Security, and the Freedom of Information Act', *Yale Law Journal* 115 (2005) 628.

Prosser, William, 'Privacy', *California Law Review* 484 (1960) 383.

Radcliff, Deborah, 'A Cry for Privacy', *Computer World*, 17 May 1999.

Ramraj, Victor V (ed), *Emergencies and the Limits of Legality* (Cambridge: Cambridge University Press, 2008).

Ramraj, Victor V, Michael Hor, and Kent Roach (eds), *Global Anti-Terrorism Law and Policy* (Cambridge: Cambridge University Press, 2005).

Ramsbotham, David, 'Analysis and Assessment for Peacekeeping Operations', *Intelligence and National Security* 10(4) (1995) 162.

Randall, James G, *The Civil War and Reconstruction* (Boston: DC Heath, 1937).

Rascoff, Samuel, 'Domesticating Intelligence', *Southern California Law Review* 83 (2010) 575.

Rawls, John, *A Theory of Justice* (Oxford: Clarendon Press, 1972).

Reinisch, August, 'Developing Human Rights and Humanitarian Law Accountability of the Security Council for the Imposition of Economic Sanctions', *American Journal of International Law* 95 (2001) 851.

Reisman, W Michael and James E Baker, *Regulating Covert Action: Practices, Contexts, and Policies of Covert Coercion Abroad in International and American Law* (New Haven, CT: Yale University Press, 1992).

Rempell, Scott, 'Privacy, Personal Data and Subject Access Rights in the European Data Directive and Implementing UK Statute: *Durant v Financial Services Authority* as a Paradigm of Data Protection Nuances and Emerging Dilemmas', *Florida Journal of International Law* 18 (2006) 807.

Renninger, John P, (ed), *The Future Role of the United Nations in an Interdependent World* (Dordrecht: Martinus Nijhoff, 1989).

Richelson, Jeffery T, *A Century of Spies: Intelligence in the Twentieth Century* (Oxford: Oxford University Press, 1997).

—— *The US Intelligence Community*, 4th edn (Boulder, CO: Westview, 1999).

Richelson, Jeffrey T and Desmond Ball, *The Ties that Bind: Intelligence Cooperation Between the UKUSA Countries, the United Kingdom, the United States of America, Canada, Australia, and New Zealand* (Sydney: Allen & Unwin, 1985).

Risen, James, *State of War: The Secret History of the CIA and the Bush Administration* (New York: Free Press, 2006).

Ritter, Scott, *Endgame: Solving the Iraq Problem—Once and for All* (New York: Simon & Schuster, 1999).

Rockwood, Laura, 'The IAEA's Strengthened Safeguards System', *Journal of Conflict and Security Law* 7(1) (2002) 123.

Rosand, Eric, 'The Security Council's Efforts to Monitor the Implementation of al Qaeda/Taliban Sanctions', *American Journal of International Law* 98 (2004) 745.

Rossiter, Clinton Lawrence, *Constitutional Dictatorship: Crisis Government in the Modern Democracies* [1948] (New Brunswick, NJ: Transaction Publishers, 2006).

Rousseau, Jean-Jacques, *The Social Contract* [1762], translated by GDH Cole (London: JM Dent, 1923).

Rule, James B, *Private Lives and Public Surveillance: Social Control in the Computer Age* (London: Allen Lane, 1973).

——*Privacy in Peril* (Oxford: Oxford University Press, 2007).

Rusbridger, James, *The Intelligence Game* (New York: New Amsterdam, 1989).

Russell, Richard L, *Sharpening Strategic Intelligence: Why the CIA Gets It Wrong and What Needs to Be Done to Get It Right* (Cambridge: Cambridge University Press, 2007).

Sandoz, Yves, Christophe Swinarski, and Bruno Zimmerman (eds), *Commentary on the Additional Protocols of 8 June 1977 to the Geneva Conventions of 12 August 1949* (Geneva: Martinus Nijhoff, 1987).

Schauer, Frederick, *Profiles, Probabilities, and Stereotypes* (Cambridge, MA: Harvard University Press, 2003).

Scheuerman, William E, *Carl Schmitt: The End of Law* (Lanham, MD: Rowman & Littlefield, 1999).

Schlesinger, Stephen, *Act of Creation: The Founding of the United Nations* (Boulder, CO: Westview, 2003).

Schmidt, Regin, *Red Scare: FBI and the Origins of Anticommunism in the United States, 1919–1943* (Copenhagen: Museum Tusculanum Press, 2000).

Schmitt, Carl, *Political Theology: Four Chapters on the Concept of Sovereignty* [1922], translated by George Schwab (Cambridge, MA: MIT Press, 1985).

Schooner, Steven L, 'Contractor Atrocities at Abu Ghraib: Compromised Accountability in a Streamlined, Outsourced Government', *Stanford Law and Policy Review* 16 (2005) 549.

Schulhofer, Stephen J, *The Enemy Within: Intelligence Gathering, Law Enforcement, and Civil Liberties in the Wake of September 11* (New York: Century Foundation Press, 2002).

Schumpeter, Joseph A, *Capitalism, Socialism and Democracy* [1942] (New York: Harper, 1975).

Schwartz, Jack, 'The "Hearing Tom" Is Everywhere', *Newsday*, 9 January 1965.

Schwartz, Paul M, 'Reviving Telecommunications Surveillance Law', *University of Chicago Law Review* 75 (2008) 287.

Scott, Cmdr Roger D, 'Territorially Intrusive Intelligence Collection and International Law', *Air Force Law Review* 46 (1999) 217.

Sergienko, Alexander, Saverio Pascazio, and Paolo Villoresi (eds), *Quantum Communication and Quantum Networking* (Berlin: Springer, 2010).

Setear, John K, 'Responses to Breach of a Treaty and Rationalist International Relations Theory: The Rules of Release and Remediation in the Law of Treaties and the Law of State Responsibility', *Virginia Law Review* 83 (1997) 1.

Shetler-Jones, Philip, 'Intelligence in Integrated UN Peacekeeping Missions: The Joint Mission Analysis Centre', *International Peacekeeping* 15(4) (2008) 517.

Shils, Edward A, *The Torment of Secrecy: The Background and Consequences of American Security Policies* (London: Heinemann, 1956).

Shorrock, Tim, *Spies for Hire: The Secret World of Intelligence Outsourcing* (New York: Simon & Schuster, 2008).

Shue, Henry, 'Torture', *Philosophy and Public Affairs* 7 (1978) 124.

Shumate, Brett A, 'From "Sneak and Peek" to "Sneak and Steal": Section 213 of the USA PATRIOT Act', *Regent University Law Review* 19 (2006) 203.

Silver, Daniel B and (updated and revised by Frederick P Hitz and JE Shreve Ariail), 'Intelligence and Counterintelligence', in John Norton Moore and Robert F Turner (eds), *National Security Law* (Durham, NC: Carolina Academic Press, 2005) 935.

Simester, AP, 'Necessity, Torture, and the Rule of Law', in Victor V Ramraj (ed), *Emergencies and the Limits of Legality* (Cambridge: Cambridge University Press, 2008) 289.

Simma, Bruno (ed), *The Charter of the United Nations: A Commentary*, 2nd edn (Oxford: Oxford University Press, 2002).

Simpson, AWB, *Cannibalism and the Common Law: The Story of the Tragic Last Voyage of the Mignonette and the Strange Legal Proceedings to Which It Gave Rise* (Chicago: University of Chicago Press, 1984).

Singleton, Susan, *Tolley's Data Protection Handbook*, 4th edn (London: Lexis-Nexis, 2006).

Slaughter, Anne-Marie, *A New World Order* (Princeton: Princeton University Press, 2004).

Slobogin, Christopher, 'Public Privacy: Camera Surveillance of Public Places and the Right to Anonymity', *Mississippi Law Journal* 72 (2002) 213.

——*Privacy at Risk: The New Government Surveillance and the Fourth Amendment* (Chicago: University of Chicago Press, 2007).

Smist, Frank, *Congress Oversees the United States Intelligence Community*, 2nd edn (Knoxville: University of Tennessee Press, 1994).

Smith, DJ, *The Sleep of Reason: The James Bulger Case* (London: Century, 1994).

Smith, Hugh, 'Intelligence and UN Peacekeeping', *Survival* 36(3) (1994) 174.

Smith, Michael, *New Cloak, Old Dagger* (London: Gollancz, 1996).

——*The Spying Game: The Secret History of British Espionage* (London: Politico's, 2003).

Solove, Daniel J, 'Conceptualizing Privacy', *California Law Review* 90 (2002) 1087.

Solove, Daniel J, *The Digital Person: Privacy and Technology in the Information Age* (New York: New York University Press, 2004).

—— '"I've Got Nothing to Hide" and Other Misunderstandings of Privacy', *San Diego Law Review* 44 (2007) 745.

—— *Understanding Privacy* (Cambridge, MA: Harvard University Press, 2008).

Solzhenitsyn, Aleksandr, *Cancer Ward* [1968], translated by Nicholas Bethell and David Burg (New York: Noonday, 1991).

Stevens, G and C Doyle, *Privacy: Wiretapping and Electronic Eavesdropping* (New York: Novinka, 2002).

Stewart, Jonathan D, 'Balancing the Scales of Due Process: Material Support of Terrorism and the Fifth Amendment', *Georgetown Journal of Law & Public Policy* 3 (2005) 311.

Stimson, Herny L and McGeorge Bundy, *On Active Service in Peace and War* (New York: Harper and Brothers, 1947).

Stone, Geoffrey R, *Perilous Times: Free Speech in Wartime from the Sedition Act of 1798 to the War on Terrorism* (New York: WW Norton, 2004).

Swire, Peter P, 'Proportionality for High-Tech Searches', *Ohio State Journal of Criminal Law* 6 (2009) 751.

Sykes, Charles J, *The End of Privacy: Personal Rights in the Surveillance Society* (New York: St Martin's Griffin, 1999).

Tarallo, Mark, 'Hayden Wants Fewer CIA Contractors', *Federal Computer Week*, 25 June 2007.

Theoharis, Athan, *The Quest for Absolute Security: The Failed Relations Among US Intelligence Agencies* (Chicago: Ivan R Dee, 2007).

Tran, Van Dinh, *Communication and Diplomacy in a Changing World* (Norwood, NJ Ablex, 1987).

Turner, Admiral Stansfield, *Secrecy and Democracy: The CIA in Transition* (Boston: Houghton Mifflin, 1985).

Urquhart, Brian, *Hammarskjöld* (New York: Knopf, 1972).

Valencia, Mark J, *The Proliferation Security Initiative: Making Waves in Asia*, Adelphi Paper 376 (Abingdon: Routledge, 2005).

Wadham, John, 'The Intelligence Services Act 1994', *Modern Law Review* 57 (1994) 916.

Wark, Wesley K, *The Ultimate Enemy: British Intelligence and Nazi Germany, 1933–1939* (Ithaca, NY: Cornell University Press, 1985).

Warner, Michael, 'Wanted: A Definition of Intelligence', *Studies in Intelligence (Unclassified Edition)* 46(3) (2002) 15.

Warren, Samuel D and Louis D Brandeis, 'The Right to Privacy', *Harvard Law Review* 4 (1890) 193.

Watkins, Frederick M, 'The Problem of Constitutional Dictatorship', *Public Policy* 1 (1940) 324.

Wedgwood, Ruth, 'International Criminal Tribunals and State Sources of Proof: The Case of Tihomir Blaskic', *Leiden Journal of International Law* 11 (1998) 635.

Weiner, Tim, *Legacy of Ashes: The History of the CIA* (New York: Doubleday, 2007).

Wendel, W Bradley, 'Legal Ethics and the Separation of Law and Morals', *Cornell Law Review* 91 (2005) 67.

Westin, Alan F, *Privacy and Freedom* (New York: Atheneum, 1967).

——(ed), *Information Technology in a Democracy* (Cambridge, MA: Harvard University Press, 1971).

Whaley, Barton, *Codeword Barbarossa* (Cambridge, MA: MIT Press, 1973).

Whitman, James Q, 'The Two Western Cultures of Privacy: Dignity Versus Liberty', *Yale Law Journal* 113 (2004) 1153.

Whitney, Craig R, *Spy Trader: Germany's Devil's Advocate and the Darkest Secrets of the Cold War* (New York: Random House, 1993).

Wiebes, Cees, *Intelligence and the War in Bosnia, 1992–1995* (Münster: LIT Verlag, 2003).

Williams, Bernard, *In the Beginning Was the Deed: Realism and Moralism in Political Argument* (Princeton: Princeton University Press, 2005).

Woods, Michael J, 'Counterintelligence and Access to Transactional Records: A Practical History of USA PATRIOT Act Section 215', *Journal of National Security Law & Policy* 1(1) (2005) 37.

Woodward, Bob, *Plan of Attack* (New York: Simon & Schuster, 2004).

Wright, Lawrence, 'The Spymaster', *New Yorker*, 21 January 2008, 42.

Wright, Peter, *Spycatcher: The Candid Autobiography of a Senior Intelligence Officer* (New York: Viking, 1987).

Wright, Quincy, 'Legal Aspects of the U-2 Incident', *American Journal of International Law* 54 (1960) 836.

——'Espionage and the Doctrine of Non-Intervention in Internal Affairs', in Roland J Stanger (ed), *Essays on Espionage and International Law* (Columbus, OH: Ohio State University Press, 1962) 12.

Yoo, John, 'Transferring Terrorists', *Notre Dame Law Review* 79 (2004) 1183.

——'The Terrorist Surveillance Program and the Constitution', *George Mason Law Review* 14 (2007) 565.

——*Crisis and Command: A History of Executive Power from George Washington to George W Bush* (New York: Kaplan, 2010).

Zegart, Amy B, *Flawed by Design: The Evolution of the CIA, JCS, and NSC* (Stanford, CA: Stanford University Press, 1999).

Zegart, Amy B, 'Cloaks, Daggers, and Ivory Towers: Why Academics Don't Study US Intelligence', in Loch K Johnson (ed), *Strategic Intelligence* (Westport, CT: Praeger, 2007) 21.

——*Spying Blind: The CIA, the FBI, and the Origins of 9/11* (Princeton: Princeton University Press, 2007).

Zittrain, Jonathan, *The Future of the Internet—and How to Stop It* (New Haven, CT: Yale University Press, 2008).

# Index